KNOWING
with
the
heart

RELIGIOUS
EXPERIENCE
& BELIEF
IN GOD

Roy Clouser

InterVarsity Press
Downers Grove, Illinois

InterVarsity Press
P.O. Box 1400, Downers Grove, IL 60515
World Wide Web: www.ivpress.com
E-mail: mail@ivpress.com

InterVarsity Press® is the book-publishing division of InterVarsity Christian Fellowship/USA®, a student movement active on campus at hundreds of universities, colleges and schools of nursing in the United States of America, and a member movement of the International Fellowship of Evangelical Students. For information about local and regional activities, write Public Relations Dept., InterVarsity Christian Fellowship/USA, 6400 Schroeder Rd., P.O. Box 7895, Madison, WI 53707-7895.

All Scripture quotations, unless otherwise indicated, are taken from the Holy Bible, New International Version®. NIV®. *Copyright ©1973, 1978, 1984 by International Bible Society. Used by permission of Zondervan Publishing House. All rights reserved.*

Cover photograph: Dale O'Dell/The Stock Market

ISBN 0-8308-1507-4

Printed in the United States of America ⊗

Library of Congress Cataloging-in-Publication Data

Clouser, Roy A., 1937–
    Knowing with the heart : religious experience and
belief in God / Roy Clouser.
        p. cm.
    Includes bibliographical references.
    ISBN 0-8308-1507-4 (paper : alk. paper)
    1. God—Proof, Empirical. 2. Experience (Religion)
I. Title.
BT102.C56 1998
231'.042—dc21   98-27689
                                                                                   CIP

21	20	19	18	17	16	15	14	13	12	11	10	9	8	7	6	5	4	3	2	1

16	15	14	13	12	11	10	09	08	07	06	05	04	03	02	01	00	99

*This book is lovingly dedicated to my dear parents
from whom I first learned of God*

Introduction

The subject of this book is the question whether we can *know* God is real. The answer it gives is yes. It is written in the style of a dialogue and is primarily addressed to two audiences: those who believe in God but are confused about their intellectual right to that belief, and those who do not believe in God but are willing to inquire as to whether there is more to such belief than blind faith. It will also be of interest to anyone who is simply curious about the subject.

Neither the question posed nor the answer given is considered a topic for polite conversation these days. Religion has changed places with sex as a taboo subject in public. It's all right to acknowledge that there are such things as religious beliefs, but only so long as we go into no further detail. The least acceptable form of going into further detail would be a discussion such as the one that takes place here—that is, a consideration of how to tell which, if any, of those beliefs are true and which are false.

In fact, even the thought that some may be true and others false is regarded by many people nowadays as reprehensible. People who know very little about the religious tradition they are most familiar with, and absolutely nothing about other traditions, nevertheless purport to know with the utmost certainty both that all religious beliefs may be true at once and that no one can know for sure whether any is true. They're also quite sure that the word "faith" *means* accepting a belief without knowing it's true. As a result, they see a Berlin Wall between faith and all that we can truly be said to know—such as science.

Another thing a great many people are sure of is that religious belief was invented as a scare story to be tacked onto ethics. The ethic found in the Bible is OK; who would disagree with the Ten Commandments that murder, theft, dishonesty and so on are wrong? But on the other hand, who needs the scare story? Why suppose that people won't be ethical unless they're told that there's a big umpire in the sky who'll penalize them in the next life even if they escape reprisal for wrongdoing in this life? After all, the reasoning goes, we know firsthand that *we* are ethical without the scare story. Therefore the importance religious people attach to their belief is simply irrational. So let's keep reinforcing that Berlin Wall and hope that one day the advance of science will cause religious beliefs—all of them—to fade away and relieve the world of a needless source of contention.

The only trouble with these gems of popular wisdom is that they are all wholly false. This book shows how clarifying the nature of religious belief allows us to see that under the right circumstances it can be a basic belief grounded on the same kind of justification enjoyed by beliefs traditionally regarded as among the most certain we have. Thus if justified certainty warrants us in saying we have knowledge, then belief in God can also be knowledge. In that case it is not merely wishful thinking, blind trust or a scare story invented to promote ethics.

What is more, clarifying what distinguishes religious belief makes it plausible that no one can avoid it, though this fact goes unrecognized for two reasons. The first is that such a belief can be an unconscious assumption, and the second is that many people call it by another name, thereby disguising its religious character. In both cases people think they have no religious belief when they actually do.

The clarification of what counts as religious belief also makes it possible to see why religious belief can't be walled off from the rest of knowledge. It's actually one of the most influential beliefs people hold, affecting not only their conceptions of human nature and destiny but also their ideas of society, justice and ethics, and even how they do science.

I wish to thank a number of people who read the manuscript in whole or in part and made valuable suggestions for its improvement. These include Professor Martin Rice (University of Pittsburgh), Professor George Mavrodes (University of Michigan), the Reverend Dr. Walter Hartt (Christ Church, Toms River, New Jersey), Dr. Kenneth Wolfe, my IVP editor Rodney Clapp, and my dear wife Anita, whose editing of the first and final drafts was invaluable.

1

What Is Religious Experience?

*W*HEN I ASKED YOU TO TALK WITH ME ABOUT HOW ANY EDUCATED *person in this scientific age could still believe in God, I expected you to start our discussions with arguments for God's existence. Instead you start by talking about religious experience! Does that mean you're kissing off the proofs for God's existence? Are you conceding right away that none of them work?*

Yes. I'm skipping the arguments for God's existence, first, because in my opinion none of them succeed. Let me hasten to add that I don't believe their failure matters much. I totally reject the view that belief in God is justified only if proven and that otherwise it's blind faith. Proving is actually an inferior way of coming to know something, a way we resort to when we can't directly experience what we want to know. That's why proving is standard procedure in philosophy and the sciences. Both seek information we can't get directly from experience. So we make hypotheses (educated guesses) and then construct arguments and weigh evidence to prove or disprove them. But genuine belief in God doesn't regard God as a hypothesis, and it doesn't need proof. *It's a belief that is both acquired and justified by experience.*

The second reason for skipping the arguments is that you asked me why *I* believe God is real and is the sort of being the Scriptures say God is. If I am to answer candidly, my answer has to be a confession—an admission—of my real reasons. If I instead invent arguments intended to make that belief look good to you, they won't be *my* reasons for believing, since I don't believe in God because of any arguments (and I don't know of anyone else who does either). So that's why I want to start our discussions by talking about religious experience.

Fair enough. I did ask how you can believe something that sounds like a convenient fairy tale. But to be as candid with you as you want to be with me, I have to say that I'm at least as skeptical about an appeal to religious experience as I am about the proofs of God's existence. I've never had any such experience nor do I know anyone who has.

Anyway, most of the claims I've heard about such experiences sound a lot like the reports of people who claim to have been kidnapped by aliens from outer space! So even if belief in God is "acquired" by some sort of experience, I don't believe it can be justified *by it!*

Perhaps no other topic is in as much need of having its name explained as is "religious experience." So before we go any further, I need to clarify the meaning of that expression. That will take some doing, but when the dust clears I hope to have shown you that it does not refer only—or even primarily—to weird events such as mystical states of consciousness, visions or miracles; an experience isn't religious only if the furniture flies around the room.

Of the two terms in the expression, the meaning of "experience" is easier and can be cleared up pretty quickly. I'm going to use it in the broadest possible sense: An experience is being aware of anything whatever, regardless of the nature of what is experienced or the sort of ability by which we become aware of it. The content of experience, then, is everything of which we are in any way aware; acts of experiencing are all the ways we are aware of anything. Thus the expression "religious experience" refers to *any experience by which a religious belief is acquired, deepened or confirmed.*[1] For the rest of these discussions we can concentrate on the experience by which religious belief is acquired, since that is what you specifically asked about. So from now on I'll only be speaking about experiences that generate belief in God rather than those that deepen or confirm it.

Hold on a moment. You seem to be switching back and forth just now between talking about religious belief in general and about belief in God in particular. Which one are we going to discuss?

The account I'm going to give will first be general and then focus on belief in God in particular. To be clear about *what* religious experience is, we have to inquire about its role in the acquisition of any religious belief whatever. Once that is clear, we'll be in a position to examine its role in relation to belief in God specifically. After that we can go on to discuss belief in God in comparison to other religious beliefs.

OK, I think I understand what you're up to. We start by taking experience in the broadest sense, concentrating on experiences that generate religious beliefs. Then we examine how such experience constitutes the basis for belief in God.

But doesn't that mean we have to be able to tell whether a belief is or is not a religious belief in order to be able to tell whether or not an experience is?

Exactly! As I said, clarifying the term "experience" is the easy part. It's a lot harder to differentiate religious beliefs from nonreligious beliefs. But we must do exactly that if the meaning of the expression "religious experience" is to be clear enough to guide the rest of our discussions. So our first task has to be to arrive at a definition of religious belief. I wish this could be defined as easily as "experience." But there is a lot of confusion about religious belief, and some of the most deeply entrenched popular ideas about it are the most misleading. For that reason we need to talk about why some of these widely accepted ideas fail, and try to come up with a definition that successfully covers all religious beliefs. This means tackling some of the most difficult issues first.

If you can really give a definition of religious belief that covers all religious beliefs, it will be worth the effort. But why is that hard? What's so bad about the popular ideas?

Before we tackle the popular ideas of religious belief, let's take a moment to recall what's involved in arriving at the sort of definition we need. We have to identify the list of features that are true of all religious beliefs and are true of only religious beliefs. This is the hardest sort of definition to get, so often in philosophy and science we have to settle for other ways of delimiting what we mean by a term. Nevertheless, this type of definition would be the most helpful to our subject if we could get it—and I think we *can* get it!

Any attempt to form this sort of definition must overcome two main difficulties. On the one hand, if it fails to cover certain beliefs that are obviously religious, then it is too narrow; on the other hand, if it covers all religious beliefs but also applies to clearly nonreligious ones, then it's too broad. These difficulties can often baffle our best attempts. But even when one can be formulated, there are still other difficulties that plague its acceptance. Since it can be disturbing to pare back the characteristics of a type of thing till we're left with only the features that are shared by all of them and only by them, such definitions are often both surprising and disappointing. And they are frequently rejected for those reasons.

Take the case of defining what counts as a tree. Everyone easily recognizes trees, of course, and yet it is hard to state just what features are shared by all trees and are shared only by trees. The definition can be disappointing because so much that is obvious or valuable about trees is not included—their beautiful foliage, shade, or uses as wood, for example. Likewise, the definition may be surprising. Did you know that there are mature trees only a foot tall? So we need to recognize at the outset that this sort of defining often has such results. In fact the more initial confusion there is about the definition of a type of things, the more certain it is that formulating a definition to clear up the confusion *will* have such results.

Consider an actual example of this. Many years ago whales were classified as fish. Their bodies were shaped like fishes' bodies, they lived their lives in the oceans, and they swam. But as time went on, they were reclassified as mammals. There were good reasons for this. Whales have four-chambered hearts and are warm-blooded; lacking gills, they breathe air with lungs; and they bear their young alive and nurse them. So despite their very fishlike tails and fins, despite the fact that they can't live on land but spend their lives swimming in oceans, whales are defined as mammals. Perhaps this redefinition was disappointing or surprising to some people when it was first put forward, since it means that whales have more in common with humans than with fish! But it was not wrong for that reason.

I get it. You're about to drop a definition on me that's disappointing and surprising, so you're saying in advance that it doesn't matter.

Exactly right! The task of identifying the defining features of religious belief is no different in these respects from defining trees or whales. The process must inevitably leave out many of the most prominent and treasured features of *each* religious belief in order to state what is common to *all* of them—hence the disappointment. At the same time, the only definition I know that really covers every sort of religious belief also results in many beliefs' turning out to be religious that are not popularly thought to be—hence the surprise. Yet neither the surprise nor the disappointment is, all by itself, a good objection to this definition. The issue is only whether the essential core of what is being defined has been identified correctly. So please remember that we're not now trying to define religion as a whole, nor are we yet addressing the question of how to tell which religious belief is true. For now, we are only trying to *distinguish* religious belief from nonreligious belief.

OK. I've buckled my seat belt. So what exactly is wrong with popular ideas about religious belief?

One of the most widespread ideas about religious belief takes it to be the same as belief in God or a supreme being. Many people even suspect that all religions actually believe in the same supreme being under different names. This idea seems plausible in Europe and North America because the three most widely held religions on those continents—Judaism, Christianity and Islam—all believe in one God who created the universe (though they have different beliefs about how to stand in the right relation to God so as to obtain his favor). In other words, this definition would be quite right if these three were the only possible religions. But that is far from being the case.

Many religions are polytheistic, which means that they believe in many gods and goddesses. Some of these religions do not recognize any one god as supreme. If belief in a supreme being were the right definition of all religious belief, we would have to say that such a polytheism is not a religious belief at all. Still other religions are literally atheistic and do not believe in any gods. Brahmin Hinduism and Theravada Buddhism are examples.[2] According to Brahmin theology, the gods of popular Hindu worship and practice are but mythological ways of thinking that accommodate religious truth to the level of the average person. The divine, called Brahman-Atman, is not a person or even an individual being. It is rather being-itself, which alone is real, in contrast to our everyday world, which is an illusion. Teachings such as these show that religious belief cannot be defined as belief in a supreme being. If it were, Brahmin Hinduism, Theravada Buddhism and polytheisms with no supreme god would all be ruled out as religious beliefs. So I reject this definition as too narrow.

Interesting! I know the U.S. Supreme Court has ruled more than once that U.S. laws do assume the existence of "a Supreme Being," although there is no official religion in the United States. So that ruling actually doesn't allow for complete religious freedom?

I'm afraid it doesn't. It's biased toward Jews, Christians and Muslims.

Another widely accepted idea holds that religious belief is any belief that induces or supports worship or worship-related rituals. But insisting on worship in the definition is also defeated by the counterexamples of Brahmin Hinduism and the Theravada form of Buddhism, since neither practices worship. Nor are they the only counterexamples. The ancient Greek philosopher Aristotle believed in a being he called both the "prime mover" and "god." But he also held that this god neither knows nor cares about humans, so he neither advocated worship of that god nor engaged in it. Similarly, his later compatriots the Epicureans believed in many gods but never worshiped them for the same reason; the gods, they thought, neither know nor care about humans. So the trouble with making inducement of worship the defining feature of a religious belief is that there are forms of two major world religions that lack worship, as well as other cases in which belief in gods also lacked worship.[3]

But if the beliefs central to those forms of Hinduism and Buddhism are not religious beliefs, what are they? And why should we suppose that Aristotle's and Epicurus's beliefs in gods were not religious beliefs when they themselves thought they were? It seems clear that belief in a god must count as a religious belief. So I'm going to insist that any definition that makes belief in a god turn out to be nonreligious is implausible.

What happens if we don't concentrate narrowly on worship but look instead for whether a belief induces rituals of all kinds?

That sounds more promising but still leads to a dead end because there are a lot of rituals that are not religious. Think, for example, of swearing-in ceremonies, graduations, inductions into clubs, national anniversaries and even birthday celebrations. All involve ritual. Gathering around a cake with candles on it and singing "Happy Birthday" is surely a ritual, but not a religious one. If there were a specific list of rituals that accompanied only religious beliefs, this might work. But there's a long list of activities that are at times religious but at other times not: burning down a house, setting off fireworks, fasting, feasting, having sexual intercourse, singing, chanting, cutting oneself, circumcising an infant, covering the body with manure, washing, killing an animal, killing a human being, eating bread and wine, shaving the head and many more. It seems clear that the only way to characterize certain rituals as religious and others as nonreligious is to determine what those who take part in them *believe* about them. Without that, even an act of prayer can't be distinguished from fantasizing or talking to oneself. This is why we need to know whether the beliefs that motivated the ritual actions were religious in order to know whether the actions were. And it's also why we'd be trapped in a vicious circle if we tried to determine which beliefs are religious by looking at the rituals to which they give rise.

But suppose we expand our idea of what must accompany a belief to make it religious. Suppose we include an ethical code as well as either worship or ritual. Wouldn't that work?

There can be no question that most religious traditions actually include those things. The question is whether such accompaniments *make* a belief religious. I think the examples of Aristotle and Epicurus already show that the answer is no, since those thinkers never connected any ethical teachings to their belief in the prime mover or the gods. Nor are those the only examples. Ancient Roman religion had no moral code or ethical teachings connected to its belief in the gods, and neither does the Shinto tradition. So the resulting definition still looks too narrow.

By the way, depending on just what sort of relation to ethics is supposed to render a belief religious, this definition can also be too broad. Surely there are many beliefs that are clearly not religious but are importantly connected to ethical teachings. Many clubs and other organizations have a code of behavior as well as rituals (think of the Boy Scouts), and even some criminal enterprises have both initiation rituals and an unwritten code of "honor among thieves." But these don't make a criminal's acceptance of the purposes and code of his organization an article of religious belief.

I must admit that I'm surprised at how badly these ideas have turned out. But none of these objections defeats another idea I've read about. Some scholars think the most plausible proposal is that a religious belief is whatever a person believes to be of supreme or highest value. Is there anything wrong with that?

Yes, there is. This definition appears more plausible than it really is due to the way we sometimes speak of peoples' obsessions as their "religion." For example, we say that golf is a golf fanatic's religion or that a workaholic's career is his religion. But just because such expressions have value as metaphors doesn't mean that they can provide a definition. It's true that there are ways in which someone's love of golf or career can be *like* the devotion and fervor of saints or prophets, but that won't make it true that whatever people value most is their religious belief. And there are good reasons to suppose this is not true.

For starters, we can notice that there are polytheistic traditions whose gods are counterexamples to this definition because they are little valued or even hated. If belief in these gods is religious belief, then this definition can't be right.

Christianity provides another counterexample. To be sure, what a person values most figures importantly in Christian teaching. A Christian is one who believes that God's favor is to be valued above all else. Jesus himself said that a person's highest value should be the kingdom of God and the righteousness God offers to those who believe in him (Mt 6:33). Therein lies the difficulty, however. Belief in God is belief in a divine personal being, not in a value. Belief in God is neither itself a value nor the belief in a value, but the *basis* for the proper ordering of all values. Unless a person already believed in God's existence and in the faithfulness of his covenant promises, that person could not possibly value God's favor and kingdom above all else. As the New Testament says, to properly approach God one must believe that he exists and rewards those who seek him (Heb 11:6). The belief that God is real and his promises trustworthy is thus the precondition for valuing God's favor above all else. To put the same point another way: God's favor is to be valued above all just *because* God is the divine Creator on whom humans and their destiny depend. So belief in God is not religious because of what a Christian values most; rather, what a Christian values most *is a result of* believing in God. For that very reason the belief in God and the valuing that results from that belief cannot be identical.

This is not to deny that what people value most can often be an indicator of what they believe to be divine. But the fact that a person's highest value can reflect his or her religious belief does not mean that it always does, let alone that the belief can be *defined* that way.[4]

I see what you're saying. But it still seems to me that there's a sense in which a believer can be said to be valuing God, not just the right relation to God. We do really value other humans, don't we? I know I value my wife, for example.

OK. But in that case I'm going to say that "value" is too weak to describe the believer's relation to God. Remember, belief *in* God is much more than belief *that* God exists. Belief in God is a wholehearted love for God that commits the believer's entire being to God in unconditional trust. That's not simply a value. It goes beyond all valuing and is different from valuing our loved ones. In the case of valuing people, the valuing is still a combination of appreciation and preference. But God is never just a preference, not even the one that outranks all others. The commandment to have no other gods "before" the Lord doesn't mean "have nothing ahead of God on your list of other gods and values." In Scripture, the term "before" signifies a covenant relation between God and his people: to "swear before the Lord" or "eat a meal before the Lord" means to ratify or reaffirm unconditional trust in God's covenant promises.

Look, maybe we're on a wild-goose chase here! If religious belief can't be defined as belief in a god or a supreme being, as belief that induces worship or ritual, sanctions ethics or concerns what is valued most highly, what can possibly work? There are such wide differences among religious beliefs that I don't see any way to pick out something they, and only they, all share. Perhaps religious belief can't be defined this way at all, and we should try some other sort of definition to delimit it.

That suggestion puts you in distinguished company! In recent years a number of scholars have tossed in the towel, giving up on any essential definition of religion at all.[5] They were attempting a slightly different task, of course, since we're concerned only with religious *belief* and not with religion as a whole. Yet their conclusion—that religions have only family resemblances—is one they would surely apply to our quest too. And its easy to see why they feel driven to say that.

Suppose, for example, we were to reply to them that every religious tradition regards something or other as divine. That seems true enough but is not very enlightening; it simply shifts the problem to defining the term "divine." How, they would ask, can we find a common element among the ideas of divinity, even if we confine that search only to the major world traditions of the present? What common element can be found in the biblical idea of God in Judaism, Christianity and Islam, in the Hindu idea of Brahman-Atman, in the idea of Dharmakaya in Mahayana Buddhism, and the idea of the Tao of Taoism? To isolate a common element among just those few seems daunting enough, but if we could do it we would then also have to be able to discover that same common element in all the other ideas of divinity: those of ancient Egypt, Babylon, Palestine, and Greece; the divinities of China and Japan, of the Pacific islands, of Australia, of the Druids, and of the tribes of Africa and North and South America. So, they would ask, isn't it painfully obvious that there is no common feature to the divinities of all these traditions, and no single belief they share in common?

Part of this point I agree with. If we look for a common element in what each tradition regards as divine, then it's true that the natures of those divinities are so diverse as to have no feature in common. But I now want to suggest there is another way to go at the matter, a way that succeeds in finding something common to all religions. Suppose that instead of looking for common features among the *natures* of all the various putative divinities, we were to seek the common denominator in the *status* of divinity itself.

Since this seems to be an important point for you, I want to be sure I'm understanding it. Can you be a bit more precise about the difference you're pointing to?

The difference between these two approaches is like the difference between two possible ways we could answer someone visiting the United

States who asks, "Who is the president of this country?" We could answer by naming the person who holds that office, then going on to describe that person by giving the president's sex, height, build, political affiliation and other distinguishing features. Or we could answer by describing the responsibilities, powers and limitations of the office of the presidency. The difference is important. Even if an election were in dispute so that people did not agree on *who* is really president, they would still agree on *what it means to be the president.* In a parallel way, it is possible that although the ideas of *what* is divine are so diverse as to have no common element, there could still be common agreement among all religions as to *what it means to be divine.* If this were the case, the disagreements among religious beliefs would be disagreements about who or what has divine status; they would all still agree about what it means for anything to have that status.[6]

Now this is exactly what I find to be the case. In all my reading and study I have never found a single exception to this: *In every religious tradition the divine is whatever is unconditionally, nondependently real.* It is whatever is believed to be "just there." By contrast, everything nondivine ultimately depends for existence on (at least some part of) whatever is believed to be divine.

Please do not misunderstand this point. I am not saying that there are no disagreements whatever about what having divine status means. There are. But although there are disagreements over what *else* may also be true of divine status, all ideas of it include nondependence. Nor am I saying that every myth or body of teachings has used the expression "nondependence" or its equivalent. Some trace everything nondivine back to an original something, the status of which is not emphasized or not explained. But in such accounts that original something is still spoken of as though it has independent reality; there is nothing that it is said to depend on. Thus, at the very least, that reality is tacitly given nondependent status; it is nondependent so far as the teaching goes.

Does this definition really cover every known religion, though? It sounds plausible, but so did the others till a few minutes ago.

It seems to me that it does succeed. For openers, it can locate a common element among beliefs in the biblical God, Brahman-Atman, the Dharmakaya and the Tao, which was the brief list that appeared so daunting just now. Moreover, it also covers such conceptions of the divine as Nam in Sikhism, Ahura Mazda (Ohrmazd) in early Zoroastrianism or Zurvan in its later development, the soul-matter dualism of the Jains, the high god in the myths of the Dieri aborigines, the belief in Mana among the Trobriand islanders, Kami in the Shinto tradition, the Raluvhimba of Bantu religion, and the idea of Wakan or Orenda found among various Native American tribes. It also holds for the ancient Roman idea of Numen, and for Chaos or Okeanos found in the myths of Hesiod and Homer.

I can't, of course, claim to know about every religion that ever existed or to know that there's no religion yet to be discovered that doesn't have this idea of divine status. But I can say that no idea of divinity I have ever come across fails to regard the divine as the nondependent reality all else depends on.

Your proposal is clear enough and seems plausible. But as I said, so did several other definitions until a few minutes ago. Can this one really stand up to criticism?

I believe it can. For one thing, it simply avoids the sorts of difficulties we found with the other definitions (which is perhaps the reason it keeps getting rediscovered).[7] More than that, it both covers and helps clarify some of the most important differences and unique features of various religious beliefs.

For example, it is well-known that in Judaism, Christianity and Islam there is but one God who is the only divine reality, so that God and divinity are identical. In these traditions everything other than God is creation, and the creation is not divine. By contrast, however, many religions believe there to be a difference between divinity per se and the gods. They believe in a divine reality that is the source of the gods and goddesses as well as of humans and the rest of the nondivine world; for them every nondivine thing is partly divine. The ancient Greek and Roman myths are examples of this. Hesiod and Homer called this divine reality Chaos or Okeanos, whereas it was called Numen in ancient Roman religion. And there are similar beliefs in many other polytheisms, both ancient and contemporary.

This explains why the gods of these religions do not fit the definition just given for "divine." The gods of these traditions are called divine only in the sense that they have more divine power than humans have; they do not have unconditional existence. Their religious importance lies in their superhuman powers and in their being the ones through whom humans can approach and relate to divinity.

This definition also sheds light on why it is that in certain polytheisms where there is more than one divinity or god, and where the divine and the gods are not identical, there are idle or evil divinities or gods: ones that have no important relation to human affairs or are malevolent.[8] Some scholars have puzzled over how belief in such divinities or gods could persist despite the fact that they aren't valued and aren't thought to do anything good for those who believe in their existence. The definition makes it clear why such belief is possible. It is not beneficence or usefulness to humans that is the defining characteristic of divinity or of a god, but nondependence that characterizes divinity and greater participation in divine power that characterizes a god. Thus the definition allows for the possibility that either a divine principle or a god can be one on which nothing, or nothing important to humans, depends. The significance of this point is that it is a confirming feature of our definition that is able to allow for, and make sense of, the fact that idle divinities or gods occur in certain teachings.

Yet another feature of the different conceptions of the divine that this definition accounts for is the large variety of ways the nondivine can be thought to depend on the divine.[9] For example, there are religions that believe in two or more divine principles and understand every nondivine thing as partially dependent on both divinities simultaneously. By contrast, others hold that one range of nondivine things depends on the first divinity while another range of nondivine things depends on the second divinity. Still other religions believe in a whole realm of divine beings, thus increasing the number of ways these can be thought to relate to one another and to the nondivine world—including that some of them are idle with respect to humans.

So it appears that this definition not only isolates a common element in all ideas of divinity but also allows for the great diversity of ways the nondivine is thought to depend on the divine.

No doubt belief in divinity is crucial to religion, but you now seem to have made it everything! Even if worship and ethics and values can't define religious belief, surely they shouldn't be left out altogether. Aren't such beliefs also religious in some sense—at least when attached to belief in a divinity?

Absolutely! We've already noticed there's more to religious belief than just holding something or other to be divine. I alluded earlier to beliefs about *how to stand in proper relation to the divine* as religious. So the full statement of my definition is as follows: A belief is religious provided that it is (1) a belief in something as divine or (2) a belief about how to stand in proper relation to the divine, where (3) something is believed to be divine provided it is held to be unconditionally nondependent.

Perhaps this helps make clear the main problem with the popular definitions of religious belief that I found to be faulty: they focus almost entirely on the second part of the definition. In a way that's understandable since those are the most obvious, public features of religious traditions: their creeds, rites, rituals, holy days, meditations, pilgrimages, codes of behavior and range of values. Important as these are, however, they are not the most fundamental aspects of religious belief or practice. They are secondary for the purpose of definition. What is fundamental is identifying what is divine, since every belief about how to stand in proper relation to the divine is determined by what is taken to be divine and how the nondivine depends on it.

OK, so you allow that beliefs about the right way to relate to the divine are also religious. This still seems to demote them somehow in a way that doesn't sound plausible. After all, doesn't the word "religion" literally mean "reconnection"? Isn't it essential, then, that religious belief be about the human connection to the divine? And doesn't the whole business have to be more personal than you're making it?

Oh, I see what's bothering you. You are thinking more of actual, personal religious belief and practice than of the task of defining it. In that case you're right on target. I didn't mean to say that the proper relation to the divine is secondary in actual lived belief and practice, but only for the purpose of definition. And our relation to the divine is *never* without personal importance. Let me try to clear that up.

Identifying the unconditional nondependent reality is never just a matter of intellectual curiosity. Human beings cannot help but want to know about that on which everything depends, since that includes us. For the same reason, the divine is also what determines our destiny—however that is conceived. What's more, our idea of the divine strongly influences the view we take of human nature and that, in turn, influences what we believe about values and many other issues ranging over the entirety of our experience. For these reasons, a belief in something as divine is intensely personal. We can't help but think of our relation to it in ways that far exceed mere dependence.

This side of religious belief is no less important than identifying the divine. In order to get a definition, we needed to distinguish belief in something as divine from beliefs about how to relate properly to it so as to see that the idea of the divine is logically basic to ideas about how to relate to it. But distinguishing these two points in thought is not the same as *separating* them in practice. From the standpoint of religious experience, belief and practice, the idea of the divine is always encountered embedded in a context of teachings about how to relate to the divine. Both are grasped simultaneously; they are intertwined and inseparable. So although it is true that (1) the divine is whatever is basic to the existence of the rest of reality and (2) belief in something as divine is logically basic to beliefs about how we *should* relate to the divine over and above dependence, it is also true that (3) a belief in divinity is almost always acquired in conjunction with, and remains embedded in, beliefs about how to relate to it. As far as actual experience and belief are concerned, these are equally important.

Plausible as all that sounds, there is an objection that seems more plausible. It's the very one you mentioned earlier: the definition makes beliefs that are not religious into religious beliefs, so it's too broad.

For example, I know of a number of theories in philosophy and the sciences that assert or assume something as nondependent. Matter, for example. But surely belief in the nondependence of matter is not a religious belief, so your definition is too broad. If you try to say that it is a religious belief, then what difference is left between religion, philosophy and science?

I am indeed saying that such beliefs are religious regardless of what is regarded as divine and regardless of the context in which they occur. To see why this is so, let's consider your example of materialism and use the teachings of Epicurus as our example. For Epicurus there is a distinction between the divine, which has independent reality, and what he called gods. In his theory, only atoms of matter (and space) are self-existent; all things other than atoms are combinations of them. This includes the human soul and the gods; they too are combinations of atoms.

You seem to be willing to concede that this theory gives matter the same status that is called "divine" in religions, but you want to say that it's not a religious teaching despite that fact. Have I got you right?

Exactly! I want to say that beliefs in something as nondependent are only religious when they're accompanied by other beliefs about how to relate properly to what is nondependent.

In that case it's important to notice why even Epicurus's theory could not avoid beliefs about how humans should relate to the divine. The most important element in the relation was, of course, simply to *know* that matter is divine. That knowledge then served as a guiding presupposition to Epicurus's view of human nature, destiny, values and ethics, since he clearly believed that human happiness depended on that knowledge. In all these respects his teaching exactly mirrors religious traditions.

The same is true of modern materialisms, not just Epicurus' version. Most people think that being a materialist is the reverse of being religious. But why think that? Every materialism asserts a belief about what has independent existence.[10] It's just a *different* idea of divinity from the ideas held by a Christian, a Hindu or a Shintoist. Materialism also delimits a distinctive range of acceptable conceptions of human nature, of destiny and of what can or can't be done to improve the human condition. And it includes an idea of human happiness. At the very least it prescribes that all other conceptions of the divine are to be rejected as false and that people will be better off knowing that to be the truth. In other words, the secondary beliefs that religions emphasize (and which you say make a divinity belief religious) can't be utterly absent from any belief in divinity, even one that occurs in a theory. So even on the view you're defending, there is no denying the religious character of materialism's belief that matter is nondependent. It's not religious only if its adherents sing hymns to force fields or offer prayers to quarks. It's religious both because it regards matter as nondependent and because that belief implies other beliefs about human nature, happiness, values and destiny.[11] Needless to say, these implications are highly personal and so are like the secondary beliefs found in cultic traditions.

Can't we strip away the personal stuff if we just try harder? Why can't we just drop every idea of human destiny, for example?

Maybe materialists of the past were too influenced by the religions of their culture and allowed their theories to be larded with religious trappings. Even if that has persisted into the present day, it doesn't have to be unavoidable.

How will you strip away all the implications for human destiny? Doesn't materialism require that when we die we rot and that is the end of us? Isn't that just as much a conception of human destiny as the Hindu belief in nirvana or the Christian belief in the resurrection of the body? It's just a *different* idea of human destiny. The same goes for ethics or the idea of happiness. Doesn't materialism require either that there are no distinctly ethical properties and laws or that they all have a physical basis? Doesn't that make a difference to one's ethical beliefs? And doesn't materialism require a view of happiness that is very different from a view derived from beliefs based on nonmaterialist ideas of what is divine?

This is really weird! I've always thought of materialism as the reverse of religion. Now you're saying it is *one!*

It should be clear by now that thinking of atheism and materialism as the reverse of religion is narrowly culture bound. It reflects the fact that the religions you are most familiar with denounce materialism. But the truth is that there have long been religions in which matter is believed to be divine. Some of the Greek mystery religions, for example, referred to the divine as the "everflowing stream of life and matter." There is still a branch of Hinduism that regards Brahman-Atman as matter.

But then is there no difference at all between a theory and a religion? This almost sounds as though everything is religion!

I'm not saying that everything is religion or that there's no difference between a religion and a philosophical theory. Beliefs in divinity occur in both. But such beliefs are used differently in theories than they are in cultic religious traditions. In theories they form the basis for constructing *explanations;* they become the basic assumptions guiding the formation of hypotheses. Religious traditions, by contrast, emphasize the actual acquisition of the proper relation to the divine in order to obtain present happiness and/or an ultimate destiny not otherwise obtainable. That is an enormous difference which is not canceled by the fact that belief in a divinity doesn't lose its religious character when it occurs in a theory.

Perhaps this all looks more convincing than it should. Maybe the theories you picked as illustrations fit your definition better than others would have.

Why think that? I started with materialism just because it seemed to you, as it does to most people, to be the great counterexample to my definition.

All I can add here is something parallel to what I said about religions. I said I couldn't claim to have read about every single religion that ever existed but that in all my years of study I've not come across one that lacks a central belief in something divine. Likewise, although I can't claim to have read every theory of reality ever written, I've yet to come across one in which a belief in something as divine doesn't play a pivotal role in guiding the hypotheses that get constructed, adopted or rejected. What's more, I can't imagine how any theory of reality could possibly avoid such a belief insofar as they all try to identify the basic nature of reality.

But surely most theories don't try to do anything as esoteric as "identify the basic nature of reality." Maybe I'm more upset about this point than I really need to be; maybe all you've shown is that one small set of (strange) philosophical theories may have an involvement with religious belief in an obscure way!

It's true that most theories don't explicitly concern themselves with the basic nature of reality. Some even go out of their way to avoid anything that even sounds like that—especially anything that could be construed as a teaching about what is nondependent. Nevertheless, despite the intentions of their backers, those theories can't avoid *presupposing* something as having divine status, even if they never mention what it is. Suppose a theory uses a certain kind of facts and laws to explain everything else, while saying nothing about the status of those explainers. Then that theory would be a counterpart to the myths that fail to explain the precise status of what they say all else depends on, and the same point made about those myths would apply to the theory: whatever is presented as the explanation of all else is tacitly being given divine status. Just as in the case of those myths, so far as the theory tells us its explanatory principles don't depend on anything whatever.

Besides, the most influential philosophical theories have been very explicit about their candidates for divine status. A list of just a few of their more famous candidates would include numbers, space, space/time and energy, space and matter, matter alone, forms and matter, souls (or minds) and material bodies, sensations, logical laws plus matter, monads and logical categories plus sensations. What is more, a great many scientific theories also presuppose one or another of them. So the point I'm making has very far-reaching consequences. To the extent that any theory presupposes a view of the nature of reality, it would thereby also be presupposing some religious belief! This would hold not only for the physical sciences but also for theories arising in other fields, for example, mathematics, politics, law, psychology and sociology.[12] Once again, these theories would not thereby be *religions* any more than theories of reality are. But they are unavoidably and importantly influenced by some religious belief.

Your admission that your definition would have surprising and disappointing results was an understatement. I find this to be downright offensive. Instead of the theories of philosophy and the sciences being able to help us judge religious beliefs, you expect me to accept that theories are themselves controlled by religion!

No matter how surprising or disconcerting this result may be, it doesn't show the definition to be mistaken. Remember that it has been derived from an enormous empirical base including every major world religion of the present, a great many influential religions of the past, and tribal myths from all over the globe, both past and present. It includes doctrines that have been given an extensive theological elaboration, those that are embodied in simple myths or stories and those that are both. It can't claim to be based on my having canvassed every religion, of course, as I already admitted. But then it is rare that any definition can claim to have canvassed every instance of the type of things being defined, and no one supposes that we don't have a good definition of trees just because we haven't seen every tree.

What is more, the definition appears to have identified the only element that is common to religious beliefs; if that is correct, it is then the only feature that *could* define them. And the common element I've identified is not an oddity at the fringe of religious belief and practice, but is central to each *in the view of each*.

But simply being true of all religious beliefs is not enough to show it isn't also true of nonreligious ones, and that's what is at stake here. Surely this definition is too broad when it forces nonreligious beliefs to be religious.

Remember, the definition can justly be accused of being too broad only if it covers beliefs that are *clearly* not religious.[13] So I ask: is it really clear that the beliefs in something as nondependent that occur in theories are not religious? You suggested yourself that regarding something as divine would be truly religious only if it were conjoined with beliefs about how to stand in proper relation to the divine, beliefs that were personal and implied a way of life. But surely that's true of beliefs in divinity when they occur in theories. They unavoidably imply beliefs about human nature, destiny, ethics and values. So what reason can there be for insisting that they aren't religious just because they occur in theories?

Isn't this objection a holdover from one of the popular views of religion? Or isn't it based on the assumption that there must be a specific set of ideas or practices about how to relate to the divine that are the only truly religious ones? We've already seen why that can't be right: there's no limit to which ideas or practices can be religious.

This sounds to me like a great slander on the neutrality and reliability of science. It's bad enough to say that philosophical theories can't avoid religious assumptions, but to extend that to science is intolerable!

What you're saying now sounds like the objection that whales just *couldn't* have more in common with humans than with fish because it's disappointing or offensive to think so.

No, my reaction is not just emotional. There's still something about this definition that bothers me a lot—even aside from its consequences for theories. But I'm having a hard time putting my finger on what it is.

While you try to think of it, consider one more point in favor of my case that the definition isn't too broad. Any belief in divinity advocated or presupposed by a theory is the logical denial of every contrary belief, no matter what the context in which the others occur. How, then, could any such belief fail to have genuinely religious import? If any one is true, then every other one that disagrees with it is false. It wouldn't matter whether the others occur in cultic religious traditions or not. The others would all be alternative, competing religious beliefs. Denying this is like claiming you alone speak with no accent: just as having an accent is any difference in diction, having a distinctive view about what is nondependent is having a different religious belief.

I'm now going to try to come at this from a different angle. I'm going to say that it's not consistent with the biblical teaching about God. After all, it's belief in God that we're ultimately concerned with here, so this is an important issue: Is it really part of biblical teaching to say that God's being creator is basic to everything else it says of God?

I think it is. For example, when Moses asks God for his name—his self-identification—God tells him that it is Yahweh. The eminent archaeologist and biblical scholar William Albright said that the best translation of this is "the one who causes to be."[14] The prophet Isaiah makes the same point another way. He quotes God as saying, "I will not yield my glory to another" (Is 48:11 NIV). What is the glory that belongs to God alone? Isaiah answers the question in a passage that is well-known because it has become part of the Christian liturgy. Because it is so familiar, however, we need to notice that it has entered the liturgy in a translation that is not quite accurate. The familiar rendering is "Holy, holy, holy is the LORD God of hosts; the whole earth is full of His glory" (Is 6:3 NKJV). Translated more precisely, the last clause should read "the fulness of the whole earth is your glory."[15] In other words, the glory God will not share with any other is that he alone is the One who fills heaven and earth with creatures, the One on whom all else depends; attributing that status to any other is idolatry, says Isaiah, because it replaces God with a false divinity. (Of course, by the same token, from other points of view God would be the false replacement for Brahman-Atman, the Tao, Mana or Wakan, just as any of them could be viewed as false replacements for numbers, matter, space, sense data or logical forms.)

This same point is explicit in the New Testament when it says that all people either believe God to be the sole and true divinity on which all else depends or replace him with something from creation that they regard as divine in his stead (Rom 1). And the point is repeated with specific reference to the famous "four elements" of ancient Greek meta-physical theories (earth, air, fire, water) when it says that it is not these elements but God in Christ on which the entire cosmos depends (compare Gal 4:3, 8-9; Col 2:8).[16] The point is that any belief in something as nondependent has genuine religious significance, if only because it is an alternative to God. And finally, the New Testament explicitly says that God is worthy to receive glory and honor because God is the One by whose will all things exist and have been created (Rev 4:11).

This is really hard to take. It makes something I find repugnant pervade human experience—even down to corrupting theories of science.

I realize that many people have such a strong antipathy to the whole subject that there is nothing that would ever convince them to accept a definition that entails this sort of importance for it. A fellow graduate student once said to me, "Show me that any belief I have is religious in any sense and I'll give it up on the spot." And a faculty colleague once commented that the only way religion should be taught is "with great hostility." It may surprise you to hear me say that there is a sense in which I sympathize with this attitude. The history of religious institutions has been such an abysmal panorama of bigotry, persecution and cruelty that I can see why it could lead someone to wish to be rid of the whole business.

But as much as I can sympathize with those reasons, they do not count against the definition. Failing to acknowledge the power and pervasive-ness of religious belief will hinder and not help the restraint of its worst consequences. Please bear in mind that the definition defended here does not seek to praise religious belief as something good in itself; it only recognizes it for what it *is*. Some of the worst evils plaguing the human race derive from distorted or fanatical religious belief, but these cannot be corrected by pretending to avoid it altogether.

Wait a minute! If this is right, wouldn't you then have to say that everyone who holds a theory that assumes a divinity belief is therefore a religious person? You can't want to say that! So surely your definition is too broad in at least this way.

What's more, if you try to escape this by biting the bullet and accepting that result, then you're going to end up with nothing more than a cheap trick that tries to make everybody religious overnight merely by definition! But who can really believe that everyone has become religious just by rearranging words on a page?

The definition does not perform the magic trick of making everyone religious in the sense you mean. There are indeed many people who completely reject the dominant religion(s) of their time and place. They adhere to no community, practice no worship or other rites and may have no conscious, fervent commitment about what is divine or about how to relate to the divinity. So they are not "religious" in the sense you're placing in opposition to my definition. You're using it to describe a person who has a conscious conviction about what is divine and joins others in adhering to a tradition that cultivates a life of devotion to the divine. There certainly are many people not like that. But that doesn't show that the people who are nonreligious in your sense are nonreligious in the minimal sense I'm pointing to. To be utterly nonreligious in my sense a person would have to lack even an unconscious, vague notion of what everything depends on. I think all people are religious only in the minimal sense of having some such belief.

Maybe what I pointed to doesn't show that there are people who don't have any such belief, but nothing you've said shows they all do. Aren't there many people who just never think about this issue at all? Isn't it true that there are even scientists and philosophers who, if you ask them what they think everything depends on, would honestly answer that they haven't a clue?

That's quite true. I was trying to acknowledge that point when I said that such beliefs could be unconscious assumptions as well as fervent convictions, and vague ideas as well as precise concepts.[17] What I meant was that many people's beliefs as to what has divine status are very imprecise. They locate the divine in a certain "region" of their experience without ever sharply formulating that belief. For example, they may have a vague sense that what everything depends on is roughly spatial/physical, or is something like a mind, or is the universe as a whole. And they can do this without even articulating these ideas to themselves, let alone trying to refine them into sharply drawn concepts.

In theories that make explicit what is taken to be divine, on the other hand, great care is usually taken to elaborate the idea of divinity as sharply as possible. Often that takes the form of a hypothesis about how best to conceive it (a fact that has misled many thinkers into supposing that beliefs in divinity are always theories and therefore to be evaluated as such). So it is important to notice that even where a precise concept of divinity really is a hypothesis, the vague sense of divinity it tries to refine is not. For example, a materialist may be ever so tentative about how to conceive of exactly which physical entities have divine status but will not budge from the conviction that it is something physical that has that status, however it is to be conceived!

If we keep these distinctions in mind, then it seems to me quite plausible that everyone has some divinity belief. This is especially so if my point is right about theories presupposing something as divine. Virtually everybody believes theories on a wide variety of topics: the proper role of government, how to raise children, whether a particular behavior should be illegal and what sort of education is best, for example. It's hard to see how any of these could avoid assuming some view of reality, and it's hard to see how any view of reality could avoid assuming something as nondependent. If that's right, then it's another reason to think that everyone has some religious belief, whether consciously held or not, and that the only plausible candidates for people *totally* without religious belief would be those who hold no theory whatever.

But let's not get bogged down on this point. It's not essential to what I want to say right now about religious belief that you agree that everybody has one. We can come back to this later.

While you were answering my last question, I finally put my finger on what it is that's been bothering me about your claim that all beliefs in independent reality are religious, even when they occur in theories. And it's a decisive objection!

Even if it's true that belief in an independent reality is central to religion and occurs in theories, and even if such beliefs have implications for the whole of life both in religious traditions and in theories, it still won't follow that the belief is religious in both cases. I can concede your definition of divinity and still maintain that when such a belief occurs in a theory it isn't religious, since in a theory it's justified by reasons and arguments, whereas in religion it's taken on faith. So even the same idea of divinity—say, that it's matter—would be religious if taken on faith but not if supported by rational arguments and evidence. In that case all you were saying about the theory of Epicurus, about materialism, and about theories of reality and the scientific theories that presuppose them is defeated!

This is perhaps the best objection to my position, and I want to do it justice. As a result, my reply will have to have several parts, so we can only start it here. In fact, the full answer is going to extend throughout the rest of our discussions.

To begin with, let me remind you that philosophers and scientists aren't the only ones who have given arguments for their beliefs about what everything depends on; religious writers and theologians have done that too. Do you really want to say that if someone were to defend his or her belief in God with an argument, then that belief would thereby become nonreligious? If so, that would mean that all the Jews, Christians and Muslims who ever accepted an argument for their belief have thereby rendered their belief in God nonreligious! Does that make any sense? And if you say it does, then notice your position also requires that those people are therefore not really *religious* Jews, Christians or Muslims. Is that even plausible? I think not.

That aside, there are powerful reasons to doubt that any divinity belief can ever really be justified by evidence and argument. These reasons show that in fact people don't have good arguments for their divinity beliefs, although they may think they do. If this is right, then either (1) every such belief that ever occurred in a theory is a sheer mistake or blind faith or (2) there's some other ground for them. Since I started today by saying I think divinity beliefs are grounded in religious experience, it won't surprise you to hear that I don't think they're all sheer mistakes or blind faith. Their real ground is experience, whether or not arguments are appended to that experience. So the reasons I'm about to sketch briefly are intended to support that position by showing you why its alternative is wrong—why divinity beliefs can't be justified by reasons and arguments.

The first of these goes back to what I had been saying about the way theories presuppose some such belief. This was easy to show for theories of reality, but I went on to argue that other theories—including those of the sciences—do this too. The position I took was that the influence of religious belief extends to these other theories indirectly: theories of reality either explicitly assert or tacitly assume that something is divine, whereas other theories presuppose some view of reality. In this way religious belief directly impacts theories of reality and indirectly impacts the other theories through whatever view of reality they assume.

I now want to apply that same point to theories of knowledge. There are many views of what counts as knowledge, and the differences between them lead to competing views of what it means to justify a belief. They disagree about the kinds of premises they regard as basic, as well as about what argument procedures they accept as convincing. The crucial point about these differences is that they appear to derive from assumptions about the nature of reality.[18] In other words, what you see as divine guides your view of reality, and the view of reality you take makes a crucial difference to the view of knowledge you subscribe to. At the same time, your view of knowledge includes standards for what counts as rationally justifying a belief! The upshot is that attempts to justify a belief about what it is that has nondependent reality will be circular; they will subtly assume what they are trying to prove.

My second argument has to do with the process by which theorists have arrived at the various candidates for divinity that have been defended by most theories. The slate of these candidates is usually acquired by abstracting them from our everyday experience. That is, we find the objects of experience to exhibit quantitative, spatial, kinematic, physical, biotic, sensory, logical and other kinds of properties. And we find that each kind of property exhibits orderliness, which we call its laws. Theories of reality all single out some one (or combination) of these kinds of properties and laws, and select it (them) as the nature of the independent reality everything else depends on.

Now there is a powerful reason for rejecting the possibility that *any* such selection can be justified. The reason takes the form of a thought experiment. This means that in order to grasp the argument you actually have to perform the experiment, and to perform the experiment you have to try to think of something. In this case the something is the theory's divinity belief.

Let me see if I've got this right. The experiment is to try to think of whatever a theory says has independent reality as though it really does. Is that it?

Exactly. We're going to try to conceive of these kinds of properties and laws in isolation from all the other kinds because the theories claim they exist (or could exist) that way. If a theory claims that candidate X can exist apart from everything else, we're going to see if we can think of X apart from everything else. Fair enough?

I guess so. But where will that get us? I mean, suppose we can't? So what?

Well, if it turns out you can't—that you can't even conceive of one candidate apart from all the other candidates—then that's a powerful reason to think you can't give an argument in favor of thinking it really is independent of the others. How are you going to produce an argument to show something is a fact when you can't even conceive of the alleged fact? How can you produce evidence for a belief you literally can't conceive?

I think I get it, but I'm not sure. How about an easy example?

OK. Let's take Plato's quest to find what he calls "justice in itself." He says he's not trying to find out which acts or people possess the quality of justice, but what that quality is apart from anything that has it and apart from all other qualities. Try the experiment on that. Can you conceive any meaning for "justice" when that idea is divorced from all other kinds of properties? Think of justice; and then strip away everything having to do with number, space, matter/energy, biotic life, sensation/feeling, logic and social relations. What do you have left?

I've got nothing left. But what if I said I did? What would you say then?

I'd say that this argument would have no force for you, and we'd go on without it. The force of the argument lies in your own self-reflection. If you find you have nothing left to the idea of justice once it's stripped, it shows you really have no idea whatever of that quality in splendid isolation. Your idea is of justice *in relation* to other properties and laws. Therefore as far as you can ever know, that's the way justice is. You have no idea of it apart from everything else, so even if it could exist that way you could never know it.

OK, suppose that's right. How does it affect, say, materialism? Surely matter is more substantial than something as ethereal as justice.

Let's take materialism, then. If that theory is correct, either all reality is purely physical or all nonphysical realities depend on purely physical ones: physical reality is divine because it's entirely nondependent. Either it does exist without any other kinds of properties, or it could do so. That's the reason for enthroning it as divine.

But can we conceive of what it would mean for anything to be exclusively physical in complete isolation from all that is nonphysical? Try it. Do the same thing you did for "justice in itself." Try to form an idea of matter or energy as *purely* physical: subtract from your idea every element of quantity and spatiality, every property and law of sense perception and logic, everything of language and of social relationships. Now tell me: what do you have left?

Whenever I try this, I get literally nothing.

I got nothing too. But then how could I have anything left? Without logical and linguistic properties nothing can be so much as identified or named.

Exactly right. And that's why I get the same result no matter which of the traditional theories' candidates for divinity I test this way.

What, for example, is left of the idea of sense perception when it is deprived of all connection to number, space, matter and logic? What, indeed, is left of logic if there is nothing nonlogical to which it can apply? Even its famous axiom of noncontradiction says that nothing can both be true and false *at the same time in the same sense.* Thus it includes an essential reference both to time and to other "senses" (kinds of properties) to which it applies.

But you admit this doesn't show that reality couldn't actually be just physical or whatever. The experiment just shows we can't think of it that way.

Right. The experiment doesn't show that no theory's candidate for divinity could possibly be right. We weren't trying to see whether any of these ideas of divinity could be true, but whether any of them could be justified by argument. I think the experiment succeeds in undermining any way to argue for any of the candidates, even indirectly. Suppose, for instance, that instead of offering specific arguments that conclude with "X is what everything else depends on," a theory's backers argue that awarding divine status to X yields great explanatory advantages across the board. The trouble is that all the explanatory power they can point to will never demonstrate X's independence, since that explanatory power is derived from conceiving X as essentially related to all the other candidates rather than as isolated and independent of them![19]

This seems to destroy the neutral rationality of theories, so I'm not about to accept it on the spot! It's deeply disturbing, and I'll need to think about it.

Meanwhile, I'm afraid I've forgotten where we were going with all this. Remind me how we got into this experiment and why it's important.

Let's recap. We started by asking what religious experience is, and that led to finding a definition for religious belief. You objected that my definition of divinity is too broad because it would mean that (at least many) theories argue for or assume something as divine. So you suggested that belief in divinity is not religious when justified by arguments and evidence rather than taken on faith.

I pointed out that this would make clearly religious beliefs nonreligious, and then briefly sketched two arguments to show that no one can ever really justify a divinity belief with arguments and evidence. People may, of course, *think* they have this sort of justification for them, but they don't. And this opens the way to take more seriously the possibility that divinity beliefs are grounded in religious experience. Thus it's all the more important to examine that experience, as I intend to begin doing at our next meeting. It's all the more important because even though there are people who hold a religious belief on blind trust or wishful thinking, it's not plausible that all philosophers and scientists did so. That fact supports the likelihood that there's another source for these beliefs—at least as they occur in theories. In that case it's no longer reasonable to insist that divinity beliefs be proven, and it is unlikely that all theorists were engaged in blind trust or wishful thinking. Together these points strongly suggest that those beliefs have an experiential basis. But if that's so, there's no reason to suppose that *only* philosophers and scientists ground their belief about what is nondependent on experience.[20] There may be many people whose divinity belief is held in a traditional cultic setting but is equally grounded in experience.

OK, I'm back on track.

It's more than a little upsetting that you are able to put religious belief in general on a par with beliefs in divinity that occur in theories. I'm going to think about that between now and our next session. But I can tell you that I'm going to keep looking for some way to distinguish the two. I don't think religious belief at large is reliable, but I don't want to demote theories to being equally unreliable.

Before we quit for the day, let me add one more thing in favor of the view that religious belief is based on experience. The experiential view is better able to account for why religion has always been one of the most widespread and persistent features of human life. Humans everywhere and at all times have been drawn to the question of their origins, not just in the sense of *how* they originated (the processes that produced them) but in the sense of *what* it is they ultimately depend on. In fact I would say that, from its subjective side, religion is an innate impulse in humans to direct themselves to what they take to be that which everything else depends on, and to understand their own nature in light of whatever they take that to be.[21] So even without thinking up any arguments to justify these beliefs, people have in all times and places instinctively formed beliefs about what they, along with everything else, depend on. It is only within the last two hundred years that the idea has been entertained on a large scale that it is possible to be free of all religious belief and that people would be better off if they were. (The massive incoherency in that claim is that the arguments for it assume views of reality and human nature that presuppose something as nondependent and thus divine.)[22]

But why insist on calling all beliefs in anything as nondependent "religious"? Why not say that when they occur in theories they are "metaphysical" beliefs or some other less objectionable term? After all, you must admit that beliefs about what is nondependent that occur in theories have a different "feel" to them than those that occur in religious traditions.

Sure they do. That's because cultic traditions concentrate on showing believers how to stand in proper relation to the divine for their personal benefit, whereas theories concentrate on how to explain phenomena of all kinds by their relation to the divine. The difference, however, seems to me to be one of emphasis and not of exclusion, because theological doctrines also seek to explain, and philosophical theories also have implications for how we should live. I am not suggesting that everyone has a reli*gion* in the full sense of that word but only that people have at least one belief that is reli*gious* in an important sense.

Of course we could refer to divinity beliefs by some other name. If someone were determined not to admit having a belief that is religious in *any* sense whatever, there is nothing to stop such a person from calling a belief in ultimate reality "metaphysical" or from coining a new term for it. I'm not simply arguing for one word rather than another here. There's a sense in which it doesn't matter what you call such beliefs so long as you see that they are all contrary ideas of what it is that has unconditional reality and that identifying that reality is central to religious belief. In that case even if you insist that whatever you believe to be divine isn't religious for you, you'll have to admit that for those of us who hold such a belief and admit its religious character, your belief is going to appear to be religious for reasons that are far from arbitrary.

Moreover, there are reasons why I don't think "metaphysical" is a good term for these beliefs. First, because even when they occur in theories, they carry the same freight: implications for human nature, destiny, values, happiness and so on. Second, because it would give the impression that these beliefs are a result of making theories or that they arise in the context of theory making. That's not true. Beliefs about ultimate reality can be refined and sharpened in the context of a theory, but they arise in ordinary experience whether or not we engage in theories; they are *brought to* theory making, not derived from it. Beliefs about what is divine are not invented out of nothing in order to explain certain things we experience but are formed in response to whatever is experienced to be divine. Missing this point is what's wrong with the popular idea that religious belief arose because primitive people were puzzled about this or that and so invented religion out of the blue to explain their puzzlements. That's not even plausible.

No doubt ancient people did invent gods, but in order to think of specific beings as bearers of divine power those people would already have had to believe in the existence of a divine reality. In other words, inventing gods depends on prior religious belief, even if only of the vague type I mentioned earlier. The same is true about the relation of religious belief to theories. Belief in divinity is not the product of theorizing but is one of many beliefs we bring to that task. It guides theorizing as one of its unavoidable presuppositions, and the history of theories bears witness to that fact. (Surely there's no question which came first historically: humans have held beliefs about what is divine for over a hundred thousand years, whereas theories have only been around for the last twenty-seven centuries.)

In short, the fact that religious beliefs play a role in theories doesn't make them products of those theories. The belief there is a real world, the belief that other people have minds, and the belief in logical consistency also come up in theories but are not inventions of them. Like divinity beliefs, they are also *brought to* theory making from our pretheoretical experience. They are all beliefs everyone already had—and needed to have—in order to live in the world as well as to construct theories about the world.

I'm going to have to think about all this between now and our next discussion. Although I find your definition of religious experience unobjectionable, I'm still not convinced I should accept your definition of divinity. But since I can't think of a rebuttal right now, I think we should just go ahead; I want to hear what you're going say about religious experience.

2

Types of Religious
Belief & Experience

*W*E NEED TO COVER TWO DISTINCT AREAS TODAY. THE FIRST IS TO distinguish the major types of religious belief, and the second is to discuss the ways religious experience is usually classified into types.

As I said, I need to keep thinking about your definition of divinity because I'm not prepared to accept it yet. But that needn't prevent us from examining the ways religious belief can be classified, and I'm very curious about what you're going to do with the notion of religious experience.

Despite your reservations about it, my definition of religious belief includes an important ancillary benefit: it affords a way to classify types of divinity beliefs which is extremely helpful in understanding the major religious traditions. Given that "divine" means the ultimate reality, however that is conceived, we can then classify religious beliefs according to how they understand the nondivine to depend on the divine. This simplifies things, as well as casting into sharp relief some important commonalities and contrasts between the major traditions. The fact is that virtually every extant religion subscribes to one or another of only three possible ideas of that dependency, although there are a great many ways it could be thought of.[1]

Let's take the most familiar type first—the one that holds the divine to be distinct from (transcend) the rest of reality. This is the view of the three theistic[2] religions: Judaism, Christianity and Islam. They all hold that God alone is divine and that everything other than God depends on God. Another way to put the same point is to say that God's Being is not the being of creation; God is not what creation is made of, since God's own being is unconditional and self-existent, whereas the existence of everything else is dependent on God.[3] A diagram can help clarify this dependency relation. Using a solid line to represent the divine and a dotted line to represent all that is not divine, this type of religious belief can be schematized as in figure 1.

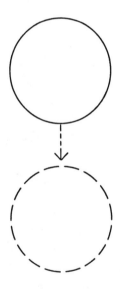

Figure 1

As the diagram shows, the theistic idea of dependency sees a basic discontinuity at the heart of reality. This discontinuity has been beautifully expressed by Will Herberg. Referring to the theistic idea as Hebraic and the other ideas as Greco-Oriental, Herberg says:

> Hebraic and Greco-Oriental religion, as religion, agree in affirming
> some Absolute reality as Ultimate, but differ fundamentally in what
> they say about this reality. To Greco-Oriental thought, whether
> mystical or philosophic, the ultimate reality is some primal unper-
> sonal force . . . some ineffable, immutable passive divine substance
> that pervades the universe or rather is the universe insofar as the
> latter is at all real.
>
> Nothing could be further from normative Hebraic religion. . . .
> As against the Greco-Oriental idea of *immanence,* of divinity per-
> meating all things and constituting their reality, Hebraic religion
> affirms God as a transcendent person, who has indeed created the
> universe but who cannot without blasphemy be identified with it.
> Where Greco-Oriental religion sees a continuity between God and
> the universe, Hebraic religion insists on discontinuity.[4]

This doesn't mean that God can't share qualities with creatures, can't act
in creation to make himself known, or can't be present in creation. These
are points all theists affirm, and we can deal with them in more detail
later. For now the important thing is to make clear the contrast between
this dependency idea and its rivals.

*I have a question about this diagram. Why is the arrow between God and
creation also dotted?*

It indicates that even the relations God bears to creation are themselves
created by God. Only the being of God is unconditionally real, so the most
fundamental relation God has to creation is to be its Creator. But God is not
a creator apart from there being a creation. So God brought into existence
the relation being-the-creator-of-the-world along with bringing the world
into existence. God, then, really has the property of being the Creator even
though it is a property God called into existence.

Now contrast this theistic idea with another one, the one traditionally
called pagan. The term "pagan" refers to religious belief that identifies the
divine as part of the world, that is, part of what a theist calls "creation."
Notice that the term is not meant to be derogatory. Its essential feature
is the belief that the divine is some part, force or principle in the universe.
On the pagan view, there is therefore no discontinuity at the heart of

reality. There is but one continuous reality, part of which is the divine element on which all the rest of it depends. The schematic for this view would look like figure 2.

Figure 2

A wide variety of religions fall into this type, worshiping a divine reality variously manifested in the sun, the sea, the earth, fertility and so on. Either these objects were regarded as gods or it was believed that gods inhabited or ruled over them. Religions of this type generally recognize a difference between what is divine per se and gods and goddesses, who are beings with more divine power than humans—a point we noticed briefly last time. This makes sense from the pagan view, since its dependency idea requires all nondivine things to be partly divine; the divine permeates the nondivine in a way that makes it part of the being of each nondivine reality.

To fully appreciate the influence of this type of belief, we should also recall another point we discussed last time, namely, that religious belief need not involve worship. It's important here because cultic, ritual paganisms that actually worship aspect(s) of the world as divine are no longer major players in Western culture. Whereas the *worship* of some aspects of the natural universe has been on the wane for centuries, the *belief* in the divinity of one or another of them has not. Few people now worship matter, space, mathematical truths, sense data or combinations of them, yet many believe them to be divine.[5] Thus while the ritual forms of pagan belief have been fading from villages and towns, various nonritual versions of it still flourish in theories which have able and vocal defenders in colleges and universities.

I can see why on your definition of "divine" that would be true.

Historically, one of the most influential forms of this type of belief was the one held by the ancient Greeks. In that version there were two divine principles, which came to be called "form" and "matter." Matter was the name for the stuff of which all nondivine things are made, and form was the name for the principles that organized matter into a tree, a horse, a planet, a human or whatever. Although form and matter were both eternal and nondependent, the things that were composites of them came into being and passed away. Humans are among these composite beings, with matter making up their bodies and form making up their rational souls. And although both form and matter were regarded as divine, form was the source of good in the world whereas matter was the source of evil. The schematic for this version of the pagan dependency idea would look like figure 3.

Figure 3

Finally, contrast the theistic and the pagan ideas of dependency with the pantheistic idea found in the Hindu and Buddhist traditions, which recognizes only one reality: the divine. Anything that appears to be a distinct individual—to be limited, to change, to have different qualities—is in fact unreal. Strictly speaking, then, the relation in this case is between the divine and what only *appears* not to be divine. The difference between them is the difference between the ways we experience and conceive things to be and the way reality is. In Hinduism the divine reality, which is the only reality, is called Brahman-Atman; in Buddhism it is called the Void, Dharmakaya or Suchness. For both traditions the way we naturally experience and conceive of things is the realm of illusion called "maya."

This type of dependency relation may be diagrammed as in figure 4.

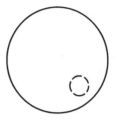

Figure 4

I should add, however, that the circle for the divine in this schematic is misleading because in this view the divine is infinite; it is unending and there is nothing that is not contained within it. But since it's not possible to draw an infinitely big circle, this finite one will have to symbolize an infinite one.

This is very interesting, but I'm not sure why you've taken the time to deal with it. How does it contribute to our examination of religious experience?

It may help in several ways. First, contrasting the types of religious beliefs makes us better able to recognize them when and where they appear in literature, plays, essays, theories and everyday life. Second, it can help us be more open to seeing as religious a number of beliefs that are very different from the religions we are used to. Because we are used to the theistic traditions, we are prone to discount the religious nature of many teachings that take some part or aspect of the natural world to be divine, as do the various forms of the pagan type of belief. And finally, it may help clarify something we began to discuss last time: the way divinity beliefs are presuppositions to other beliefs, such as those about human nature, happiness and destiny. Contrasting these dependency ideas can help make that point clearer by allowing us to see how each of these ideas implies a distinctive view of these other beliefs. In fact, I can illustrate that right now by briefly contrasting the view each takes of human nature, specifically, its view of what's wrong with humans.

On the theistic view, humans are creatures of God and will never be anything else. The biblical story of humanity's fall into sin portrays that sin as the human desire to deny our creaturehood and instead regard ourselves as (at least partly) divine. What is wrong with us from the theistic view, therefore, is not that we have bodies and feelings (the fall into sin was not the discovery of sex); it is not that our bodies are naturally evil; it is not that we regard the world around us as real when in fact it is an illusion. What is wrong with us is that we don't love God with all our heart nor our neighbors as ourselves. The order in which I listed those last two items is important. Sin, in biblical teaching, is primarily a *religious* idea and secondarily a moral one. Fundamentally it is substituting anything whatever for God, especially because the substitution allows us to pretend we are either partially or wholly divine. Our failure to love our neighbor, who is the created image of God, is secondary in that it is both a sign and a result of our failure to love God.

By contrast, the pagan view sees humans as either partly divine and partly nondivine or as composed partly of the good divinity and partly of the evil divinity. What is wrong with us is that we often allow the nondivine or evil part of our nature to get the upper hand over the divine or good part. In the Greek version, this meant that having a body and emotions is what leads people to do evil, whereas having a soul and thinking rationally is what leads them to do good. Thus Plato called the body "the prison house of the soul." The Greek belief in life after death was also tied to this dualistic view of human nature: since the soul can know rational, everlasting, changeless truths, it might be enough like those truths to be everlasting itself.[6]

The pantheistic view, over against pagan and theistic views, sees humans as encompassed in the one divine reality. We are already divine; what is wrong with us is that we don't believe it. Our individual identifying characteristics are as illusory as the differences in the things around us. What is wrong with us, therefore, is that we take the illusion to be real; we value, plan and care about the illusory world. As long as we do that, we continue to suffer, since our attachment to the illusory world dooms us to be reborn into one lifetime of suffering after another. The deliverance from this is a mystical experience that leads us to reject the world of ordinary perception and thought as illusory and detach ourselves from all concern with it. This is the experience of spiritual enlightenment, which alone can set us free from the cycle of rebirth. When that happens, our individuality and all else about us that is illusory is absorbed into the divine "as a drop of water is absorbed into the ocean." This is the state called nirvana.

The purpose of the foregoing sketch was to illustrate two points: (1) there are a number of ways of conceiving of the divine and of the way the nondivine depends on the divine, and (2) how we think of the divine and of our dependence on it underpins our conception of human nature. Conceptions of human nature, in turn, influence a wide variety of other beliefs. If that much is now clear, I think we can proceed to examine the types of religious experience that are usually distinguished.

Yes, it's clear enough and I'm anxious to get on to religious experience. Before you go ahead, though, there are some things about religious experience I want to get out on the table so that they don't slip by us. Let's start with the thought experiment argument you made last time. If I understand it correctly, it shows that belief in anything selected as nondependent reality can never be justified by argument. I don't see any way to rebut that, so I'm going to let it stand for now. But it leads me to make several points about what I think I see coming.

First, since you intend to appeal to some sort of experience to justify belief in God, won't you then be doing the same thing the thought experiment criticizes? Won't an appeal to religious experience have to say that something experienced is divine or shows what is divine?

That's true enough. But remember, I don't claim that belief in God can be justified by argument and evidence. I maintain it is justified by experience itself without argument.

OK. That's what I thought you'd say, and it leads to several worries I have about the very idea of justifying belief in God by experience. First, any appeal to experience will have difficulties that pagan candidates for divinity don't have. For one thing, candidates for divinity drawn from the world are known to be real by our ordinary experience, whereas the whole notion of experience seems fishy in relation to God. You don't claim to have tea with God on Tuesday afternoons, do you? See what's bothering me? I'm afraid what you're going to appeal to won't be anything like ordinary experience, so that the meaning of "experience" will get stretched in a way I'll find completely implausible.

And that's not all. There's another problem with the notion of experience in relation to God. Since God is supposed to be a transcendent Creator, it seems to me that taking transcendence seriously creates grave problems for appealing to any sort of experience. In fact, I'm inclined to say that anything we could experience would thereby not be transcendent!

Those are all legitimate concerns and I promise to address them. But there are no short, easy answers I can give to them right now that are independent of the analysis of religious experience we're about to launch into. I will say, however, that what I take to justify belief in God will be an element of our ordinary experience, not some implausibly stretched notion of it.

That's some relief. But even so, your project still looks doomed for yet another reason. I don't see how experience alone could ever show any particular religious belief to be true, since it generates incompatible beliefs. It seems obvious that since these beliefs all appeal to experience but can't all be true, experience alone can't show us which (if any) is true. This alone seems fatal to what you propose to do!

I promise to deal with that issue as well. But like the other questions you've raised, the answer to it needs preparation and must come later. Let's first address what is at the core of religious experience and then ask whether it can justify the beliefs it produces and how to deal with the conflicting beliefs it produces.

Let's start by looking at the usual ways religious experiences are sorted into types. The major classifications I'm about to review are based on William James's classic work *The Varieties of Religious Experience*. I'll be drawing on *Varieties* for several of the types and for its wide survey of experience reports, though I won't follow James in distinguishing types of experiences according to the sorts of people who have them or according to the different ways those who had them were affected by them. I'll also be drawing on the suggestions of other scholars,[7] and I'll add my own modifications wherever they seem helpful. I must say right away, however, that we'll be reviewing these classifications only as a point of departure. I'm starting with them partly because they're so widely accepted and partly because it's an easy way of introducing a lot of data about religious experience. But in the end I'll mainly use them to make my position clear by contrasting it to them—not so much because they are patently wrong as because their emphasis is misleading in a way I think it important to correct. The usual classifications start with any dramatic, strange and unusual episodes or experiences that were regarded as religious by those who had them. My own focus is going to differ from this in a way that parallels what I tried to do with religious belief: I want to see if there's anything all religious experiences have in common. I mean, of course, what they all have in common besides generating beliefs in something as divine. I'll do that by looking for what is essential to the experiences themselves rather than in their specific contents or outcomes.

Because you frequently express concern about where our discussion is headed, I'll say right now that all such experiences have discernible features which are the source of their religious significance and which, I will argue, attach to quite ordinary experiences as well as to those that are weird, miraculous or mystical.

I think I see where you're going. The prevailing way of breaking religious experience into types takes only strange experiences to be religious and takes every strange experience as religious as long as the person who had it thinks it was. In that case there's no way to say that an experience wasn't really religious when the one who had it thought so. Is that it?

That's one part, yes. The other part is its converse: on the prevailing view there's also no way to say that anyone had a religious experience but failed to recognize it as such. My view will allow for both possibilities.

I'm surprised that your view allows ordinary experiences to be genuinely religious. I still think of them mainly as events such as seeing visions or hearing voices.

Well, that's certainly one type: those that involve the faculties of ordinary sense perception—especially seeing and hearing. When they involve the normal organs of perception, they're not utterly out of the ordinary, as is the mystical experience emphasized by the pantheist traditions. Rather, these experiences are classified as religious because of *what* is seen or heard. The objects of such perceptions may be observable publically or may be restricted to the one who sees or hears them. They are so varied that they defy any simple blanket characterization other than their being experienced as coming from and revealing the divine or a divinity. For example, they may be an appearance of God, a god, or a messenger from God such as an angel, a saint or someone who has died. Sometimes what is seen is just a great light. They may include verbal messages such as commands to action or information about the future.

Then this would include biblical examples such as Moses' seeing a burning bush and hearing God's voice, or Paul's being blinded by a great light and hearing the voice of Jesus?

Yes. But such experiences are also reported by ordinary folk. The case of Sadu Sundar Singh is an example. Singh had been a devout Sikh all his life. Eventually he became discouraged with Sikhism and embarked on a deliberate quest to find God. His quest was open to everything except Christianity. Early one morning he was praying, when

> I saw something of which I had no idea at all previously. In the room where I was praying I saw a great light. I thought the place was on fire. I looked around, but could find nothing. Then the thought came to me that this might be an answer that God had sent me. Then, as I prayed and looked into the light, I saw the form of the Lord Jesus Christ. It had such appearance of glory and love. If it had been some Hindu incarnation I would have prostrated myself before it. But it was the Lord Jesus Christ whom I had been insulting a few days before. I felt that a vision like this could not have come out of my own imagination. I heard a voice saying in Hindustani, "How long will you persecute me? I have come to save you; you were praying to know the right way. Why do you not take it?" The thought came to me, "Jesus Christ is not dead but living and it must be he himself." So I fell at his feet and got this wonderful peace which I could not get anywhere else.[8]

Virtually every religious tradition includes reports of such experiences. Many describe gods appearing to humans or visions of animals that represent gods. In all of them the visions and voices are experienced as communicating genuine information about the divine, whether the recipients of the messages are asleep or wide awake and whether the visions are spontaneous or induced by disciplines such as fasting, prayer or meditation. Here's another example, a report from a village chief of the Apinaye tribe of eastern Brazilia about his encounter with the sun god:

> I was hunting near the sources of the Botica creek. All along the

journey I had been agitated and was constantly startled without knowing why. Suddenly I saw him standing under the branches of a big steppe tree. . . . I recognized at once that it was he. Then I lost all courage. My hair stood on end, and my knees were trembling. . . . When I had grown somewhat calmer, I raised my head. . . . I pulled myself together and walked several steps toward him, then I could not go farther because my knees gave way. I remained standing a long time, . . . lowered my head, and tried again to regain composure. When I raised my eyes again, he had already turned away and was slowly walking through the steppe. . . . At night while I was asleep he reappeared to me. I addressed him, and he said he had been waiting . . . to talk to me, but since I had not approached he had gone away.

Today I know I was very stupid then. I should certainly have received from him great self-assurance if I had been able to talk to him.[9]

Also included in this type are perceptions of miracles[10] as reported in every tradition—those that are publicly accessible as well as those that are private to a particular person. Witnessing someone being raised from the dead, water being changed into wine, or a serious deformity or disease being healed instantaneously is an example of a public miracle; a sudden transformation of character or a spontaneous recovery from an addiction would be an example of a private one. They are all experienced by means of the senses.

Does that mean there are religious experiences that are not perceived via the senses? How then could they be experienced at all?

The second type of religious experience involves becoming aware of the presence of divinity when that presence is *not* sensorily perceived. That is not to say that the person having the experience isn't perceiving anything at the time, but it does mean that he or she becomes aware of something not perceived in conjunction with whatever is perceived. This experience occurs in both a personal and an impersonal form.

The impersonal version of this type of experience was perhaps best described by Rudolf Otto, who called it an encounter with the "holy," the "numinous," the "uncanny" or the "mysterious." It is an experience in which a person is perceptually confronted with something ordinary but becomes aware of the presence of divine power in addition to what is sensorily perceived. Otto stresses how such experiences often produce reactions of "fascination," "awe" and even terror.[11] He says:

> It may burst in sudden eruption up from the depths of the soul with spasms and convulsions, or lead to the strangest excitements, to intoxicated frenzy, to transport, to ecstasy. It has its wild and demonic forms and . . . may become the hushed, trembling and speechless humility of the creature in the presence of—whom or what? In the presence of that which is a mystery inexpressible and above all creatures.[12]

Notice, by the way, that Otto confirms that what is experienced is divine in my sense of that term when he speaks of it as "above all creatures." In fact, he adds that the experience is at its heart one that produces "creature consciousness"; what is experienced is mysterious, but it is known to be that which creatures depend on.[13]

This type of experience has long been valued in many pagan traditions, in which priests and shamans are considered experts in (nonperceptually) sensing the divine presence in particular objects, locations or occasions. There are many expressions of it in poetry as well; Wordsworth's "Tintern Abbey" is an instance:

> And I have felt
> A presence that disturbs me with the joy
> Of elevated thoughts; a sense sublime
> Of something far more deeply interfused,
> Whose dwelling is the light of setting suns,
> And the round ocean and the living air,
> And the blue sky, and the mind of man:
> A motion and a spirit, that impels
> All thinking things, all objects of thought,
> And rolls through all things.

The personal version of this type is one of the most frequently reported of all religious experiences. In it too the experiencer is aware of the presence of the divine without perceiving it sensorily, but the divine is sensed as personal. The experience is like the nonreligious experience people often report of feeling the presence of another person or of someone watching them, when they neither see nor hear anyone. Such experiences are often called "sensing" the presence of another person, but no conscious perception is involved—just as Wordsworth said he "*felt* a presence" to indicate his sense of it without any actual, conscious sensation or emotion.[14]

The religious experience of sensing a presence differs from a nonreligious sensing of another person not only in that the personal presence is experienced as divine but also in that the experience is much more definite. There is certainty about being in the presence of another person and about the person's being a divine spirit or, more specifically, the Spirit of God. The descriptions of these experiences are remarkably alike over thousands of reports. The following example was reported to me by a person who was a dedicated atheist at the time the experience occurred:

> I was alone for the evening and decided to try reading the Gospel of John as you had suggested, convinced it could make no difference to my skepticism about God. I'd picked up the Bible and turned to John, when suddenly I was overwhelmed by a presence that filled the room. I was startled and jumped up, closing the book at the same time. It seemed to be gone, so I decided my mind was playing tricks on me; I'd get a shower, calm down and try again. Refreshed by the shower, I was surprised at the way I'd let the simple suggestion of reading the Bible spook me. "It's just a book!" I said, laughing at myself. But when I opened the Bible again, the presence was far more overpowering than the first time. Although it was not threatening—and in fact was powerfully loving—I was really scared. I threw the Bible across the room and yelled, "Go away and leave me alone! I like my life the way it is!" But it persisted; it would not let me go. Now in tears, I picked up the book again and began to read John chapter 1, and suddenly it all looked undeniably true.

James reports another experience which, though slightly different, is of this same type:

> I remember the night, and almost the very spot on the hilltop, where my soul opened out, as it were, into the Infinite. . . . I stood alone

with Him who had made me, and all the beauty of the world, and love, and sorrow, and even temptation. . . . The darkness held a presence that was all the more felt because it was not seen. I could not have any more doubted that *He* was there than that I was. Indeed, I felt myself to be, if possible, the less real of the two.[15]

And Simone Weil has written of such an experience this way:

I had never foreseen the possibility of that, of real contact, person to person, here below, between a human and God. . . . Moreover, in this sudden possession of me by Christ, neither my senses nor my imagination had any part.[16]

Of course not all experiences of this type are so powerful and dramatic; many are quiet and calm, and some come on gradually.

A third type of religious experience is called "mystical" to emphasize its radical difference from anything even close to ordinary experience. In it nothing is sensorily perceived at all, nor is there an awareness of an individual personal presence. Rather, a person experiences a closeness with the divine which involves a direct communion that is not like any other relationship humans experience. There are several varieties of such experience,[17] according to the most radical of which the mystic is said to be absorbed into identity with the divine. All distinctions seem to be canceled and the divine becomes the only reality. Usually this experience takes place in a trancelike state, which James describes as having four main characteristics.[18] The first is ineffability: it defies expression in words. The second is certainty: truth is conveyed about the divine so that it is indubitable. Third is transiency: the state never lasts long and often cannot be repeated. When it is repeated, however, it is always recognizable as the same type of experience. Finally, it is passive, in two senses. The onset of the experience is never in the person's control, although he or she may have engaged in meditation and other disciplines to induce the experience. And once it has begun, the person feels in the grasp of something vastly superior; the person is helpless or, in the most extreme subtype, unreal.

This type of experience is especially emphasized and sought in the

Hindu and Buddhist traditions, which take it as the ultimate authority concerning the divine. Though achieving it usually takes years of discipline and meditation, it can also occur spontaneously. One name for its spontaneous occurrence is "Zen." Experiences of mystical communion with the divine are also reported in Judaism, Christianity and Islam but are rarer in those traditions. There are even occasional claims of actual union with God, but they are highly problematic in these traditions.

To summarize, the main types of religious experiences include (1) perceptual phenomena such as voices, visions and miracles, (2) the sense of a presence (both impersonal and personal) and (3) mystical communion or union. The types are not intended to be mutually exclusive, and some reported experiences cut across these categories. Neither should the list be taken as exhaustive, since there are other experiences that produce belief in something as divine but don't fall into any of these types, as James himself admits.[19] Even so, this is enough to introduce the types of experiences most discussions of this topic follow.

I must say that your description of these experiences does nothing to allay my suspicions of them. My initial reaction is that they all seem best explained as psychological abnormalities. But whatever happened to your claim that religious experiences are not all weird? Nothing you've said so far seems to allow that any ordinary experience could be religious.

Many scholars share your suspicions and dismiss the strange sorts of experiences classified here as abnormal. Others, however, do not, including James, who was a psychologist himself. But my purpose here is not to defend them as normal. As I said, they serve to introduce the usual way the subject is discussed so that I can contrast another approach. And since you've pressed me about that point, I'd like to get right to it.

Rather than dwell on the strangeness of the types we just noticed, I want to get past that by seeking, as I forewarned you, what they all have in common. I don't mean that we should look for what the *objects* of those experiences have in common, since the answer to that is "nothing." The most radical form of mystical experience doesn't have any object as such, since in it even the difference between subject and object seems to disappear. Rather, I want to call attention to specific features common to them all as far as the mode of the experience itself is concerned.

At first glance, the task of finding anything common to them all looks almost as daunting as the task of finding an element common to all religious beliefs. Not only are they all strange in comparison with ordinary experience, but they are strange in very different ways. The first mode uses ordinary faculties of perception to see or hear very nonordinary things; the second doesn't use those faculties at all but becomes aware of something anyway; and in the third all distinctions seem to be obliterated, even the one between the person having the experience and the all-encompassing reality being experienced. Nevertheless, I think they do indeed have common features, and the shared features are essential to their being religious experiences. One of these I've already argued for: they all produce belief in something or other as divine, where the divine is the unconditional reality on which all else depends.

Another feature is that the beliefs these experiences produce are noninferential. What is experienced is experienced *as* the voice of God, the presence of God, divine power, unity with the divine and so on. It is not that the person has a weird experience and then reflects on it, ponders over it and draws conclusions about it that lead him or her to *decide* to interpret it as God, Brahman-Atman, nirvana or whatever. Rather, the experiences *produce* those beliefs directly without any mediating steps of reasoning. For this reason those who have had them, and scholarly reflections on them in every major religious tradition, often refer to them as "intuitions" rather than the products of reasoning.

This doesn't mean that those who have these experiences never subsequently think about them, or never later draw any additional conclusions about them. I am simply pointing to the fact that the experience reports of each type include the point that beliefs were produced which were directly intuited without being inferred.

Another feature that these experiences share is both hugely important and sorely neglected by those who have written on the subject, including James. I don't mean that James and others miss this feature altogether, but that they fail to give it its due. I'm referring now to the quality of *certainty* that attaches to the belief that the experience generates. Moreover, this quality is experienced as compelling, so that the experiences have the quality of revealing truth about the divine in such a way that the beliefs they produce have the quality of irresistible certainty.[20]

James and others do notice that such certainty is part of the description of every one of the types of experiences cataloged above. At one point James says:

> One may indeed be entirely without them; . . . but if you do have them at all strongly, the probability is that you cannot help regarding them as genuine perceptions of truth, as revelations of a kind of reality which no adverse argument, however, unanswerable by you in words, can expel from your belief.[21]

But although he recognizes this, he treats it as just an interesting additional observation. And that just won't do. That these experiences generate certainty is a central feature of them, not just an interesting sidelight.

Supporting evidence for this point is provided by cases in which people had something *like* one of these types of experiences, but its content was unclear and no certainty was produced. The result was that those reporting such experiences did not then regard them as religious at all. For example, there are reports of people being suddenly overwhelmed by a presence that they could not identify. They subsequently regarded the experience as strange but not as religious; no belief in anything as divine was produced, and no certainty about it was conveyed. There are also reports in which the presence was thought at the time to be divine, but in the absence of certainty that perception later became subject to doubt: "I had a strange experience which *might* have been God, but I'm just not sure."[22] Again, no abiding religious conviction was produced.

To sum up, my first conclusion is that to be religious, an experience must generate belief in something as divine; my second conclusion is that the experience directly (noninferentially) produces that belief; and my third conclusion is that the belief carries the quality of certitude.

But if this is right, there is no longer any reason whatever to confine the study of religious experience to experiences that are strange, miraculous or mystical. James admits at one point that certainty attaches to experiences that produce religious belief but are not strange at all.[23] Amazingly, he never seems to realize the importance of that point. Its importance is this: *The strangeness of an experience is irrelevant to its being religious. Its being an experience of noninferentially recognizing truth about what is divine, where that carries certainty, is what is essential.*

But how does this view of religious experience show that we're not restricted to strange experiences? The very idea of "experiencing something to be divine" itself sounds strange!

I'm saying that certainty about what is divine does not attach only to experiences having strange contents or taking place in unusual ways. It does not attach only to the weird and the miraculous; in fact, it does so less often than it does to such ordinary experiences as reading about the belief, hearing it taught or preached or seeing it lived out in the lives of those who believe it. So my point is that cataloging only strange, miraculous and mystical experiences as religious is seriously misleading. The vast majority of religious experiences do not fall into those classifications at all, so it's not surprising that most of the people who consciously hold a belief in something as divine have never had any strange experiences.

And that's not the only correction in the idea of religious experience that results from this point. If the direct apprehension of truth about the divine is all that need occur for an experience to be religious, even if it comes about quietly and with no mystical or miraculous elements, then neither is there any good reason for insisting that only distinguishable *episodes* of seeing religious truth should count as religious experiences. To see why this is so, compare the experience of apprehending the divine with that of recognizing aesthetic beauty. Our appreciation of beauty is often connected to special episodes that are memorable. We may marvel at a great performance of music, dance or drama, for example. But our experience of aesthetic value is just as real when it is a steady, continuous background that is woven into the rest of our experience without issuing in an intense episode. A case in point would be the quiet, continuous appreciation of a beautiful, well-designed building. Many people's reports of their recognition of truth about the divine have more in common with a continuous appreciation than an intense episode.

Additionally, religious experience need not be sudden. It can develop gradually. Again, consider the analogy to our experience of art. We may be exposed to a particular work of music or a painting but not think much of it at first. As time goes by, however, it strikes us more strongly; we say it "grows on us." Similarly, belief in God can come on gradually as well. The certainty I've been pointing to can be the end result of a lengthy chain of experiences as well as occurring as suddenly as turning on a light switch.

In confirmation of this, there are many reports from people who recognized the truth about God gradually, as an element running through a prolonged tract of experience. Many say that they were exposed to teaching about God in their youth, but as they grew older concerns about education, work, marriage and family came to dominate their attention in such a way that the whole issue of religion took a back seat. Often they jumped to the conclusion that belief in God must be false for no other reason than that they seemed to be able to get along without it.

But then something happened to raise the question of God's existence again. For some it was the death of a close relative; for others it was their own close shave with death. For still others the aging process brought them face to face with their mortality. It's not always connected with death, though. Sometimes the experience was initiated when they began to notice little incidents that seemed to be too meaningful to be only coincidences. Perhaps they were considering a religious issue when the words of a song on the radio perfectly answered a question, or they heard a sermon or recalled a Scripture text that did the same thing. After a number of such incidents, they began to wonder whether God was trying to reach out to them and thus started to think seriously about the Scriptures again or even attend worship occasionally. Upon discovering that others were reporting the same sorts of things, they began to take the matter even more seriously and began studying Scripture and attending worship regularly. In time, the truth of the biblical message came to be a certainty.

This is only one way of gradually coming to experience full certainty concerning the love of God; there are many other ways it can happen. And still other people find that religious certainty does turn on like a light switch. A woman I know had been an outspoken atheist for years. She surprised me one day by speaking about God. When I asked how she came to believe, she said, "Nothing really happened. I just woke up one morning and it all looked true. I have no explanation."

Clearly, then, religious experience is highly variable not only as to precisely *what* is experienced or *how* it is experienced but also as to whether it occurs as an episode or results from a prolonged stretch of experience. In the light of all this, we can now draw yet another conclusion, a conclusion I call the "democratization of religious experience": There is no reason to think that only religious leaders, prophets and mystics have religious experiences. This is not to deny that there have been and are those who have remarkably intense experiences. It is only to insist that the commoners of religious belief have religious experience as well as the nobility. Simple, quiet, noninferential certainty about what has unconditional reality is actually as prevalent among average pew-dwellers (and even supposedly secular academic theorists) as it is among religious leaders.

But don't those who report the strange types of experiences put great stock in their very strangeness? Isn't that what is supposed to make their experiences convincing?

Not at all! In report after report, those who had them go to pains to say that it was not the strangeness of the experience that was important, although it served to get their attention. While they often marvel at its strangeness and feel privileged to have had such an experience, they insist that what was really important about it was precisely its element of *truth recognition* and the certainty of the belief they acquired. It has not been those who had the experiences who placed great stock in the strangeness of them, but the scholars of religion who downplayed the certainty of truth they conveyed and concentrated on cataloging the types of strangeness that accompanied the experiences. In fact, those who had the experiences often go further. Many add that whereas the experience was fleeting, the truth they gained was abiding; though the experience never came back, the truth they realized stayed with them for the rest of their lives and changed them.[24] So again, although the reporters of strange experiences stress the truth conveyed to them, the scholars of religion focus on cataloging their strangeness and on establishing whether they are pathological. There's something perverse about that, even aside from its having the effect of shutting the majority of religious experiences out of the discussion.

Thus my last conclusion is that the vast majority of religious experiences don't consist of episodes that are strange in mode or content, and many are not episodes at all. They are simply the experience of seeing something to be divine, without inferring it from any other belief, and having that belief appear irresistibly certain.

I am relieved to hear you downplay the strange experiences, but I'm still nervous about this business of simply recognizing something as true. Lots of people claim to "just see" that all sorts of crazy things are true.

The key issue here is not whether people have experiences that convince them of various beliefs. Who doubts that? People have all kinds of experiences and are convinced by them of all sorts of beliefs, some of which are as irrational as anything you can imagine. The key issue is whether there are experiences that not only produce beliefs but justify *them, which is how you described your position.*

This brings me back to something I said last time. I proposed that beliefs about ultimate reality weren't religious when they were argued for, but only when taken on faith. That still looks good to me, though right now I don't know how to rebut your criticisms of it. Even if beliefs in something as divine initially arise from the experience of having them look right (and I don't think they all *do), at least philosophers and scientists then try to justify them by arguments, whereas in religions people are content simply to have them look right. I think that puts each case in a different category.*

I'll put the same point another way: even if you distinguish two senses of the term "faith," one referring to blind trust or wishful thinking and the other referring to a belief that arises from experience, that alone does not make the second a justified belief. You seem to speaking as if it does.

I agree with a great deal of what you have just said. I agree that not all who adhere to a religion do so because of a genuine religious experience. And more important, I agree that you've put your finger on the crucial question: is there any sort of experience that can justify as well as produce belief? I, along with the vast majority of thinkers dealing with the study of how we acquire knowledge, think the answer to that is yes. The two types of experience that the vast majority have held to confer justification are normal sense perception and the rational intuition of self-evidency.

I further agree that we need to distinguish "faith" as it refers to wishful thinking, blind trust, cultural conditioning, and so on, from faith that refers to a conviction arising from the experience of seeing for oneself that the belief is true. Virtually every major religious tradition agrees with that point and insists that the first sense is not genuine religious belief. What they all require is the experience of being "enlightened" so that the believer sees the truth of that divinity belief for himself or herself. This noninferred truth recognition is what I said they often call "intuition."

Please don't read anything weird into the meaning of "intuition." After trying to demystify religious experience, I am not now reintroducing something strange or mysterious. It doesn't mean merely having a hunch, as we sometimes use it in ordinary speech. In theories of knowledge the word "intuition" is often used to mean apprehending a truth without the mediating steps of reasoning, evidence weighing, arguing and so on. As I said last time, those mediating steps are at the very heart of theories because hypotheses have to be judged in those ways. But as I also said in our last discussion, there are many beliefs we form without engaging in those processes—beliefs that are necessary in everyday life and are pre-conditions for making theories in philosophy and science.

Normal sense perception is one of these. We don't perceive a tree and then engage in reasoning or weighing evidence in order to draw the conclusion that there's a tree before us. Under normal conditions seeing the tree triggers our belief-forming faculties, which produce in us the belief that a tree is there. There are also truths of mathematics and logic that we don't believe on the basis of proofs or evidence, such as $1 + 1 = 2$ or the axiom "Things equal to the same thing are equal to each other." These are examples of what philosophers call "basic beliefs," to signify that they are not derived from other beliefs. The ability to form these is what I mean by "intuition." It is our capacity to recognize a state of affairs as in fact the case and to form the belief that it is so without any mediating process of reasoning.

This is also what I want to say the about that second sense of "faith," the sense that's not blind trust or belief beyond the evidence but a reference to the experience of intuiting truth. Since this claim strikes you as odd, let me add that using "faith" in connection with religious belief is not new but has been pointed out again and again for a long time. Calvin and Pascal did it, for example, and a more recent theologian put it this way: "Faith [is] that function of the soul . . . by which it obtains certainty directly . . . without the aid of discursive demonstration. This places faith over against 'demonstration' *not* of itself over against *knowing*."[25]

But you can't really think I'll let you get away with simply defining "faith" so that it turns out to be on a par with, say, normal sense perception or self-evident truths! If that's what you want to maintain, you're going to have to do a lot more than just say it. And then—as I already pointed out—you're going to have to deal with the fact that these experiences yield conflicting beliefs and so can't all really be experiences of recognizing truth! Although these experiences produce beliefs, that's still a million miles from showing they can intellectually entitle anyone to them.

As I see it, then, you'd need to do both tasks in order to convince me I'm wrong in saying that some beliefs about what is nondependent are religious because they are taken on faith whereas others are not because they have arguments to support them. To defend what you just said, (1) you'd need to show that religious beliefs are formed by the same intuitive capacity that enables us to form beliefs such as axioms, and (2) you'd need to explain how such intuitions could justify those beliefs in the face of the fact that they lead people to form conflicting beliefs.

Fair enough. I had no intention of just *saying* that truth recognition with respect to what is divine is on a par with self-evidency, though that's exactly what I plan to show. Again, I promise that I will deal with the problem created by the fact that such experiences produce conflicting beliefs about what is divine.

I propose, then, that we get right to those issues at our next session by examining the whole notion of what it means for a belief to be self-evident. That seems appropriate because they're the standard case of basic beliefs considered to be justified without evidence or argument. Since the experience of a belief as self-evident is one we've all had and can reflect on, we should then be able to compare what we find about cases of nonreligious self-evidency with the certainty produced by religious experience.

To prepare for that discussion, I'd like you to read an essay I wrote for my students on the idea of self-evidency. It surveys what a number of the most influential writers have had to say about it and critiques certain parts of their views in order to come to a clearer understanding of it. Please don't be put off by its references to philosophers and scientists; there's nothing in it that requires any technical background, and I think it will help to give us a common point of departure when we meet again.

3

Self-Evident Knowledge

*W*HAT'S YOUR PROOF OF THAT?" HOW MANY TIMES HAVE WE heard this question? Of course, it makes sense. It's only fair to demand proof from anyone who claims to know the right answer in a controversial matter. In addition to being fair, this question has been endorsed by any number of enormously influential thinkers. John Locke and David Hume, for example, have reminded us again and again that "the wise man tailors his belief to the evidence." And more recently W. K. Clifford put the point forcefully, declaring that "it is wrong always, and everywhere, and for anyone to believe anything upon insufficient evidence."[1]

If all this were not enough, we could further point to the sciences, which are constantly engaged in trying to prove their theories. If scientific theories need evidence and proof, must not every other sort of belief then need it too? After all, science is the best route to knowledge, isn't it? So it's obvious that if we don't have proof for something, then we don't really know it. We might hold a belief without proof, but in that case it is at best mere opinion and we have no intellectual right to say we know it is true.

The view just stated is so widespread and so deeply entrenched nowadays that it is hardly ever questioned. The vast majority of my students arrive in class already taking it for granted, since the popular press, cinema, TV and literature disseminate it continuously.

Please! Don't jump to the misunderstanding that I'm about to advocate blind acceptance of beliefs, reject science or condemn the questioning turn of mind that asks for reasons, evidence and proof. What I'm about to argue against is only the overestimation of the role of evidence and proof in gaining knowledge. I want to show why evidence and argument are not needed for every belief, although they are indispensable for establishing the truth of many beliefs. I'll begin by examining what goes into a proof. This will enable you to see why there are self-evident beliefs that don't need proof and why they are necessary in order to get proofs. Then I'll examine how we obtain this unproven knowledge.

Once that is done, we'll go on to discuss some of the more influential interpretations of unproven knowledge. This is needed because many thinkers have, I believe, gone to the opposite extreme from the popular view, claiming too much for unproven knowledge and trying to make it carry burdens it cannot bear. So I'll try to expose the exaggerations about self-evident knowledge just as I'll try to expose its neglect. In fact, these two aims are closely related: rescuing it from its overzealous admirers is part of showing its indispensability.

What Is a Proof?

Any reference to "unproven knowledge" strikes many people as self-contradictory. "How can we really know something unless it is proven?" they ask. But this question betrays a lack of understanding of what goes into a proof, since it is *impossible* that the only beliefs we have the right to be certain about are the ones that we have proven. So let's begin with what goes into a proof.

At its core, a proof is a form of inference, and inference means deriving new information from information we already have. When we infer, we come to see that if such and such beliefs are true, then some other belief must also be true. Here is an SSE (Super Simple Example) of what I mean:

1. Joe drives 49 miles one way to his office.
2. Joe drives to his office over 220 times a year.

---

3. Joe drives over 21,560 miles to his office each year.

In this SSE, statements one and two (above the line) assert the beliefs already known and from which the inference is drawn to statement three. You should be able to see for yourself that if statement one and statement two are true, there is no way statement three could be false. The relationship between the starting beliefs and the belief inferred is called entailment, and it operates according to rules (of arithmetic) which show that statement three must be true if statements one and two are true. It is this seeing-that-something-else-must-also-be-true that lies at the heart of a proof.

The inference in the following SSE should be just as obvious:

1. All horses are mammals.
2. Mammals all nurse their young.

---

3. Horses all nurse their young.

Once again it should be obvious, even to someone lacking knowledge of the rules of logic, that statement three is entailed by the combination of statements one and two.

Proofs have their own terminology. The statements of the starting facts are called *premises;* the statement of the inferred fact is called the *conclusion;* the *rules* by which the inference is drawn are those of logic or math, and the premises together with the conclusion are called an *argument.* Most arguments are not the short, two-step affairs that these SSEs are. Most have a number of premises and thus require a chain of inferred steps to reach their conclusion. When an argument is stated along with the rules used to draw each inferred step, and the steps end with the argument's conclusion, we have a *proof.* All proofs have this structure, no matter how complex they are.[2]

This structure shows that constructing a proof requires information that is not proven, for two reasons. First, if everything needed to be proven, then the premises of every proof would also need to be proven. But if you needed to prove the premises of *every* proof, you would then need a proof for your proof, and a proof for the proof of your proof, and so on—forever. Thus it makes no sense to demand that everything be proven because an infinite regress of proofs is impossible.[3] So when the premises of an argument are themselves in need of proof, the series of arguments needed to prove its premises must eventually end with an argument whose premises are all "basic," that is, not in need of proof. If that cannot be done (as is the case much of the time), we may have amassed a lot of supporting reasons for the original conclusion, but we cannot say it has complete certainty. The arguments may make a good case for it, and people may be justly convinced by them, but we do not have proof beyond all doubt. Thus room for disagreement will always remain.

Notice that I am not saying we can never claim to know a belief is true unless we can trace its inference back to premises that don't need proof. In ordinary speech we don't use "knowledge" only of beliefs that don't need proof or are derived from others that need no proof; we use it for beliefs we're nearly certain of as well as those we're fully certain of. Thus a cumulative case made up of evidence and arguments that do not rest solely on basic beliefs can still be quite overwhelming (think of atomic theory, for example). But even in such cases of near certainty, the arguments involved still depend on our having at least *some* basic premises that do not need proof. There are no exceptions to this point: not all beliefs need proof, and proving anything depends on having beliefs that don't need it.

A second reason why not every belief needs proof is that the rules for drawing inferences correctly, the truths of logic and mathematics, cannot themselves have proofs because they are the very rules we must use in order to prove anything. If we were to use them to construct proofs of themselves, the proofs would already be assuming the truth of the very rules we would be trying to prove![4] So proofs need beliefs in unproven *rules,* as well as *premises* which can be known without proof. This is why the most fundamental rules of logic and mathematics were called "axioms": they were taken to be self-evident and therefore basic. So once again, even though gathering evidence and formulating it into arguments is very important, especially in the sciences, which debate hypotheses, it just cannot be true that all knowledge is obtained that way. Framing a proof is *needed* only for a belief that is not obviously certain already, and it is *possible* only when we already have some premises and a set of rules that are not in need of it. Even then, a proof serves its purpose only when it's error-free[5] and all the premises for its conclusion have more certainty than the conclusion. If the premises of a proof have no more certainty than the conclusion they're supposed to support, how could they add to our certainty about that conclusion?

If you are accustomed to thinking that only what is proven counts as knowledge, you may be surprised to hear that what I have just said is not controversial in science or philosophy. The major theories about what counts as genuine knowledge have long acknowledged this conclusion. Some theories hold that a belief can be knowledge without proof if (1) it is about what is evident to the senses or (2) it is self-evident (Aquinas, Locke, Hume, Clifford). Otherwise it needs proof to be knowledge. Others, such as Descartes, have dropped the "evident to the senses" part. But either way, there has always been and still is general acknowledgment that while some beliefs need proof, many others don't.

So how do we get beliefs that we can know to be true without proof? Since there is controversy whether these include what is "evident to the senses," I will start by considering the nonperceptual beliefs conceded by most thinkers to be self-evident; later I will return to the question of whether those based on normal sense perception should be included among them.

The Experience of Self-Evidency

One central characteristic of beliefs that don't need proof has already been touched on: they are beliefs that strike us as being certain without having been inferred (derived) from other beliefs.[6] These are the beliefs we call "self-evident." They have often been described as beliefs we need only understand to see that they are true; but that is a slightly misleading way of putting the point, for two reasons. First, saying we need *only* understand a self-evident belief to see its truth makes it sound as though this sort of truth recognition always happens as soon as the belief is understood. Although this is sometimes true, it isn't always true. It doesn't always happen the first time someone becomes acquainted with such a belief, let alone immediately. There are cases in which its truth is recognized only after much exposure.

Second, this definition is misleading because of its inclusion of the term "only." To be sure, a self-evident belief is known without its being inferred from any other beliefs; but that is not at all the same as saying that nothing but understanding it is needed in order to have the experience of recognizing its certainty. To experience the self-evidency of a particular belief, a person often needs to have acquired other beliefs, to have had certain other experiences, to be in a certain frame of mind, to have acquired certain skills, or even to have become an expert in some field. (Surely there are beliefs that are self-evidently true to experts that are not to nonexperts![7]) So I'm going to stick with the definition that a self-evident belief is one that appears compellingly certain without being inferred from any other belief. And I'm going to use the traditional term "intuition" for such noninferential recognition of truth.[8]

Perhaps you wondering how we can know that there really is self-evident knowledge at all, and why the things I just said about it are correct. The answer is simple. You can know that we acquire beliefs by intuition of their self-evidency because you can confirm that fact by reflection on your experience—both past and present. You can begin to test this point right now by asking yourself whether you have ever had the experience of having a belief appear obviously true without reasoning to it, and whether this description of it is accurate (that is, the description of it as the experience of having a belief appear certain without inferring it from any other belief). Doing this is only the beginning of the test, however, since your answer won't depend solely on your being able to remember such beliefs from the past. You may also have such an experience now, simply by thinking again of any truth that is self-evident to you. If your reflection shows this to be the case, then both my claim that we have self-evident beliefs and the brief description offered of them will not need proof. That is, what has been said so far about self-evidency will itself be self-evident; it will be self-evident to you when you reflectively compare it to your present and past experiences of self-evident beliefs.[9]

Earlier I mentioned 1 + 1 = 2 and the axiom of equals as self-evident, so let's stick with them for now and make them our representative examples of self-evident truth. Notice that they both confirm the definition I just gave of self-evidency: they are beliefs whose certainty is intuited, since we do not discover it by deriving it from other beliefs. All we need in order to be convinced of their truth is that our understanding of the statements of them be accompanied by the intuition of their self-evidency. And that is not the only feature of self-evident truths we may notice by considering these examples. We may also confirm by self-reflection that self-evident beliefs are experienced not only as true but as compelling. That is, not only do we arrive at them without inference, but we do not initially choose to believe them. Under normal circumstances, the experience of intuiting a truth as self-evident is such that it triggers in us the response of believing it. I will call this part of the experience that of finding the belief to be prima facie compellingly certain.[10]

This is not to say that it is impossible ever to raise doubts about such truths and come to revise or even reject them later. We can confirm this point also by reflecting on past and present experiences of self-evidency. Reflection confirms that we do not see a belief to be self-evident and then never question or think about it further. Rather, we notice how it comports both with our perceptions and with our other beliefs. We are also concerned with how it compares with experiences reported to us by other people. The more we find that the newly acquired truth does not conflict with these three external checks, the greater its negative confirmation. And the more we find that it actually contributes to understanding our perceptions and our other beliefs, and is shared by other people, the greater positive confirmation we have of it. So our examples, $1 + 1 = 2$ and the axiom of equals, are beliefs that both appear self-evident and have great confirmation both negatively and positively.

Can someone intuitively experience a belief to be true and then find it disconfirmed? For example, can a belief be experienced as self-evident but conflict with normal perception? This is not common, but it can and does occur (we will return to this point later). More often conflicts arise between one self-evident abstract belief and another than between any of them and our perceptions of objects and events. Where a conflict does arise between an intuition of self-evidency and perception, it usually results in the rejection of whatever is at odds with the self-evident belief. When a belief seen as self-evident is inconsistent with another that appears equally self-evident (or logically follows from beliefs that are self-evident),[11] the dilemma created can be severe. There really are cases of such conflicts, so this is not merely hypothetical. Although I can't give you a rule for what *ought* to be done to resolve them, I can tell you what people (almost always) in fact *do:* they continue to hold whichever belief they take to be more encompassing, that is, to have the greater scope of application to reality.

The possibility of such conflicts forms another constraint on what I called the "irresistibility" of the intuition of self-evidency. We noticed that under normal circumstances the experience conveys certainty in a way that initially simply produces belief (provided its acquisition isn't blocked).[12] But as was pointed out earlier, we must also acknowledge that this prima facie irresistibility can later be defeated if the belief produced generates conflicts with perceptions and/or other self-evident beliefs. What Donne said about humans is true of beliefs: none of them are islands that stand on their own. They must survive scrutiny as to how well they integrate into the rest of our experience, so their irresistibility has constraints. Even after having been acquired and having survived an initial integration into the rest of our experience, a self-evident belief is still not utterly immune from revision or rejection, though it would take very powerful reasons to force us to do so.

Three Theories About Self-Evidency

So far we have been confining what we say of self-evidency and what we say of its role in the larger context of our total experience to what we can know of them by our own reflection. I have approached the matter this way deliberately in order to be clear about which features of the experience we can know directly, as opposed to other features that thinkers have wanted to impose on it. Of course, there's nothing wrong with proposing that self-evident beliefs have more features than the ones they exhibit to our experience, as long as we recognize at the start that these are theories about it and not features we can directly confirm by self-reflection. This needs to be said for two reasons: first, theories are not confirmed by self-reflection but need arguments to back them; second, the theories we're about to examine have had such wide acceptance for so long that it's often been forgotten that they are theories. As a result, the arguments for them have rarely been examined closely. This is important because I find all three of these theories to be unacceptable.

Theory one: Self-evident beliefs are infallible. This theory has been held by some of the most outstanding thinkers to write on the subject. For example, Aristotle said that the intuition of self-evident truth is "unfailingly true,"[13] and Descartes insisted that "there can be no falsity in the bare intuition of things."[14] "Intuition is that non-dubious apprehension . . . born in the sole light of reason [which] is surer than deduction (although, as we have already noted, deduction can never be wrongly performed by us)."[15] This is a theory because it goes well beyond what our experience of self-evidency exhibits. When we experience beliefs to be self-evidently true, they appear to be irresistibly certain and they produce belief in us. We may subsequently reflect on the fact that many of these beliefs have been confirmed by a large number of people for thousands of years. Such reflection can serve to reinforce the general reliability of the experience of self-evidency. But neither the experience itself nor any subsequent reinforcement can ever justify the claim that anything known to us by an intuition of self-evidency *cannot possibly ever* be mistaken. In other words, when we intuit a belief as certain and find that it comports with the rest of our experience, we have as good grounds for believing it as humans can attain. It is thereby justified and warrants us in asserting that we know it. But that is not the same as an unconditional guarantee that our intuitive capacity can never err so that no belief it yields us could possibly be false. In fact, there are excellent reasons to believe the reverse.

The main reason for saying the experience of self-evidency is not infallible is that there are conflicts between self-evident beliefs. These conflicts have occurred between one person and another, and even for one and the same person at the same time. Since incompatible beliefs can't both be true, such conflicts are enough to show that there are cases in which people experience two beliefs to be intuitively certain when they can't both be true.[16]

As an example of one and the same person's experiencing such a conflict, there is the case of the great mathematical logician Gottlieb Frege. Frege was attempting to develop a system of logic that could account for the whole of arithmetic without using any concepts of quantity or number. He thought he could show that all the concepts of arithmetic could be derived from logical concepts if they were given sufficiently explicit definitions, and that all the theorems of arithmetic could be derived from logical axioms by purely logical deduction. Thus the axioms of the system he constructed were to be purely logical, self-evident truths. But not long after he worked out his theory, Bertrand

Russell constructed a proof that there was an inconsistency within the set of Frege's axioms![17] So despite the fact that each axiom considered by itself had appeared to Frege self-evident, they couldn't all be true!

This is not the only case of a first-class scientist or philosopher's finding an apparently self-evident belief that just couldn't be true, but it's unnecessary to multiply examples. For if this can happen at all, then self-evidency—however valuable—is not infallible. Here it is appropriate to remember Russell's remark that the basic concepts in mathematics all seem self-evident but there has been great merit in checking out their consequences all the same:

> Since people have tried to prove obvious propositions, they have found that many of them are false. . . . For instance, nothing [seemed] plainer than that the whole always has more terms than a part, or that a number is increased by adding one to it. But . . . most numbers are infinite, and if a number is infinite you may add ones to it as long as you like without disturbing it in the least.[18]

Examples of conflicts between beliefs experienced as self-evident by different people are even more plentiful, but perhaps the most striking is one that has arisen concerning a belief long held to be a basic axiom of logic itself. I refer to what is called the "law of excluded middle." This law says that for any belief whatever, it must be either true or false (whether or not we're able to find out which it is). This means that statements we have no way of deciding, such as those about the future or about how the past would have differed had a certain event not taken place or whether there are infinitely many prime pairs, are nevertheless really either true or false. This law has been regarded as a basic law of logic for centuries and has been held to be self-evident by a host of distinguished logicians, including Aristotle, who regarded it as one of three fundamental axioms of thought and reality.[19]

Starting in the twentieth century, however, a number of thinkers have denied that this is a universal law. The denial first gained adherents in a group of mathematicians led by Luitzen Brouwer. For Brouwer and his associates, the law of excluded middle not only isn't self-evidently certain, in some cases it is false. They developed an impressive system of mathematics that omits the law, and its denial has now spread beyond mathematics. Recently their position was the subject of a close examination and defense by philosopher Michael Dummet.[20]

Please notice that these examples of the fallibility of self-evidence are drawn from mathematics and logic, which are precisely the kinds of beliefs infallibilists have regarded as the best examples of infallible knowledge. So if there is disagreement about even these beliefs, then surely the capacity by which they were formed is not immune from error. In fact such disagreements are not only widely known but are (in part) responsible for the rise of the different "schools of thought" in math which have been so intractable. As one historian of mathematics has put it:

> The current predicament of mathematics is that there is not one but many mathematics and that for numerous reasons each fails to satisfy the members of the opposing schools. It is now apparent that the concept of a universally accepted, infallible body of reasoning—the majestic mathematics of 1800 and the pride of man—is a grand illusion. . . . The disagreements about the foundations of the "most certain" science are both surprising and, to put it mildly, disconcerting. The present state of mathematics is a mockery of the hitherto deep-rooted and widely reputed truth and logical perfection of mathematics.[21]

At this point you may wish to object: Even if self-evidency isn't *always* infallible, it may sometimes deliver specific truths that are. What of the logical law of noncontradiction? What of my belief that I am conscious? Aren't these beliefs ones that we can be certain are not false?

The answer to this is that we must not confuse two different but similar issues. All along I have been trying to point to the difference between asking whether we possess a capacity for obtaining truth that is infallible (cannot deliver anything but truth) and asking whether there are beliefs of which we can be so certain that it makes no sense to deny them. I've been arguing that the answer to the first question is no: we are not entitled to claim that our intuitions of self-evidence cannot possibly be mistaken. I've been pointing to reasons for thinking that we are fallible creatures who have no infallible powers for ascertaining truth. Surely we don't have any pretheoretical pretensions to infallibility; the very fact that we check our intuitions of self-evidency against the rest of our experience is already a tacit admission of this point (which reconfirms my contention that infallibility is a theory imposed on the experience).

But saying that a mode of experience is not infallible is not the same as saying that every belief obtained through it is therefore in real doubt. We may indeed have the best of reasons for saying that a particular belief is certain without having to say that one of those reasons is that it was obtained in an infallible way (the best reasons would include the belief's being self-evident and having excellent negative and positive confirmation).[22] And the two beliefs just cited above as prime candidates for infallibility are, I believe, examples of what I've been maintaining: their certainty has the best justification we could want, without assuming or entailing our infallibility. Let's consider them separately.

The first is the principle of noncontradiction, the logical axiom that no belief can be both true and false at the same time in the same sense. This, to be sure, is experienced as self-evident by almost everyone and has often been cited by philosophers, scientists, mathematicians and logicians as the most certain of all truths. But the grounds for claiming such an exalted status for it do not lie in its self-evidency alone. Simply in regard to its experienced self-evidency, the law of noncontradiction is not experienced as any more certain than $1 + 1 = 2$, the axiom of equals, or the perception of our immediate surroundings (since we are completely certain of all of them).[23] The fact that this law is experienced as equally—rather than more—certain is reflected in the way the claim for its supreme status is defended. The usual arguments for it are that (1) without it we could make no inferences, form no concepts and draw no distinctions, including the distinction between what is true and what is false, and (2) the very assertion that it is false assumes its truth. Those are powerful reasons indeed; but notice that they appeal to factors over and above its bare self-evidency. They are reasons gleaned by reflection on its role in the whole of our experience and not on its self-evidency alone. So even though the principle has a special status, that status is not accurately described as "the most certain of all truths" but "the most indispensable of all truths." It is the belief that carries the biggest price tag for rejecting it. These reasons plus its self-evidency make the law of noncontradiction as certain as anything we could want, but even they don't add up to making the experience of its self-evidency infallible. Here's why.

In several forms of Hinduism and Buddhism the experienced self-evidency of perceptual beliefs and of mathematical, logical and other axioms is relativized to the doctrine of maya. This doctrine teaches that the certainty we experience attaching to many normal perceptions and to the truths of mathematics and logic is wholly deceptive. The real truth depends on having a mystical experience that produces the only genuinely self-evident (and infallible!) belief—the belief that there is only one thing: the divine reality. Because perception and logic lead to and/or support belief in the existence of many things, all percepts are rejected as illusions and all concepts are rejected as false. (Thus the very beliefs that thinkers such as Aristotle and Descartes took to be infallibly true are said to be infallibly false!)

The reason for mentioning this is that it's another case of conflicting experiences of self-evidency: the Hindu or Buddhist mystic experiences a belief to be self-evident which requires that even the self-evidency of the law of noncontradiction is spurious. The conflict shows, therefore, that even with regard to this law the experience of self-evidency isn't infallible. Although many people experience the law to be self-evidently true, mystics have a different experience that they say denies and trumps it.[24]

This example and the earlier one concerning Frege show that intuitions of self-evidency can produce conflicting beliefs in the same person and between different persons. Such conflicts do not show that no intuitions ever deliver truth or that we are never warranted in regarding the beliefs they generate as certain. But they do show that the intuitive experience of self-evidency is not itself infallible. A direct result of this is the conclusion that the certainty to be derived from self-evidency is person-relative. What one person can be justified in taking as certain may be different from what someone else is equally justified in taking as certain. This has always been obvious for justification when it consists of weighing arguments and evidence, but the point here is that it applies equally to intuitions of self-evidency. For a person who has no such experience as those reported by Hindu and Buddhist mystics, the self-evidency of the law of noncontradiction—along with the dire consequences of rejecting it—surely justifies its being taken as certain. But those who have such a mystical experience report that it overrides those reasons in a way they cannot communicate.

But what of the second example, the belief that "I am conscious"? This seems even tougher to deny than the laws of logic. It is one of a class of beliefs known by introspection that are called "incorrigible" because there is no way to show them false. Others in this class include such examples as "This looks green to me" and "I have a headache." They simply report how our subjective states *seem* to us. Even the mystic who denies that these beliefs report reality will have to admit that they seem to be true; the mystic claims that nothing we perceive or conceive is really what it seems to be but could hardly claim that we have no experience of things seeming to be that way. (If he did, what would he then be rejecting in favor of the mystical experience?)

But even here I want to maintain that the capacity for introspection is not itself infallible, although such introspective self-evident beliefs are ones that we are justified in regarding as certain. It is not the case that all introspective beliefs are formed by a power in us that simply cannot ever get anything wrong. Introspection can at times be mistaken even if it appears self-evident. For example, we can deceive ourselves about our motives or intentions. And even where a belief is not only known by introspection but is also incorrigible, simply being unable to find out whether it is mistaken is not the same as knowing that it is infallibly right.[25]

To sum up, I find that the attempt to declare that our intuitions of self-evidency are infallible fails. There is nothing that could be said in its favor that could override the plain fact that there are disagreements over what is self-evidently certain, so that its intuition is not a capacity that is incapable of producing false beliefs. This remains so even in cases in which it attaches to incorrigible introspection.[26]

Theory two: The everybody requirement. Defenders of the infallibility theory have, of course, realized that their claim would be defeated if the experience of self-evidency yielded contrary beliefs. For this reason many of them have appended to it a second theory, which I call *the everybody requirement.* This theory tries to avoid admitting that there are ever disagreements about self-evidence by insisting that (except for introspective incorrigible beliefs) a genuinely self-evident belief is one that *all* normal adults see as true once they understand it.[27] This means that no matter how obvious a belief may seem to one person, it's not *really* self-evident unless every other normal adult also sees its truth upon understanding it.

One part of this theory can be dispensed with out of hand: we have already seen why it's a mistake to define a self-evident belief as one that needs only be understood to be seen as true, so I'm not going to repeat all that here. Let's concentrate on the other part, the part that requires all normal people to intuit the truth of a genuinely self-evident belief. What are the grounds for this claim? Haven't we already seen reasons for concluding that intuiting a belief to be self-evident is person-relative, so that the truth of a belief can be obvious to some people but missed altogether by others? Wouldn't this alone be enough to show that the everybody requirement is false?

The defenders of this theory could reply that we are misunderstanding them if we think that their theory is defeated by the fact that some so-called self-evident beliefs are not shared by all people. They might tell us they did not mean to say that whatever anyone thought self-evidently true is a belief everyone else will agree with. Rather, they meant to say that only those experiences of self-evidency on which everyone agrees are genuine. On this view, then, any experience of self-evidency not shared by other normal adults is to be rejected as spurious; only those producing beliefs all normal adults agree with are really experiences of self-evidency.

To evaluate this claim, let's start once again by comparing this theory with the description of the experience of self-evidency we've seen to be confirmed by self-reflection: A belief is self-evident if its truth is not inferred from any other belief but is intuited as irresistibly certain. That description, I pointed out, is itself self-evident. Now compare that with the theory's proposal that everyone who understands the statement of such a belief must see it as irresistibly true. Is *that* self-evident? You will have to answer that question for yourself. But however you answer it, I can tell you honestly that the proposal is not self-evident to *me*. And in that case even if the theory is correct, it is not self-evident and is therefore in need of argument and defense. So the question is, are there good reasons for believing it is true?

The answer is no. For openers, this is a requirement that we could never be able to tell is satisfied! How could we ever know whether *all* normal adults intuit, say, the truth of the axiom of equals upon understanding it? We can't canvass the entire population of the world at any given moment, and even if we could that wouldn't show whether there ever *was* anyone who failed to see it as self-evident or ever *will be* any such person; we can't canvass the dead or the unborn. And that means it is simply impossible ever to apply the requirement since we can never know whether any belief meets it. So if this is really a necessary condition for knowing whether any belief is a genuine case of self-evidency, then we can never know that *any* belief is self-evident. Thus the everybody requirement defeats every candidate for genuine self-evidency in the same way as the examples of mystics defeat the everybody requirement!

But that is an utterly absurd consequence. We do know that we experience some beliefs, such as $1 + 1 = 2$ and the axiom of equals, as self-evident; it is self-evident that we do! (If you were a mystic these wouldn't be good examples, but you would have other examples.) Notice that it won't help to water down this requirement so that it insists only that "most people" or "most people now living" must see the truth of a particular belief for it to count as genuinely self-evident. The objections that count against simply insisting on "everybody" would also count against those watered-down versions; how could we ever tally the majority, for example? Nor would it help to lower the requirement still further so that it reads "most experts." First there is the problem of how to tell who counts as an expert. And even if we could solve that, there could still be real disagreement among experts with no clear majority party to the dispute. In that case would no one's experience count as genuine? And if there did emerge a slim majority for one particular view, should that fact alone make the experience of those people genuine? What if that majority shifted over time? Would we have to keep revising our belief about whose experience of self-evidency is genuine? And why would the mere number of experiencers determine the genuineness of their experience? Clearly this theory is hopeless.

Nevertheless, it has been taken very seriously and has done great mischief. For one thing it has encouraged the reductionist view of self-evidency so typical of philosophy since Descartes. By "reductionist" I mean that it reduces the number of self-evident beliefs by reducing the *kinds* of beliefs allowed to count as self-evident. Traditionally only those of introspection, math and logic (and a few others) were allowed to count, so that the very possibility of self-evident beliefs' arising in physics, biology, psychology, economics, sociology, aesthetics, ethics and so on was ruled out. The effect of this reduction in the kinds of beliefs allowed to be self-evident also reduced the *modes* of experience that genuine self-evidency was allowed to attach to: all beliefs arising from perception or memory were ruled out. And they were ruled out despite the fact that everyone experienced many of them as self-evident every day! In this way the infallibility theory, taken along with the everybody requirement, imperialistically *pre*scribed what was to be permitted to count as self-evidency instead of allowing it to be *de*scribed as we actually experience it. And they got away with this despite the fact that there are no good grounds for these theories whatever!

I conclude, therefore, that the everybody theory fails on its own demerits and thus fails to support the infallibility theory. It has no justification, it is impossible to apply, and it falls short of its goal because of the Hindu and Buddhist successes in rejecting the genuine self-evidency of math and logic. What is more, the very failure of these theories makes our actual experience of self-evidency look better and better. There seems to be no good reason to deny that we find genuinely self-evident beliefs arising in every mode of experience and attached to beliefs of many kinds.

Theory three: The necessity requirement. A third theory often appended to the definition of self-evidency is that (except for incorrigible beliefs) self-evident certainty is a quality that attaches only to beliefs that are necessary truths, that is, truths about relations that cannot fail to hold among their members because they are laws or express beliefs guaranteed by a law.[28]

What's the reason for this theory? Why should anyone want to propose that our intuitions of self-evidency are genuine only when experienced in connection with a necessary law? The answer is that just as the everybody requirement was needed to support the infallibility theory, the necessity requirement is a way to support the everybody requirement. It's simple:

if you want to make it plausible that genuine self-evidency can't be wrong, you need the everybody requirement in order to rule out real disagreements; and if you want to make it plausible that everybody really agrees about (genuine) self-evidency, then restrict it to the laws of math and logic and you'll get universal agreement! After all, who can disagree that 1 + 1 = 2 or that triangles have three sides or that things equal to the same thing are equal to each other? (Remember those who proposed this did not know about Hindu or Buddhist mystics and that the conflicts in math and logic we noticed earlier had not yet arisen.) So if what I've said so far is right about the infallibility and everybody theories, then the purpose as well as the plausibility of the necessity requirement has already been undermined. Nevertheless, it is instructive to see why it further fails on its own account.

First, let's be clear that necessity is not the same as either infallibility or certainty. The infallibility theory says we have a belief-forming power that can never be wrong. I argued that we have no such power but are often justified in being certain of particular beliefs anyway. This happens when the experience of self-evidence produces initial certainty and that initial certainty is not disconfirmed when the belief is integrated into the rest of our experience.

The necessity theory differs from both of these. It says self-evident beliefs are restricted to beliefs which, if true at all, cannot be otherwise. The best way to explain the difference between necessity and certainty is with an example from arithmetic: $74{,}928 \times 163 = 12{,}213{,}264$ is true but is not self-evident to me (if it is to you, I'm impressed!). It is not something I intuit to be irresistibly true without inferring it from anything else. To see whether it is true I need to go through the proof of multiplying and thus infer the truth of the conclusion. But it is a necessary truth, that is, the relation it expresses can't fail to be true and can't be altered. So a belief may be one which, if true, is necessarily true but still be one we're unsure of (Fermat's last theorem was such a belief for centuries). Because a belief can be necessary without our being certain of it, those two qualities—necessity and certainty—are not the same.

Our intuitions of self-evidency are, however, importantly related to necessary truths in this way: it is hard to see how we could know any belief to be necessary other than by means of intuition. We may see with our eyes that one thing and another thing make two things whenever we put them together, but no amount of doing that could ever show that 1 + 1 just *can't* equal anything else and therefore *always did and always will everywhere make 2*. So it appears that the only way to know a belief to be a necessary truth is by intuiting it or by deriving its necessity from other beliefs intuitively known to be necessary by means of rules that are also intuitively known to be necessary.[29] But even if intuition of self-evidency is the way to know necessary truths, we have seen why self-evidency and necessity are not the same quality: a belief may have necessity without being self-evident. So the question is whether the theory we're considering is right when it claims that the reverse is not true: that a belief can't be self-evident without also being necessary.[30]

Once again, what we know about the experience of self-evidency by reflection counts against this theory. From the standpoint of our experience, nothing is more obvious than the fact that at every moment at least some of our present perception generates beliefs that have the quality of self-evident certainty without being necessary truths. Of course, perception is perspectival in a way abstract concepts are not; we know that being far from an object, seeing it in dim light, being sick, and a host of other conditions can render what we perceive less than certain. But we don't experience perceptions such as those to be self-evident, whereas we have others that are as self-evidently certain as anything we could wish for. Can you now deny that you see these words on the paper in front of you? If you are holding the book, can you doubt that you have hands and that your hands are holding the paper on which these words appear? Aren't these beliefs every bit as certain to you (without inferring them) as 1 + 1 = 2? If we accept the collapse of the infallibility and everybody requirements and reject their imperialist decrees, there is no reason left to deny this. In that case the necessity requirement is also groundless.

On the other hand, if we focus on those self-evident beliefs that *are* necessary, they can help us to see confirmation of a point made earlier. That point was the reductionist nature of the traditional theories about self-evidency. One result of these reductionist theories is that perceptual beliefs were disallowed and only the axioms of math and logic (and a few metaphysical principles) were permitted to count as genuinely self-evident. But in fact reflecting on our experience of the self-evidency of necessary truths reveals that we experience many different kinds of necessity. There are necessary relations that are spatial (no plane figure can be both a square and a circle), kinematic (the law of inertia), physical (unsupported objects in the earth's gravitational field must fall to the ground), biological (any living thing with a heart must maintain a minimal body temperature and have kidneys), sensory (nothing can appear red and green all over at the same time) and many more. In other words, any view which insists that only mathematical and logical relations have necessity is a reductionist view of necessity, just as claiming that only necessary truths have certainty is a reductionist view of self-evidence.

Behind these reductionist views of certainty and necessity lies an equally reductionist view of knowledge as a whole. The champions of these theories about self-evidency held a theory of knowledge that took the laws of logic and math to be either the sole source of all truth or one of two sources of all truth (the other being sense perception). In either case, their theory of knowledge was a result of abstracting one or two kinds of truth and proclaiming them to be the winners of the "Reality Sweepstakes." They took their selection to be the source of all other truths because they believed the realities to which those truths referred to be nondependent and thus what everything else depends on. In this way their reductionist theory of knowledge assumed a reductionist theory of reality.[31]

Added to the collapse of the infallibility and everybody requirements, this point shows that there are no good reasons for the theories insisting that all self-evident beliefs are infallible, have universal assent and are necessary. More than that, it shows there are good reasons to think those theories false. Whether they are considered on their own merits, in comparison with our experience, or with respect to the more global theories they presuppose, the result is that they fail. As a consequence we are now unburdened of all of the extraneous requirements these theories attempted to impose on our experience of self-evidence. We are free to recognize the genuineness of our experience whenever and in whatever respects we find it attaches to our beliefs, no matter what they are about and no matter what mode of experience they arise in.

This conclusion is controversial in many respects, and I can't reply here to all of the objections that could be raised against it. So the last section of this essay will deal with only two of them. The first objects to my conclusion that our best perceptual beliefs are self-evident and certain and therefore constitute knowledge. A widespread view these days is that *no* perceptual beliefs have anything like certainty, and currently the most popular version of this view claims to be supported by science. It holds that only science can tell us which perceptions are reliable and to what extent.

The second objection is far broader in scope and is aimed at debunking self-evidency altogether. It is pragmatism's claim that we should believe something only on the ground that it works in practice, never because it is self-evident.

Replies to Objections

Skepticism about perception. The currently popular form of skepticism about perceptual knowledge stops short of denying that there is a real world independent of us, but it does cast doubt on just how much of what we perceive can be taken to reflect that world. It does so by raising the question as to how much of what we perceive is actually contributed by our own minds. This question has been a big issue ever since Kant (d. 1804), and over the years a number of philosophical theories have been proposed to answer it. In the latter part of the nineteenth century, however, the question began to be approached from a scientific basis instead of depending on purely philosophical arguments such as Kant's. In recent years versions of this scientific basis have again become influential, especially among some of the devotees of what is called "cognitive psychology."

One sort of evidence adduced for this skepticism lies in recent findings of psychology: we often deceive ourselves and see what isn't there. Other evidence has to do with discoveries about how the brain processes stimuli. Yet another scientific source for this partial skepticism is the theory of evolution, and it is a skepticism that stems from Darwin himself. Darwin noticed that if the human brain is a product of random evolutionary processes, then we have no reason to believe that what we conceive by means of it corresponds to reality. He said:

With me the horrid doubt always arises whether the convictions of man's mind, which has been developed from the mind of lower animals, are of any value or at all trustworthy. Would anyone trust in the convictions of a monkey's mind, if there are any convictions in such a mind?[32]

More recently Patricia Churchland made the same point:

Boiled down to essentials, a nervous system enables the organism to succeed in the four F's: feeding, fleeing, fighting, and reproducing. The principle chore of nervous systems is to get the body parts where they should be in order that the organism may survive. . . . Improvements in sensorimotor control confer an evolutionary advantage: a fancier style of representing is advantageous *so long as it is geared to the organism's way of life and enhances the organism's chances of survival.* Truth, whatever that is, definitely takes the hindmost.[33]

These comments throw doubt on all beliefs, perceptual beliefs included. So despite the fact that perceptual beliefs may be necessary to survival, evolutionary theory seems to undercut their reliability. The question before us, then, is whether the mechanics of perception, the ways brains process stimuli, and taking them both to have developed evolutionarily are good reasons to doubt that normal perception produces accurate beliefs about the objective world.

My rebuttal of this sort of partial skepticism is that it is self-assumptively incoherent. I coined this term to describe a theory that tries to deny a belief that is in fact an assumption required in order for the theory to be true.[34] Such an incoherency is a serious matter, for any theory that tries to show a belief to be false when that belief has to be true for the theory to be true is in big trouble.

Take Darwin's worries. He's troubled by the thought that if our brains (and thus our belief-forming capacities) developed by random evolution, then there is no reason to trust any of our beliefs as true. The incoherency in this worry is this: Being able to trust our belief-forming capacities is an assumption necessary to believing the theory of evolution. Unless we can trust our perceptions and belief-forming capacities to reveal reality, *there are no reasons to believe the theory of evolution at all.* In fact, if we can't trust our perceptual beliefs, there is no reason to believe that there are such things as brains or life forms to be explained.

The same sort of incoherency crops up in skepticism about perception based on discoveries about how our perceptual apparatus works. No matter what these findings may show about specific perceptions in specific circumstances, they can't possibly impugn wholesale the reliability of normal perception because normal perception is the source and (assumed) reliable ground of those very findings! It is incoherent to claim that a theory can show the unreliability of the very evidence on which it itself is based. If the theory undercuts its evidence, it undercuts itself; if it is itself undercut, it fails to undercut its evidence.

Nothing about this point is meant to deny that our powers of perception are limited, weak and subject to error. We see only a small range of the spectrum of light, for example, and hear only a small segment of the total range of sound vibrations. Our sense of smell is vastly inferior to that of many animals. And in certain circumstances our visual perception at times supplies connections between perceptions.[35] But admitting that perception is limited and fallible is not at all the same as thinking that it is (or even may be) seriously out of touch with reality. Nothing we discover about how we perceive could possibly supply good reasons to suppose our faculties are presenting a virtual reality show of their own making. And so, likewise, no discoveries about how perception works could override our experience that some perceptions yield self-evident beliefs.

If this argument from self-assumptive incoherency is correct, it will yield the same conclusion for our capacity to form nonperceptual beliefs that it did for perceptual beliefs. This is why I said that if Churchland is right in saying that the theory of evolution requires that (all) our capacities have evolved in such a way that "truth takes the hindmost," then she has no good reason to believe that very claim or the theory of evolution or anything else. Notice that I have not said that the self-assumptive incoherency of her position guarantees that her view of the relation between evolution and our capacity to acquire truth is outright *false*. That would be going too far. But what I do say is that her claim undercuts its own justification. And any theory that does that is a poor theory indeed.

For these reasons it appears that science-based skepticism about the self-evidency we experience attaching to many of the beliefs produced by normal perception does not succeed. Once we no longer insist that a belief needs to be infallible, or necessary, or seen true by everybody who understands it in order to be self-evident, there is no reason to deny the self-evidency that attaches to our best perceptions, which includes that the objects they reveal are real.

The pragmatic objection. But what about the pragmatists' criticism that no belief is ever justified by self-evidency? The pragmatist position is that beliefs are to be accepted or not depending on their results, so that we never start off being certain of any belief. This means that it is not, strictly speaking, the *truth* of a belief we come to see by trying it out, but its *usefulness*. According to this theory, there is really no such property of a belief as truth in the sense of corresponding to reality, so there is surely no such experience as the experience of recognizing a belief to be self-evidently true. And this point holds even for the most basic truths of logic and mathematics. Even 1 + 1 = 2 can't be known to correspond to reality prior to trying it out, and trying it out shows it to be "adequate" for our purposes, not *true*.

Since this may sound far-fetched, let me add that this brief description of pragmatism is not a caricature; it is not a set of accusations that I and other critics make against pragmatism, but is the way pragmatists describe their own position. Listen to the prominent pragmatist Ernest Nagel: "There is no way of ascertaining the adequacy of a logical method before we have exercised it to reveal its powers and limitations."[36] And again, "The general problem of truth . . . is thus the problem of perfecting methods of inquiry which . . . exhibit themselves as competent to do the job for which they are invented."[37]

Nagel then goes on to disparage the appeal to self-evidency by ridiculing the idea that "there must be transparently luminous universal truths which the intellect grasps as self-evident,"[38] and sums up his position this way: "The supposition that the fundamental principles of a science can be established by appeal to self-evidency is thus not even plausible."[39] Of course, if Nagel meant only to deny that self-evidency guarantees infallibility, I would have no quarrel with him. But he means to say much more; he means to say that we can dispense altogether with the appeal to the experience of self-evidency.

But it is utterly implausible that *all* beliefs and concepts are accepted because we find them useful in satisfying our needs and desires. They can't all be that because we would already have to have beliefs about what those needs and desires are in order to invent still other beliefs to satisfy them. A great many perceptual and memory beliefs, for example, would have to be held by us on some other ground than testing their usefulness in order for testing their usefulness to get started. Nor are perceptual and memory beliefs the only prerequisites to thinking up pragmatic credit checks. Any test will have to use logical reasoning and involve number concepts. And surely pragmatists, as well as the rest of us, see the truth of mathematical truths such as $1 + 1 = 2$ prior to "experimenting" with them to "find their powers and limitations."

Likewise for the logical axioms. Are we to accept as solemn fact that pragmatists really try out the axioms of logic before employing them so they can know whether they are "competent to do the job for which they are invented?" How could they actually form concepts without assuming the laws of logic or devise ways of testing the pragmatic value of a belief that didn't already presuppose that any concept, belief or test that is logically inconsistent is therefore *false?* And can we take seriously the suggestion that the orderliness expressed by logical axioms and rules is really our own *invention* rather than a kind of order we *discover* in our experience—an order that is irresistibly forced upon us both in ordinary life and in theory making? How, without assuming logical consistency, could we have invented anything, let alone the idea of logical consistency?

The force or "irresistibility" of self-evident beliefs counts against the pragmatist's position in yet another way. The pragmatist keeps telling us that every concept and belief is our own invention, created by us to satisfy our needs and desires. For that reason none can be known to correspond to reality, nor need they correspond to anything in order to "do the job for which they were invented." But if that is so, why are they so intractable? Why are they so outside our control?

I have made this point before, so now I am going to put it in a different way. Try this experiment: look at any object close at hand, such as the book in which you now see these words, and try to doubt that it is real.

Can you do it? Why not? If your belief that you are seeing these words is, as the pragmatist says, your own invention, then why can't you dismiss your own invention? The same holds for 1 + 1 = 2 and the axiom of equals. Can you get yourself to believe they're false? If they were really our own theories—hypotheses we invented for our own convenience—we should be able to revoke or replace them for our convenience as well. But we can't. And that is powerful reason to think they're discoveries rather than inventions in the first place.[40]

Another problem for pragmatism is that its highest value (usefulness) can be compatible with falsity. It is well-known that in science a theory may be shown false in the very sense the pragmatist wishes to ignore: it can be tested and its predictions shown not to correspond to reality. Yet it can still be useful within certain limits.[41] Its usefulness will not, however, remove the fact that it is still a *false* explanation. But if truth meant nothing more than usefulness, it should not be possible to discover that a useful theory is false! By abandoning truth as correspondence to reality, the pragmatist cannot explain how such a discovery is possible.

This latter point has another side, which is that the pragmatist can never avoid using an appeal to truth in the sense he rejects in the course of defending his position. For example, Richard Rorty has a version of pragmatism that focuses on language as the chief tool by which we create the rest of our reality. In the course of arguing for that view he says,

> The . . . notion of language as a tool rather than a picture is right as far as it goes. But we must be careful *not* to phrase this analogy so as to suggest that one can separate the tool, language, from its users and inquire as to its "adequacy" to achieve our purposes. . . . The attempt to say "how language refers to the world" by saying what *makes* certain sentences true . . . is, on this view, impossible.[42]

But how can Rorty claim to know that it is impossible for us to understand how language relates to the world? Isn't that a claim that purports to know something that corresponds to reality and is therefore more than just an invention of our own? This is but one example of what I find typical of the pragmatist position generally; its arguments are self-assumptively incoherent. At every turn it must assume what it is denying in order to make its arguments. And for that reason it gives us no good ground to reject our experience of self-evidency.

Conclusion

The upshot of all this is that our intuitions of self-evidency attach to more *kinds* of beliefs and are thus the ground of more of what we ordinarily think we know than has generally been recognized in traditional theories of knowledge. It does not attach only to beliefs in math and logic, to beliefs agreed on by everyone and to beliefs that are necessary truths; it also attaches to contingent beliefs, person-relative beliefs and beliefs about subject matters of all sorts. Thus there's no good reason to deny that it also attaches to many perceptual beliefs and memory beliefs. The average person's belief that she *knows* she's standing in her own doorway and *knows* her name, address and telephone number turns out to be right after all![43]

This conclusion still leaves many objections and questions unanswered, of course, as this is only a short essay. There are questions about how to elucidate further the positive and negative confirmations of self-evidency, for example, and of just how and when self-evident beliefs work in tandem with other elements of experience to provide (limited) justification for beliefs that are not self-evident. There are also questions surrounding the extent to which self-evidency is the ground—or part of the ground—for specific beliefs that have been so difficult to account for in other ways, such as our belief in other minds.

But delving into these issues would require either setting our findings in the context of an entire theory of knowledge or using them as a key element for constructing such a theory, both of which are beyond the scope of this essay. For now it is enough to show why no theory of knowledge can be adequate that cannot accommodate what we have found: the role of self-evidency is indispensable to knowledge and is experienced over the entire range of human experience.[44]

4

Belief in God &
the Axiom of Equals

*S*o DID YOU GET A CHANCE TO READ THROUGH MY LITTLE ESSAY?
What did you think?

*I thought it was pretty outrageous! When you get done rejecting the three
traditional theories about self-evidency, there seems to be no difference between
it and what you earlier argued is the core of religious experience. If you're really
claiming they're the same, I can tell you right now that I have no intention of
buying that conclusion so easily!*

Fair enough. There's more that can be said in its favor, and now is as
good a time as any to do it.

*Before you do that, I need to ask why you're saying this at all. Doesn't everyone
agree that "faith" means accepting a belief although it is not knowledge? Doesn't
the very term mean that what we take on faith we're not certain of?*

Not at all. Although many thinkers have helped popularize that use of
"faith," it has also been denied, so my position is not unprecedented.
Augustine referred to his belief in God as certainty,[1] for example, and so
did major Protestant Reformers Luther and Calvin (although Protestantism generally has not followed this part of their teaching). Calvin, for
instance, put the position this way:

As to the question, How shall we be persuaded that [Scripture] came from God? . . . it is just the same as if we were asked, How shall we learn to distinguish light from darkness, white from black, sweet from bitter? Scripture bears upon the face of it as clear evidence of its truth, as white and black do of their color, sweet and bitter of their taste.[2]

They who strive to build up a firm faith in Scripture through disputation are doing things backwards. . . . even if anyone clears God's Sacred word from man's evil speaking, he will not at once imprint upon their hearts that certainty which piety requires. Since for unbelieving men religion seems to stand by opinion alone, they, in order not to believe anything foolishly or lightly, both wish and demand rational proof that Moses and the prophets spoke divinely. But I reply that the testimony of the Spirit is more excellent than all reason.[3]

Scripture, carrying its own evidence along with it, deigns not to submit to proofs and arguments, but owes the full conviction with which we ought to receive it to the testimony of the Spirit [of God].[4]

Calvin did not use the expression "self-evident" here, but he may as well have. Nor is this position peculiar to Augustine and the Reformers. Blaise Pascal also held that belief in God is knowledge because it is grounded on the same sort of intuitive self-evidency that scientific first principles are. Since he called the processes of proving and evidence weighing "reason" and called the intuition of self-evidency knowledge of the "heart," Pascal has often been misunderstood on this point. Many writers have supposed that by "heart knowledge" he meant some sort of feeling or sentiment. This is clearly not so:

We know truth not only by the reason, but also by the heart, and it is in this last way that we know first principles; and reason, which has no part in it, tries in vain to impugn them. . . . [For example,] we know that we do not dream . . . however impossible it is for us to prove it by reason . . . the knowledge of first principles, as space, time, motion, number is as sure as any of those we get from reasoning. And reason must trust these intuitions of the heart, and must base every argument on them. . . . It is as useless and absurd for reason to demand from the heart proofs of her first principles before admitting them, as it would be for the heart to demand from reason an intuition of all demonstrated propositions before accepting them. . . . Therefore, those to whom God has imparted religion by intuition are very fortunate, and justly convinced.[5]

It doesn't make your position any more palatable to learn that some of my least favorite writers also held it! But you weren't quoting them to show that the position is true, were you? Their remarks weren't supposed to be part of the "more" you promised to say in its favor?

Certainly not. My purpose was to assure you that this account of religious belief is neither idiosyncratically my own nor, as I said earlier, a ploy to cover for the fact that proofs of God's existence don't work. There is a long tradition of thinkers who have considered attempts to prove God's reality to be a fundamentally misguided project because it differs so widely from the biblical teaching about how we come to know God.[6] Moreover, these thinkers were *not* what are nowadays called "fideists," that is, people who advocate blind, groundless faith. Instead, they pointed to experience rather than proof as the ground of their belief. They held that, as Pascal put it, "for those who believe no proof is necessary; for those who do not no proof is possible."

Oh, I understand the position all right. You don't need to go on clarifying it. What I need to see is more reason to think it's true than I've been given so far.

But before you launch into whatever it is you think can make this position plausible, let me ask you something: Can you really tell me with your bare face hanging out that your belief in God is as certain to you as 1 + 1 = 2? Isn't that hyperbole? Don't you mean instead that your belief in God is an intuition that is something like self-evidency? You don't really think it's literally the same, do you?

Absolutely I do. I find the biblical message to be the truth about God from God as certainly as 1 + 1 = 2. That's because they're both *completely* certain, and no one can be more certain than that! Of course I went through a time when I questioned that belief, as most people do. I examined the arguments for and against belief in God and found them all to fail. But the belief itself continued to look true and to make sense of life as nothing else could do.

When I reflect on it, that fact still seems pretty amazing. I find myself thinking as C. S. Lewis did when he commented that it seems preposterous that the divine Creator on which all else depends should care for people, offer them a covenant of love, forgiveness and everlasting life, and then fulfill that covenant by coming into creation incarnated in Jesus Christ. But every Christian will tell you that although it seems astounding, it's true! And whenever it appears so astounding that it seems just too good to be true, so that we're tempted to think we must be engaged in wishful thinking, all we need do is consider the other candidates for divinity to realize that they're totally implausible.

OK, OK. I wasn't looking for a sermon. So what's the "more" you can add to your claim that your belief is self-evident? Why should anyone take it seriously?

The best thing I can think of would be to give a more detailed comparison of my claim that belief in God is self-evident with that of an axiom traditionally taken to be a clear example of genuine self-evidency. So let's compare the axiom of equals with a summary of the biblical message; let's compare (1) "Things equal to the same thing are equal to each other" with (2) "God the Creator of the universe offers us a covenant of forgiveness, love and everlasting life."

Well, right away there's a difference between them in that the axiom is a law—a necessary truth—whereas the religious claim is not. But I suppose you don't think that matters much?

I don't think it matters at all. Why should it? As we've already seen, the issue here is whether a belief is self-evidently true, not whether it's necessary, infallible or believed by all rational people.

While we're at it, let's notice some other ways in which belief in the axiom and belief in God are unalike. First, although we can never observe that every two things equal to a third *always* equal each other, we can on occasion observe that it is true. But we can never observe anything that just *is* the transcendent Creator. Our experiences of God are never of his bare unconditional being but are mediated through created revelations of himself. Another dissimilarity between the two is that the axiom is an impersonal truth, whereas revelation from God is experienced as communication from him as a person. It therefore carries all the freight of a personal relationship and elicits a personal response. This means that there is an importance and an intensity to the experience of seeing the truth of God's word that can never be matched by that of the axiom. The truth of each may be alike in certainty, but beyond that the comparison seems demeaning. And finally, the consequences of seeing the truth of God's revelation extend to the whole of life, not just to doing calculations. This means that all of life is experienced as his gift so that, as Calvin once put it, "every day, in all things, we have negotiations with God." As a result the believer can't help but be overwhelmed with gratitude for God's love, forgiveness and guidance.

There are probably more differences, but it's not crucial to go on listing them. The important question here is whether both beliefs are alike in being produced by an experience of intuitively seeing them to be irresistibly true without inferring them from other beliefs. As you gathered, I think the answer is definitely yes. The basis for the comparison I'm about to offer in support of this will again be self-reflection.

Since you mean reflection on our experience, I have to say I'm still not sure about your claim that knowing the axiom should be thought of as an experience. I recall being taught it, accepting it and using it, but I don't recall its ever forcefully dawning on me in a way that would make it a distinct experience.

That may be true without its counting against what I'm saying in the least. Earlier I made the point that experiencing the truth of a belief needn't be a distinct *episode;* it can simply be the fact that the belief looks undeniably true without being inferred from other beliefs. I also pointed out that having it "look true" can arrive on us so unobtrusively as to go unnoticed, or can even remain an unconscious assumption.

In my own case, however, there was a particular episode in which I came to see the truth of the axiom. I can still remember clearly the first time I ever heard "Things equal to the same thing are equal to each other." My ninth-grade geometry teacher, Miss Collins, was explaining how proofs are constructed in geometry. She had told us that proofs require the use of axioms, which are truths so basic that they have no proof but don't need it because they are so obvious. I can still recall my reaction. I thought to myself, *Oh yeah? Like what?* As if she had heard my thoughts, Miss Collins said, "For example, things equal to the same thing are equal to each other." And instantly I thought, *Hey! That's right! How come I never thought of that before?*

Though I had never heard the term "self-evident" and the teacher hadn't used it, what I experienced that day was the intuitive self-evidency of that axiom. I didn't infer it from anything else I knew; all that was necessary for me to see that it was true was to understand it and intuit its truth; and the experience of seeing its truth was irresistible. The experience simply produced my belief in it.

It seems to me that in these respects my intuition of the truth of the biblical message is exactly the same. That's why I've continued to believe it, although I've never known of an argument I thought could prove it. (But then I don't know any for the axiom of equals either.) The truth of the biblical message was, like the axiom, something I did not infer from anything else I knew, and my belief in it was simply produced by experiencing it as the truth about God from God.

But aren't you now appealing to memory rather than self-evidency? Aren't you saying that these beliefs are based on episodes of experience you now remember?

Not at all. On the one hand, I can't recall an episode for my belief in God that is similar to the one for the axiom. On the other hand, my belief in the axiom does not now rest on my ability to recall the episode by which I initially experienced its self-evidency. It rests on the fact that every time I think of it I have the same experience of its truth (in fact I'm having it right now!). Its appearing to be self-evident has continued to be an element of my experience, and that is the ground of my belief in it, not merely the memory of the first time that ever happened. In fact, as far as my present belief in the axiom is concerned, it is not even necessary that I be able to recall the first recognition of its truth at all.

Suppose I had grown up in a home with a father who was a mathematician and a mother who was a logician. Let's say all my older brothers and sisters discussed math and logic with them every day. I might very well have absorbed the axiom by social osmosis at such a young age that I could never remember a time when I did not believe it. What difference would that make to my present recognition of its truth?

The same holds for my experience of the truth of the biblical message. We should not be misled on this point by the fact that some people, when confronted with the question as to why they believe in God, give an account of their conversion—the initial occasion on which they experienced its self-evidency. The mere memory of that occasion is not the real ground of their present belief, but the fact that it's self-evident to them *now*.

This means that those of us who find the biblical message to be self-evident are in just as good a position to know its truth as were those who met and spoke with Abraham, Moses or Jesus. It's a mistake to think that you could make a better judgment of the truth of what they had to say if only you could go back in a time machine and meet them for yourself. Unless you were to experience their message as self-evidently the truth from God, you wouldn't believe it then any more than you believe the scriptural record of it now.[7] Being with, and speaking to, those people would be exciting, of course, just as being at a ball game is more exciting than watching a videotape of it. But as far as the truth of their message is concerned, talking to them would confer no advantage over reading the scriptural record, any more than having attended a game confers an advantage over watching a videotape as far as knowing how the game went.

Since that's your position, I'm going to raise two questions that stem from my doubts as to whether belief in God arises from genuine self-evidency. The first question is, how can we distinguish such an experience from feelings of attraction to a belief? This is especially important with respect to belief in God, since it can be so seductively attractive to think that there's a Creator of the universe who loves you.

The second question is similar to the first: how can we distinguish a genuine experience of self-evidency from the effects of cultural conditioning? The fact that particular religions prevail in specific cultures is surely evidence that those beliefs are culturally conditioned. Aren't these both influences that could lead someone to think his belief is self-evident when in fact it only resembles the genuine article?

Good points. There's a lot of evidence that feelings influence the forming of beliefs, and it would be willful blindness to ignore the cultural influences that predispose us toward certain beliefs. Both points have, of course, been acknowledged by most of those who have defended religious experience as the ground of religious belief.[8] There is no question that we must seriously consider whether such influences can deceive us into thinking we have a rational intuition of noninferential certainty when we don't. What's more, I agree with you that it *is* possible.

But before I try to say how to tell real self-evidence from the effects of feelings and cultural influences, I want to preface my comments with two points. The first is that although I think it's possible to point to hall-marks—indicators—of genuine self-evidence, my doing this will not guarantee that we can ever be sure beyond all doubt whether this or that belief is a case of genuine self-evidence or not. Having the right measuring stick won't ensure that we will measure correctly, and we are not infallible about applying such indicators any more than we are about anything else. For that reason even hard and fast rules for genuine self-evidence wouldn't rule out all self-deception, and I can't give you hard and fast rules. The hallmarks I'll point to are at best rules of thumb.

The second is to notice that your questions are often raised in connection with religious belief but almost never in connection with the axioms of math or logic or with beliefs arising from normal perception. That is sheer prejudice. We have already noticed that there are disagreements among the intuitions of mathematical and logical beliefs, and that people advanced in the disciplines of Hindu and Buddhist teaching reject and repress as spurious the apparent self-evidence of both axioms and normal sense perception. So I will be answering your questions on the assumption that the answers are needed by, and apply to, all sorts of self-evident beliefs, not just the religious sort. In other words, the questions you have just raised actually focus on another way that belief in God is *like*, rather than unlike, the axiom of equals.

As to self-evidency versus strong feelings of attraction, I would say that when the feelings involved are conscious ones we can usually distinguish them from the rational intuiting of truth by introspection; they are just not the same *kind* of experience. The value of this test is enhanced whenever the truth of a belief is experienced before any feelings of attraction for it arise, or when it overcomes feelings of aversion to it. (This doesn't mean, of course, that the belief can ever be utterly divorced from feelings. Any belief will always have feelings accompany it—if only feelings of confidence in it!) The main thing here is that feelings have no significance so far as justifying the belief is concerned.[9] This is usually sufficient to distinguish real self-evidence from, say, wishful thinking. To stick with belief in God as our example, many people when questioned about it will say something like "Well, no one really knows for sure, and it would be great if it turned out to be true. Meanwhile, the temple, mosque, synagogue, church or whatever does a lot of good, and there's comfort in thinking it could be right." Talk like that is a sure sign that the speaker does not see belief in God as self-evident. The same is true if the person appeals to group loyalty or social utility. Such an answer is a clear case of *accepting* God's existence *as though* it were true rather than a case of *seeing for oneself* that it is true. But perhaps you were thinking more of the influence of unconscious feelings on our beliefs than of conscious ones?

Yes, I was.

These are more difficult to guard against, and I don't know of any way we can ever tell for sure when such feelings are a cause rather than a consequence of someone's taking a belief to be true. The best indicator I can think of is whether the belief is continuous and abiding through many changes of circumstance, time and place. That may help distinguish a genuine intuition from unconscious emotions and desires: since unconscious motives can change over time, the beliefs based only on them lose their appeal. This is reflected in the way people sometimes say that they used to believe in God, but over the years the belief just seemed to fade away.[10] If the belief is retained despite a change in its unconscious motive, its basis will tend to lapse into wishful thinking or group loyalty, which are easier to discern. But as I warned, this is pretty loose and won't rule out the possibility of cases in which an unconscious emotional motive is so powerful that it is indistinguishable from a genuine rational intuition. I just don't see how to do better. The best we can do is see whether the belief endures over a lifetime; the greater the changes through which it endures, the better the indication that the belief is not just emotionally motivated.[11]

By the way, this test appears to be what was behind the medieval Christian emphasis on the importance of how a person died. In those days the fact that someone confessed belief in God right up to death was taken as a good (though not infallible) indication of genuine belief as opposed to unconscious motives, mere wishful thinking or group loyalty.

To avoid misunderstanding, let me add right away that nothing I've said just now about the enduring character of genuinely self-evident beliefs should be taken to mean that they can *never* change. We already noticed that they can change by being trumped by another self-evident belief, that they can be repressed and that people can even be talked out of them. And they can certainly change as people's experiences of self-evidency change. That is exactly the basis of every change in self-evident belief about what is divine. To sum up: a genuinely self-evident belief is one that we experience to be certainly true without being inferred from any other belief, is prima facie compelling independently of feelings, and endures over time.

Even if what you've said is right, it still leaves me with the suspicion that belief in God isn't based on genuine self-evidency.

Not ever? Is it really plausible that everyone who claims to have had that experience is really only emotionally motivated? What of those for whom the self-evidency accompanied one of the more unusual sorts of experiences we discussed at our first meeting? What of cases in which it overcame strong feelings of aversion?

Besides, if you insist on that position with respect to belief in God, won't it apply equally to belief in the axiom? How can you defend allowing your suspicion to undermine real self-evidency for every case of belief in God, but not for the self-evidency of other beliefs?

I don't know how to answer that, so let's go to my other question. Nothing you've said so far touches the objection that religious beliefs are culturally conditioned. And I see no way you can get around the fact that in India most people are Hindu, whereas in Europe and North America most people are Christian and so on. By contrast, the axiom of equals is accepted across cultures. Isn't the cultural conditioning of religious beliefs—pardon the expression— "self-evident"? Isn't belief in God different in this way from the axiom?

If you're that sold on this point, then it's going to surprise you to hear that I think it's largely a red herring! I know it's widely accepted and has been repeated so often that it's regarded by many as a truism. Nevertheless I'm going to argue that although you've started with undeniable facts, the conclusion you've drawn from them is just about wholly misleading. To make clear why that's so, I first need to distinguish two senses of cultural conditioning.

The strong version of this claim uses "culturally conditioned" to mean that all beliefs are completely determined (forced on us) by our culture.

This is a theory that's gotten a significant following lately despite the fact that it has a peculiar and fatal flaw: It's incoherent because it cancels itself! For if all beliefs are wholly determined by the culture in which we live, then so is the belief that all beliefs are wholly determined by the culture in which we live. In that case we could never know this theory to be true even if it were true. So this attack on self-evidency goes nowhere.[12]

The weaker version of "culturally conditioned" is more plausible, since it claims only that some of our beliefs are culturally determined or that our cultural background makes us more disposed toward certain beliefs. Either way it's phrased, the suggestion is that religious beliefs are among the most susceptible to this type of determination or influence. This is probably the version that seems to you and so many others to be obvious. The reason for its appeal is that it contains a definite element of truth, though, as I said, it's taken to support a false conclusion.

First, let's get clear about the element of truth in the claim: our beliefs surely are conditioned by a host of factors, one of the most important of which is cultural. This goes for self-evident beliefs as well as for those that are not self-evident. No experience of self-evidency occurs in a vacuum. We noticed earlier that whereas self-evident beliefs are not inferred from other beliefs, the experience of self-evidency often requires that we possess other beliefs, have certain capacities, or have had some kind of training as preconditions. So do I admit religious beliefs are conditioned in this sense? Certainly. But so are *all* our other higher-level beliefs, including the learning of our native language and the finer discriminations of color needed by an artist. Moreover, there is good reason to think that this sort of conditioning is required to experience the truth of the axiom about equals as well. In his book *One, Two, Three, Infinity*, George Gamow mentions a tribe of southern Africa that has in their language only the number words "one," "two," "three" and another word meaning "many."[13] Anyone with such a limited array of number concepts would probably not find it obvious that every two quantities buried within the mysterious "many" would, if they were equal to a third, necessarily equal each other.

Likewise, it often takes extensive conditioning for a person to be prepared to see the truth of God's existence and his offer of love. But this fact is not a good objection to the truth of the biblical message. So it is not the case that if people need conditioning to be able to see its truth, then biblical faith must be mere cultural brainwashing, any more than the conditioning needed to see the self-evidency of the axiom makes belief in it mere brainwashing.

I think this same point applies as well to many other beliefs whose basis is intuition. Besides mathematical and logical axioms, there are ethical truths that have been intuited over millennia in virtually every culture. The recognition of the immorality of murder for fun is one example. The fact that these beliefs arise in a cultural context and are influenced by their setting does nothing to support the conclusion that they are *merely* the products of cultural conditioning. Even if there are cultural preconditions for their recognition, and even if there is cultural variance in their formulation, in the nuances of their interpretation and in the ways they're employed, they still have a common core. That, I believe, is powerful evidence that intuition recognizes facts that are true independently of any cultural setting—even if it always does so in some cultural setting.

Having this sort of intuition is precisely what makes the difference between being a cultural "fellow traveler" with respect to a belief and really seeing its truth for oneself. A genuine intuition sees something as irresistibly true in a way that remains, no matter what cultural changes take place. In the case of belief in God this means that intuiting the truth of God's revelation is crucially different from merely accepting belief in God out of loyalty to a way of life—loyalty reinforced by admiration for the belief's charm or beauty, or out of love for the culture in which it is embedded. This is not to deny that fellow travelers can be very tenacious and highly dedicated in their loyalty. But without the intuition of the self-evidency their "belief" is still mere acceptance and only adds up to a *hope* the belief may be true. Thus when they are pressed about the truth of their religious belief, fellow travelers usually say something like "Well, no one can really *know* that sort of thing."

By the way, I should add that being a fellow traveler is not something that comes into play only in regard to religious beliefs. If I'm to take my students seriously, many of them do not see the truth of the axiom of equals for themselves. Some even tell me they're not sure of whether 1 + 1 always equals 2! They say that they were taught it by their teachers and had to use it in their schoolwork, but they never really believed it. So apparently there are fellow travelers with respect to beliefs of all sorts. This, then, is one more way the axiom is in the same boat with the biblical message.

Even if that is so, it doesn't account for the wide differences in belief about what is divine that vary from culture to culture. Are you dismissing the masses of believers in each as merely "fellow travelers"?

Not all of them, no. But I do think it's true that in every culture there are more fellow travelers than people who see the truth of its dominant religion for themselves. And lest you take this as a slur on the sincerity of the masses, let me add that this point has been confirmed to me by Jewish, Christian, Muslim and Hindu clergy. At one time or another I have heard them say something like "If even half of those who come to worship truly believed, we'd really have something!"

The fellow traveler phenomenon is due, in part, to the fact that so many people fail to take the time or trouble to reflect deeply on what (really) looks divine to them. Their intuitive sense of divinity remains subconscious and vague, and it never gets articulated or refined. In large measure this occurs because the dominant beliefs of their culture tend to repress it. The existence of such subconscious beliefs about the divine is confirmed by cases in which people who were raised in a certain culture, and who accepted its dominant religion as fellow travelers, instantly converted to another view of the divine. They say that when they encountered the different religious belief, something about it just clicked. It just looked right. They insist that they had never *really* believed the religion they had accepted until then but had gone along with it because they'd never known of the alternative, which now looks irresistibly right. And they distinguish sharply their previous acceptance (which they often say was due to cultural and emotional influences) from their experience of what they now see for themselves to be the truth.

The fact that there are such experiences also supports the point made earlier about cultural influence not being all-powerful. If all beliefs were wholesale products of cultural forces, the surfacing of countercultural intuitions about divinity (or about anything else) would be impossible. On the other hand, if intuition outstrips its cultural setting, then countercultural beliefs are easily accounted for.

But you can't deny that there is also a much higher percentage of what you're calling "genuine" belief in a religion where it's dominant in a particular culture. How can you explain that?

It's explained by the greater exposure to the belief made available by that culture. Obviously, there will be more people who experience the self-evidency of an idea of divinity where the idea is readily available than where it isn't. The same is true of mathematical and logical truths. Most people living in the world at any given time are not going to think of the axioms of math and logic on their own. Most of those who see them as self-evident were taught them, and most of those who are never taught them never consciously articulate them. Just so with ideas of the divine. Here, once again, belief in God and in the axiom are alike.

Surely they're not in the same boat when it comes to how widely they're recognized! It seems to me that truths of math and logic have had a crosscultural recognition that far exceeds belief in God.

I'm not so sure of that. Do more people believe the axiom of equals than believe in God? Probably not. If we stick to 1 + 1 = 2, you may be right. But remember, we've been taking belief in God as our *example* of religious belief, just as we're taking belief in the axiom as our example of a nonreligious self-evident truth. So bear in mind that what I'm saying about coming to see the truth of the summary of the biblical message applies to all other beliefs about the divine. You, on the other hand, have just compared all of math and logic with only one divinity belief. The more appropriate comparison, then, would be this: whereas everyone sees *some* mathematical or logical truths to be self-evident, which ones they see can vary from person to person. Some people have told me they don't experience the axiom of equals to be self-evident, for example. Likewise, I contend that everybody sees something as divine, though just what that is varies. For many that's God; for many others it's not. So this is yet another likeness rather than unlikeness between the axiom and belief in God.

Despite these similarities, it still seems to me that our intuitions of mathematical and logical truths are different from what you're claiming for beliefs about what is divine. For example, axioms get confirmed by observation in a way that belief in God (or anything else as divine) doesn't. You mentioned this yourself earlier. We can't see with our eyes that every two things equal to a third must be equal to each other, but every time we do observe two such things we

literally see that they are equal to each other. There is no such positive
confirmation for God, Brahman-Atman, the Tao and so on.

You further opened the way for this point when you admitted that self-evi-
dent truths are not maintained in splendid isolation. You said we need to
compare them to the rest of our experience. So my point is that if you can't get
positive confirmation for belief in God as you can for the axiom, then even if
beliefs in divinity are in some sense self-evident, they're not self-evident in the
strong sense the axiom is. In that case the axiom and belief in God are not in
the same boat after all.

No way! You're begging the question against belief in God by saying
there are no observations that confirm it. We can point to a number of
observations that confirm it—that is, are what we would expect if it were
true. Think of the types of experiences we discussed at our second
meeting: Jews, Christians and Muslims all report created manifestations
of God, including visions, voices and a sense of God's presence. They all
report miracles. In addition to such individual observations, there is the
way in which experience as a whole bears being interpreted as God's
creation: theists all insist that the world really *looks* dependent on God.
As a rather literate believer once put it, "The heavens declare the glory of
God; and the firmament shows His handiwork" (Ps 19:1 KJV); and again,
"When I consider Your heavens, the work of Your fingers, the moon and
the stars, which You have ordained, what is man, that You are mindful of
him, the son of man that You visit him?" (Ps 8:3-4 NKJV).

Another important example of confirmation is that many people find
the orderliness and purpose they observe in the world to be what they
would expect from its having been created by God. I am *not* saying that
we can infer God's existence from the order and purpose we observe. It's
not that we experience order and purpose and draw the conclusion that
God exists; rather, we experience God through his revelation and then
find belief in him confirmed by our observation of order and purpose.[14]

Even if that's right, I've just thought of another way the axiom belief is
superior to belief in God. Since believers in God often speak of "growing in faith"
throughout their lives, it seems there's some weakness in their experience of its
truth that needs to be strengthened. It sounds as though they don't really
experience it as certain, and that's not true for the axiom.

This suggests to me, once again, that belief in God is dependent on feelings, whereas the axiom isn't. So even if belief in God is based on experience in some sense, it's not a genuine experience of self-evidency, as it is with the axiom.

What you're pointing to is partly correct. But I would say that for both religious belief and belief in the axiom we must distinguish between the intuition of its truth and subjective *feelings* of confidence in that truth. Our feelings can grow even when our intuition is one of complete certainty. The more we employ the axiom, the more it turns out to be just the rule we need to make coherent sense of things, and the stronger our feelings of confidence in it become. Just so, a person may experience the truth of God's offer of love and forgiveness as certain but nevertheless experience growing feelings of appreciation and reliance as the practice of faith over the years makes sense of life and confirms that God is faithful to his covenant promises.

The kinds of feelings involved in belief in God differ from those aroused by the axiom, of course. But that difference is not one that makes the apprehension of the truth of either belief dependent on feelings. The real difference is that the feelings involved in a personal relationship with God are much more complex and variable than anything evoked by the axiom. At times believers feel especially blessed, or tested, or far from God. So our feelings can vary greatly toward God, whereas they hardly seem to change about the axiom. But that shouldn't fool us into confusing the intuition of a truth with the feelings it can engender. The fact that the feelings accompanying a belief are improvable doesn't show that the intuition of its truth was—or is—in any way deficient.

Here's a quick illustration of this difference. If you show me a rope bridge across a thousand-foot gorge, my fear of heights is going to elicit a very predictable reaction: I'm not walking out on that thing unless a pack of wolves is chasing me. If you and three other people all go to the center of the bridge and jump up and down, I may have all the rational evidence I need to believe it will support me. Surely if it supports four people it will support just me after all of you have crossed over it. But I can assure you that unless I hear howling close at my heels, I'm not going out on any rope bridge no matter what weight it has already supported.

I must admit that these similarities are disconcerting; there are more of them than I would have supposed. But I'm still troubled through all of this by the fact that many ideas of divinity conflict with one another and can't all be true. I know you said you would return to this point later, but I can't help mentioning it now. Even if you're right that belief in God is held by many on the same ground as the axiom, how does that help if—as you admit—all other religious beliefs are held for the same reason?

OK, let's deal with that question now. I'll start by pointing to what mathematicians or logicians do when they disagree about an axiom.[15] They conclude they cannot both be right (provided they don't give up the law of noncontradiction[16]). Just so, in the case of contrary religious beliefs, they cannot all be correct. This does not in the least count against the fact that in each case these beliefs are still equally the products of fallible experiences of self-evidency, which are genuine sources of certainty *for those who have them.*

The result in both cases is that there is no neutral, decisive way to settle who is right. This is why those who advocate different axioms because they experience their self-evidency, like those who hold different divinity beliefs on the same ground, never succeed in persuading one another by arguments or evidence. Their disagreements cannot be settled by debating the premises of their beliefs, for the beliefs at stake have no premises. When they do debate, what happens is that each party to the disagreement tries to show that his or her belief explains things better than any alternative belief. But this rarely makes much headway, since there are almost always some things that each of the beliefs at stake seems to explain well. So in the end these debates never seem persuasive to anyone but those who already believe; and all the while no arguments will make the contrary experiences of self-evidency go away.

But you are making it sound as though reason is helpless to decide these matters! Earlier you denied being an irrationalist; what has become of your denial?

I still deny being an irrationalist, and I think that any real irrationalist who overheard these conversations would confirm my denial! We need to recall here the distinction I drew earlier between the two ways a belief may be rational. First, it may be the conclusion of reasoning from premises. Second, it may be an intuition of self-evidency needed in order to engage in reasoning. My position is that, as in the case of axiom beliefs, *no belief in something as divine is rational in the first sense, while all beliefs are equally rational in the second sense even though they can't all be true.* But this is not irrationalism. I am not saying that reason is useless or abandoning it in favor of wishful thinking, hunches or feelings. On the contrary, I'm saying that these beliefs are held on the same intuitive grounds that the principles of reason are held on, and surely reason*ing* is helpless to prove the basic beliefs that are its own axioms and rules. That was Pascal's point: reason must trust these intuitions of the heart and base all its reason*ing* upon them. In short, my position is that just as there are conflicts of intuitions about axioms, there are conflicts of intuitions about what is divine. And just as there is no neutral (non-question-begging) way to settle the differences about axioms by argument, there is no way to do that for religious ones either.

But people argue their axiom differences, don't they? There's rational debate involved as each side gives reasons for its position.

That's right, they do. But you don't mean to suggest that this doesn't happen in religion, do you? There have been centuries of debate and argument both within religious traditions and between them. There have been long debates between Hindus and Buddhists, Hindus and Muslims, Christians and Muslims, and Jews and Christians, for example. In recent years Buddhists have established an ongoing dialogue with virtually every major world religion. Clearly, the major disagreements about what is divine are debated extensively in those traditions, just as they are in the context of theories. Let me put the same point as a question. What do contrary intuitions of the divine lack when they are advocated by religious traditions as compared with how contrary intuitions are advocated in philosophical or scientific theories? And why should we think intuitive beliefs are rational, or more rational, depending on how rigorously they're argued for, *when the arguments given for them in theories have never settled those debates any more than they have in religious traditions?*

Please don't misunderstand me. I'm not saying that it's useless to discuss or debate different religious beliefs, any more than it's useless to debate different axiom beliefs. In each case, arguing can serve to bring out greater detail in the contrast between beliefs, elicit the implications of each for a host of other issues, and clear up misunderstandings. But arguments do not *settle* the question as to who is right in a purely rational way that persuades all parties to the debate.

So your objection seems to be a two-edged sword. If intuition can't count as justifying a belief because people have contrary intuitions, then how can rational arguments do it? Aren't there as many contrary beliefs whose backers claim to have justified them by argument as there are beliefs whose advocates hold them on intuitive grounds? Intuitions of self-evidency are not infallible. But neither is rational argument. When did a Hindu ever convince a Muslim by purely rational argument, or when did a Christian ever convince a Buddhist? When we look at philosophy and science, do Aristotelians convince Kantians, or materialists persuade phenomenalists? Do rationalists convince pragmatists, or existentialists convert positivists? Surely not. So why should the fact that intuitions can't all be right count against their justifying a belief for one who has an intuition of its self-evidency? Insofar as that person also conscientiously checks it against the rest of his or her experience for negative and positive confirmation, that intuition will be as justified a belief as anything we could hope to have. This conclusion may not be old-timey rationalism, but it's surely not irrationalism!

I'll tell you what *would* be irrational. It would be irrational for anyone to give up whatever he or she experiences as self-evident because of arguments. It may well be that a brilliant skeptic can cook up clever arguments to show us that we can't be sure that things equal to a third thing are equal to each other, or that we don't know that the objects we presently perceive really exist, or perhaps even that we don't really know anything at all. But we'd be fools to throw away what we directly experience as self-evident in favor of such an argument when such arguments also assume certain beliefs to be self-evidently true! An amusing illustration of this point arose some years ago when it was argued that a bee should not be able to fly based on what was known about the laws of aerodynamics.[17] Its wings were supposed to be too small and to vibrate too slowly to support the weight of its body in flight. Confronted with the evidence for this conclusion, what was the reasonable thing to do?

Give up the belief that bees fly? Raid the nearest hive for honey in the confidence that the best the bees could do would be to run after us? Surely not. Even if we couldn't detect a fault in those calculations, the reasonable thing would be to conclude they were mistaken all the same.

Are you saying that there's no way ever to argue against what someone sees as self-evident?

No. But the only time we should take an argument to defeat a belief experienced as self-evident is if it uncovers a conflict between that belief and another self-evident belief. This point is more often ignored with respect to religious belief than it is with respect to conflicts about axioms, so I want to repeat that they apply equally to both. A person who continues to believe in God despite being unable to refute a clever argument against her belief may appear simply stubborn and irrational to someone who does not share that belief and thinks his own argument is sound. But this does not show that she is doing something she has no intellectual right to do. Ironically enough, this same point was made by the great skeptic David Hume. Hume pointed out that whenever arguments "prove" what is contrary to experience, people always believe their experience and become skeptical of the arguments. And, he added, that is just what they *should* do. So I'm saying that a critic who seriously expects someone to give up belief in God because of his argument has forgotten Hume's point. He has failed to realize that producing arguments to refute what someone experiences as self-evident is as futile as trying to put Humpty together again.

I want to repeat that this point applies equally to nonbiblical religious belief as well as to belief in God. Anyone who experiences, say, matter, or the laws of mathematics or logic or Brahman-Atman or anything else as self-evidently divine would be doing something irrational to be persuaded *by argument alone* to believe that it is God who is unconditionally real. And, as with axiom disagreements, this means that insofar as these differences are the products of contrary experiences of self-evidency, *there is no way to settle them at all by reasoning.*

Although this conclusion applies just as much to axiom disagreements as to religious ones, and although it's as true of the divinity beliefs that occur in theories as much as it is of divinity beliefs in religious traditions, these cases have never been treated alike. No one seriously suggests that axiom beliefs are intellectually disreputable, and no one calls the divinity beliefs that occur in theories irrational. No one seems to feel compelled to write books suggesting that those beliefs should all be given up. So why are the divinity beliefs of the religious traditions treated that way? Why is it that when their disagreements appear to be irresolvable by argument and evidence, the question shifts to whether they are *rational* at all?

The answer, I think, is that they are treated differently because of the demands that real self-evidency must be infallible, must be confined to necessary truths, and must be the same for all rational people. Those requirements, and the accompanying pretense that axioms of math and logic meet them, have resulted in a skewed judgment of the status of beliefs about what is divine. Without these requirements, the strong likenesses between the experiential ground of religious beliefs and of axiom beliefs would have been much more apparent. In other words, what got concealed by those demands is precisely my main point: belief in God, like other divinity beliefs, can have the same ground as belief in the axiom of equals or any other intuition of self-evidency.

When we combine this point with our earlier discoveries about what religious belief is, and about what counts as religious experience, I think it makes a powerful case for recasting how we regard religious belief generally and belief in God in particular. Belief in God has especially suffered from being treated as a hypothesis—an educated guess—that has poor supporting evidence. But all such treatment is defeated where belief in God is grounded on the experience of its self-evidency. If this is denied by dismissing self-evidency generally (as pragmatism tries to do), it will also have to be dismissed as unreliable for such beliefs as normal sense perception, as well as the truths of logic and mathematics. But self-evidency is not a part of our experience that we can disregard at will. There is no way to avoid relying on it, because all the arguments anyone could give for not relying on it must make use of beliefs (such as logical rules and perceptual beliefs) that can only be known by means of it. Any wholesale denial of it will therefore be self-assumptively incoherent: its denial will assume its reliability at some point. Once again I conclude that belief in God and the axiom of equals are in the same boat whenever they are grounded in an experience of self-evidency.

This is a very disturbing position. I would like to be able to show it's wrong, and I'll try to do just that next time we meet.

Meanwhile, I will say this: even if you're right about everything up to this point, I certainly have nothing to fear! You've just admitted not only that I'm not doing anything irrational by not believing in God but that I'd be irrational to be persuaded to believe! Your view means that since I have no such experience as "seeing the biblical message to be the truth about God from God," nothing you've said has—or should have—any persuasive force for me at all!

That's right. My experience can't warrant your beliefs, and vice versa. (That's yet another way belief in God is like the axiom!)

Is that all you have to say? Look, when I asked you why you believe in God, I intended to give religion a fair shake. I wanted to see if there were arguments I'd overlooked, evidence I'd slighted or any reason that might make it seem plausible. You've given me none of those things! Instead I get an account that, even if correct, amounts to saying there's something wrong with my religious intuitions; it means that short of having a different experience of self-evidency, there's no way for me to know whether God is really there or not! Is that where you intend to leave the matter?

No, it's not. There is more to be said. But it has to do with putting yourself in a position to have the requisite experience, and I'm not sure you want to hear that yet.

What do you mean, "put myself in a position to have the requisite experience"?

Well, that's what I'm not sure you're ready to hear. To really hear it, you'd have to be convinced that the essentials of the position we've discussed so far are at least possibly correct. After all, why would anyone go to the trouble of trying to put himself or herself in a position to have a certain experience without being convinced that such an experience is possible?

I'm certainly not convinced that you're right; but do I think your position is even possible? *That's harder. I'm going to have to think more about that too before I can answer. But meanwhile I'd like to hear what you have up your sleeve. Let me worry about whether I "really" hear it.*

OK. It's simply this. Whenever someone fails to see something others claim to see, there are really only three things the others can do to help that person. One is to tell the person what to look for, another is to put the person in a position to be exposed to whatever it is the person has missed; a third is to is to lay out a conceptual framework that explains the relations of what was missed to other parts of the person's experience.[18] Consider these three in relation to the axiom of equals, for example. What would you do if you were teaching geometry and a student in your class said he didn't see that the axiom is true? You couldn't offer a proof that inferred it from other beliefs, so how could you help him? I think the answer is that you would do the three things just mentioned. You would make sure he understands the axiom and try to point out the consequences of denying it for geometry. You would get him to attend the class and see how the axiom works in doing geometry. And finally, you would try to explain how its being an axiom makes sense by the way it fits into the whole of geometry and by the way it contributes to that whole.

I'm saying the same things to you now about belief in God. Up till now I've been trying to tell you what to look for; I've been saying you should forget about proofs and look for (some part of) the biblical message to be self-evident. Now I'm going to suggest that you perform the experiment of putting yourself in a position to have that experience. The first part of this is to read the Scriptures. God can, of course, make himself known in any way he pleases, yet most people come to belief in him by some kind of contact with the message of his offer of covenant love. The primary source of that message is the Scriptures. So if you're serious about finding out whether God is real, put yourself in the position of being exposed to the biblical message.

To carry out this experiment fairly, though, you need to do the reading as open-mindedly as you can. For example, if you've read the Scriptures before, or especially if you've been instructed in them from a particular point of view in your youth, try to divorce yourself from that past and see them again on their own terms without the old associations. A good modern translation will help, as will a Bible dictionary or other reference book that can explain unfamiliar terms, allusions to strange places and so on. The main thing to remember about the reading is that you do it while regarding the writings as ordinary-language records of the covenants that reflect the time, place and outlook of their writers. If you read them with hostility to see whether you can pick holes at every turn, there is no question about whether you can pick holes; you can. The point is to read them as *possible* revelation from God.

Another piece of the experiment is that you put yourself in contact with a community of those who believe in God. You need to attend their worship and Scripture study, if only as an outside observer. Remember that in math also you can't really appreciate the spirit and nuances of its techniques in isolation from the tradition that passed it on and a community of those who know and use it. This is even more important for fully grasping belief in God because it is a belief that impinges on the whole of life in a way the axiom of equals doesn't begin to approach, and you need to see its impingement at work. Christians have always said that impingement is the power of God's Spirit applying the biblical message to people's lives, so that's something else you need to see for yourself. And finally, it's important because in addition to your own reading of Scripture, you need to hear it interpreted and applied to life by those better acquainted with it, just as a math student who doesn't find the axiom self-evident needs to have it explained and needs to see it used by those who do.

Don't misunderstand me here. I'm not at all suggesting that the skeptic about the axiom or about God should establish this sort of association in order to be enculturated into becoming a fellow traveler to the belief! On the contrary. I'm suggesting reading the Scriptures and associating with a community of those who believe only as a way of putting yourself in a position to experience for yourself the truth that God is real. Still less should you misunderstand me to be suggesting that associating with a congregation of believers will impress you with how virtuous they are or how less likely to err than other people. On the contrary! Any community of believers will be made up of quite ordinary folk with quite ordinary foibles and failings. What is more, among their failings will be failings to live up to parts of the teaching they believe. But perhaps in their very failings you will see the power of the gospel at work—how the biblical message changes the everyday lives of average people.

The third thing I said we could do for someone who failed to "see" the axiom of equals is to provide a conceptual framework showing both the internal relations among geometrical beliefs and their relations to the rest of our experience. In the case of belief in God we call such a conceptual framework "theology." So this part of putting yourself in the best position relative to its self-evidency would be to look at a theology—not as dogma but as a help to opening up your experience.[19] This last point has been well expressed by George Mavrodes:

> [Theology] may seem a cumbersome apparatus and in fact we may not need it all at once. It may also seem singularly ill supported. But if some part of it makes contact with some element in our experience so that each illuminates the other, then we will take new interest in that theology. If it goes beyond this, it serves to light up broad ranges of our experience so that we begin to see a kind of sense in our lives, then perhaps we will be more than interested. More important, if the terms and doctrines provide us a clue as to how to respond, and if, as we try that response, we find our experience continuing to make sense, then we are likely to say that [the theology] was a true one and that we also have heard God speaking to us.[20]

Finally, if you are really serious about being open-minded and "giving it a fair shake," you would try saying prior to each Scripture reading something like "If you're really there, God, show me." You would do this purely hypothetically, of course. I'm not suggesting that you say this already assuming God exists, but only to take seriously that it is possible.

That's it. That's the experiment. If you try that and nothing happens, you still won't know why any of us find the biblical message to be God speaking to us. (In that case I'd say, "Try it again!") If you do experience it to be the truth about God from God, then you'll find that you also have experienced *God* speaking to you.

Before I go near that with a ten-foot pole, I need to formulate carefully what bothers me about your position and decide whether I do think it's even possible.

OK. That's what our discussions are for. But let me add one last thing about this experiment. Short of having powerful reasons for thinking that it isn't even *possible* that God is real, refusing to make this experiment will put you in the position of rejecting a belief while failing to do what could be done to find out if it is true. In that case, your rejection will be one you're not intellectually entitled to! Consider a parallel case: Suppose you told me there is wonderful art in a certain museum and I persisted in denying it while refusing to visit the museum to see if it's true. I would not be entitled to my denial, right? Well, the same holds true concerning belief in God.

Occasionally someone replies to this point: "Oh, but I did all that as a kid. My parents took me to church, and I read the Bible. So I have already made this experiment." But that's not right. Look at how your concepts of things other than religion have changed since you were young. Your ideas about politics, sex, money and a host of other subjects have matured in ways you could not even have guessed at as a child. But have your ideas about religion also matured? Many people fail to realize that they are comparing their childish concepts of God to their mature concepts of everything else! And this mistake is compounded by the way many of the most childish misunderstandings of belief in God are perpetuated and reinforced in the popular media because those who work in them are making the same mistake. (Keep in mind that the popularization of virtually any important belief inevitably distorts it in direct proportion to its complexity, the length of time it's been popularized and the need of a given population to be corrected by it.)

Suppose someone were to tell you that Shakespeare's work is worthless and that she knows this because as a child she attended her parents' Shakespeare club each week and heard a few lines read from two or three different plays. Would you think she had given the work of Shakespeare a fair shake? Surely not. You would advise her to read *all* the plays, become acquainted with their language and historical background, study their interpretation and, above all, see them performed. You would certainly tell her that until she considered Shakespeare's work through adult eyes and stopped going only on childhood memories, she was in no position to judge it.

All the same points apply to the biblical message. To know whether it is true, you need to perform the experiment of seeking your own experience of God.

Not before I air out my objections to it, I won't! If there are good reasons to think in advance that belief in God is a big mistake, then I have no intellectual obligation to waste my time with any such experiment.

5

Objections to
Belief in God

I'*VE THOUGHT OF A LOT OF OBJECTIONS SINCE OUR LAST MEETING,
and it seems to me that they punch big holes in belief in God. Not only that, I
think they do so whether or not you're right about how to define religious belief,
whether everybody has some such belief and even whether there are people who
experience biblical teaching to be self-evidently "the truth about God from God"!*

*You do admit that an intuition of self-evidency needs to be integrated into
the rest of experience in order to stand up, right? It has to lack significant conflict
with other self-evident and well-established beliefs?*

Absolutely.

*Well, belief in God fails to pass that test in four ways, any one of which is
enough to cause it to be rejected. So you should conclude either that you're wrong
about its being self-evident or that your experience is one of the cases in which
it proves its fallibility.*

*First, the source for its content, the Scriptures, won't survive scrutiny as to
their reliability. I'm starting with Scripture because you emphasized that it's
the record of God's revelation—of the covenants God is supposed to have made
with humans. You call those covenants the biblical "message" and say it's what
looks to you to be the truth about God from God.*

I've done some reading since our last meeting that convinces me your attitude toward Scripture isn't idiosyncratic; it's widely shared in mainstream Judaism, Christianity and Islam, each of which anchors its beliefs on what it takes to be divinely inspired Scripture (Muslims even refer to Jews and Christians, along with themselves, as "People of the Book"). So wouldn't you agree that if Scripture turns out to be unreliable, so does its "message" and so does belief in the God who is supposed to have revealed it?

Yes, I would.

Second, there are biblical teachings that are flatly inconsistent with the findings of science. That means there are scientific reasons for regarding those teachings as false. Therefore your experience that they are self-evidently the truth about God is disconfirmed.

Third, the belief fails to stand up because it conflicts with the way we find the world to be. I know this is an old objection, but it still looks good: Because there's so much suffering in the world, God either doesn't have the power to prevent it or has the power but doesn't use it. If God has the power but doesn't want to prevent suffering, God is not good; if God wants to prevent suffering but doesn't have the power, he's not the all-powerful Creator. Either way God can't be what Scripture "reveals" him to be.

Finally, I'm going to come back to the point that the appeal to self-evidency equally supports incompatible—and even crazy—beliefs. That shows we can't trust self-evidency when it comes to what's divine the way we can for axioms or perceptions. Unless there are very convincing reasons to think none of these objections has any merit, I'm not about to admit that the account you've given so far is even a possible one. In that case I'm not about to try some "experiment" to see if God is real—any more than I would to see if Santa Claus is real.

For sure, your objections all deserve discussion; a large number of thinkers have written tons of books on each of them. So before I take them on, you must understand that each of them by itself would require a book-length discussion for adequate treatment. Since we can't do that now, the best I can do is begin an answer to each of them in such a way as to indicate the lines along which a fuller answer could be developed had we the time to pursue it more thoroughly.

Fair enough. Let's start with the simplest objections to Scripture and work up to the more serious ones. First, it's not clear that there is a "biblical message"

*that is just obvious to any reader. Aren't there many interpretations of
Scripture? Don't they differ radically? Look at all the denominations of
Christianity, for example. Aren't they products of conflicting opinions as to
what the teaching of Scripture is?*

Most of the denominations that divide the Christian church are not
the product of different interpretations of Scripture. Many denominations arose over what language or form of worship to use, loyalty to an
individual leader or even secular political hassles. These don't represent
any disagreements about what the "biblical message" is, let alone
whether we can say there is one at all. In fact, a recent comparison of
the creedal statements of every major branch of Christianity showed
that they agree on 98.5 percent of their teaching! This includes all the
major points of doctrine, including the creation of everything other
than God by God, the human fall into sin, God's offer of love in his
covenant, God's incarnation in Jesus Christ the Messiah, whose life,
death and resurrection fulfilled that covenant on behalf of everyone
else, and the communion of believers until Christ's return made
possible by the presence of God's Spirit in and among them.[1] This is
not to say that there are no doctrinal controversies in Christianity, of
course. There are controversies in every major religious tradition, and
Christianity is no exception: some of the divisions in the church have
been caused by disagreement over the less than 2 percent of doctrine
that remains controversial. Most of that small percentage concerns how
to organize the church itself and how to interpret the sacraments. By
the way, these differences are minuscule compared to the differences
within other traditions such as Buddhism, which has the widest
disagreements of any major tradition.

*Even if you are right about that, there's another real problem with thinking
that Scripture's "message" came from God. It's one even Sunday-school children
often ask about: How could Abraham or Moses or Jesus, or anybody else, know
that it was God talking to them? I don't know that it was; I don't see how they
could have either!*

*Here's the same question from another angle. How can you dismiss
someone today who claims God is speaking to him? Wouldn't you have to
take seriously all claims of revelation from God on your view? But if so,*

*they're all equally unpersuasive, since the contents of these alleged revelations
are inconsistent with one another!*

You just described two different objections that are closely related but
not identical. Let's take them one at a time. As to the first question—how
could those to whom God spoke know it was God speaking?—I think
the position I've already sketched for you in our preceding talks answers
this beautifully. The experiences that people had of God's revelation
included the self-evidency that it was God who was revealing himself. I
pointed out earlier that even though nothing in the universe just *is* the
uncreated Creator, God can still make himself known by mediating
revelation of himself through things, events and persons *created for that
purpose.* So no matter how God's revelation came, or whatever else
accompanied it, the experience of it always included the quality of its being
self-evidently the truth about God from God. That is exactly what
Thomas Hobbes missed in his sarcastic quip that "when a man says God
spake to him in a dream he says no more than that he dreamed God spake
to him." Those are not the same experiences, the difference being precisely
that the first has a self-evidency the second lacks.[2]

I take your second question to be about the differences among those
who believe in God: Jews, Christians and Muslims. Their disagreements concern the right way to stand in proper relation to God, and
they are disagreements that stem from what each tradition takes to be
genuine revelation. The Hebrew Scriptures are accepted by them all;
Christians add the New Testament to the Hebrew Scriptures and
Muslims add the Qur'an to the New Testament. This difference,
concerning which writings are genuine revelation, turns precisely on
which writings contain teachings experienced to be self-evidently the
revelation of God. That is why after centuries of debates they've never
made any progress toward persuading one another. Does that answer
your question?

*Not exactly. I didn't mean to ask only about why each of those traditions
disagrees with the others, but also how they could deal with anyone who ever
claimed or now claims that God is speaking to him. Obviously, you believe in
God. But can you honestly tell me that you take seriously a guy who says God
told him to run naked through the town and camp out on your lawn? No, you*

think he's crazy! So why do you and other theists take seriously Moses and the Jewish prophets, or Jesus and his disciples, or Muhammad, but not the guy who pitches his tent on your lawn?

Well, it would be presumptuous of me to answer that question on behalf of Jews and Muslims. No doubt they have their own ways of dealing with it and are far better qualified than I to say what those are. So I speak to this point only as a Christian.

The Christian answer is easy, since the New Testament explicitly deals with your question. One text in particular addresses it, though that fact isn't obvious from most English translations. So here's a more precise translation of its wording: "God, who at various times and in different ways *began and continued to talk* to our ancestors by prophets, has in the latter part of these days *finished talking* to us by a Son" (Heb 1:1-2, translation and italics mine).[3]

On the basis of this and other New Testament teachings, the doctrinal position of every major branch of Christianity is that direct revelation from God has ceased until the return of Jesus Christ. This doesn't mean that God can't make himself known in the ways we discussed at our second meeting, of course. Nor does it rule out occasions on which God's Spirit illumines the Scriptures to believers so that we see truths there we had not fully grasped before. Neither does this doctrine rule out the experience many believers have of God's guiding their judgment in a way that produces in them a conviction of his will for various matters in their lives. What has ceased is new doctrine—new information as to the terms and conditions of God's covenant required for standing in proper relation to him.

This answer is not unprecedented or ad hoc on the part of Christianity but fits with the pattern of God's revelation as recorded in the Hebrew Scriptures. Throughout history there have been periods of time in which God gave direct revelation in order to establish or administer his covenant, which were followed by periods of silence. For example, early in the story of the prophet Samuel (1 Sam 3:1) there is the remark that the word of the Lord was rare in those days because there was no ongoing revelation. The story then describes how God renewed direct revelation through Samuel. This pattern of alternating revelation and silence is also evident from the record of the way God made covenants with Adam and Eve, Noah and Abraham, as well as the one with Moses. Each succeeding covenant built on the previous ones in a way that was progressive and cumulative, until they culminated in the covenant of Jesus the Messiah, which included the promise that he will return to establish God's kingdom on earth. So Christians regard the New Testament (or new covenant) as the last revelation we can expect from God until Christ returns at the day of judgment.[4]

On that ground I am bound to reject any and all claims of new revelation. This applies to those made by Muhammad, Joseph Smith and Sun Myung Moon, as well as to the guy who pitches a tent on my lawn. The last people who can justly claim to have had such direct revelation, according to the New Testament, were Christ's own apostles.

By the way, in the light of this doctrine it's significant that the vast majority of people since Christ's apostles who report having experienced God in a perceptual way (by voices, visions and so on) do not claim to have learned any new doctrine. Even the calls to action they sometimes report are rarely anything more than what is already contained in Scripture, such as "Pray for peace."

But this position seems to mean you are accepting the teaching of Scripture on the say-so of its writers. Aren't you then taking someone else's experience as authoritative for you? Isn't that the reverse of your appeal to self-evidency?

Let me put it this way: does each and every teaching of Scripture taken by itself appear to you self-evident? Surely you don't claim that! But if not, you're taking whatever doesn't appear self-evident on someone else's authority. And that goes for the claim that revelation ceased with Jesus' apostles. It may have been self-evident to whoever wrote it that it's the "truth from God," but is that claim, all by itself, as self-evident to you as the axiom of equals? If not, you're in the position of needing evidence for the honesty, reliability and divine inspiration of whoever is your source for that belief. This difficulty is compounded by solid evidence that certain sections of Scripture were compiled from many sources, had more than one author or were written by unknown authors. If you can't even know who the writers were, how will you check up on their reliability?

What is worse, these points apply to the allegedly historical events recorded in the Scriptures as well as the doctrines built on them. How can you believe those documents to be accurate in the face of all the historical and textual criticism showing they're not? Why should the scriptural accounts of, say, the exodus or Jesus' life be taken any more seriously than the legends about King Arthur?

Taking biblical teaching on the say-so of others is just what the appeal to self-evidency avoids! Yes, the recording of the occasions on which God revealed himself depends on there being people to write it; God didn't write the Scriptures himself. But although the writing depends on there being writers, my believing what they wrote to be true is not a matter of my blindly trusting them to have been accurate, unbiased and inspired. Nor do I need somehow to *prove* they were accurate, unbiased and inspired. The truth and inspiration of the parts of what they wrote that are not self-evident are guaranteed by the parts of their message that are self-evident. This point is a bit tricky, so it needs explaining.

Go ahead.

You're right that no one who believes in God sees each and every teaching of Scripture, taken by itself, to be self-evident. Let me add that what we do see in that way can grow; teachings not at first seen to be true in that way can come to be seen that way later. It is also the case that what is experienced as self-evident varies from person to person. This is so for lifelong believers as well as those who first come to believe in God as adults. No one sees each and every teaching of Scripture to be intuitively certain, and I can't give you a specific list of teachings that appear self-evident to all believers when taken in isolation because their truth isn't learned in isolation. Rather, there are teachings that appear *as a cluster* to be self-evidently the revelation of God. And though the contents of the cluster can grow, as I said, there are specific teachings that all theists find included in the cluster (for example, God's reality and love), and teachings that all Christians find included in it (for example, the Trinity, the incarnation, Jesus' messiahship). It's only after experiencing the cluster that a believer can distinguish its individual members. But it's always the case for every believer that there are teachings that appear self-evident and others that don't; some are in the cluster and others not. The teachings that are not in it are accepted by the believer on biblical authority.

The connection between the experience of self-evidency and biblical authority is, roughly, this: Among the scriptural teachings experienced as self-evident truth from God are those asserting that God has created everything other than himself, sustains everything and continually oversees the course of events in creation. This providential superintendence is specifically said to include God's inspiring and preserving the written record of his covenant dealings with humans—the very record that the believer finds to contain self-evident truth about God! Thus the teachings that are part of a believer's self-evident cluster confer God's authority on those that are not in the cluster. In other words, since it is God who brought it about that the teachings that don't appear in the self-evident cluster are conjoined to those that do, God intended that we believe both sets of teachings; thus whatever the Scriptures teach has God's authority.

On this view, therefore, it doesn't matter to the authority of Scripture exactly what sources its writers used, whether we can always be sure who they were, or who subsequently edited or compiled Scripture texts. To be sure, the findings of textual and historical criticism can be valuable for understanding Scripture's meaning more precisely. But contrary to what some scholars have claimed, these rarely have any bearing on the truth of what it teaches,[5] and we need not await the outcome of scholarly research in order to know what to believe.[6]

Of course there are *theories*—hypotheses—proposed by textual and historical critics which, if correct, would certainly require Scriptural teachings to be false. Many of these are guesses about who really wrote what or about how history might have differed from what the Scriptures record. Some suspect that Bible writers may have had motivations that either tainted their accuracy or induced them to lie outright. But the evidence for these theories is not at all like the evidence that we have for theories in the natural sciences. For the most part these theories are based on little more than suspicion and speculations derived from it. And in fact, it isn't difficult to engage in imaginative reconstruction to suit our suspicions concerning any historical event! But simply being able to imagine another way things could have happened is not a good enough reason to believe they in fact did happen that way. Besides, there is virtually no limit to the ways things can be imagined to have been, which is why there are literally dozens of contrary hypotheses on virtually any topic connected with the Scripture texts.[7]

In addition, we need to remember that these theories, like all others, are formulated under the influence of whatever the thinker believes to be divine. It is no surprise, therefore, if scholars who do not find the biblical message to be true are inclined to invent alternative accounts that rule out teachings that theists either experience as self-evident or hold on biblical authority. The fact that they can do this is no reason to take their guesses, however well informed, over what we directly experience as self-evident or as having biblical authority. This is a point that is naively put into practice by the majority of average pew dwellers without their being able to articulate it. For this reason the faith of ordinary folk has proved impervious to critical theories, although the critics find such faith to be ignorant and stubborn in contrast to their own sophistication.

This all needs to be qualified by saying it applies to what Scripture *teaches*, not to everything it happens to mention. I am not suggesting that the Scriptures are word-for-word inerrant.[8] The only type of error they are utterly free of is teaching falsehood about God, our relation to God *and whatever else needs to be true for those to be true*. It's this religious focus that qualifies all they contain and is understood as having God's authority. (I mention this because some scholars have argued that because the Scriptures are inspired by God, they must be as perfect as possible. That won't fly. God created you and me, but we're not perfect. There is no good reason to suppose that anything God brings about must be as perfect as possible.)

OK, you can stop right there! If that is your position, it is a perfect lead-in to my next objection. You've drawn such a tight connection between what's self-evident and the rest of scriptural teaching that if any of it is false, so is whatever you take to be self-evident! But since science shows some of that teaching to be false, you must now regard your intuitive experience as misleading.

I'm referring, of course, to what has been discovered about the origins of the universe and the evolution of living things, including humans. As far as I can see, the scientific account is hopelessly incompatible with Genesis.

Before you reply, let me add this: if you're going to say that evolution is only a theory and that you are within your intellectual rights to reject it in favor of what seems self-evident to you, then you and I are wasting our time. I can see your saying that about the weakly supported and mutually conflicting hypotheses as to who wrote what, or about suspicions as to how history might have differed from what the Scriptures record. But that's utterly different from the hard evidence we have from fossils, genetics, atomic dating and so on, all of which support evolutionary theory.

I agree with you that there's a lot of evidence for evolution, and I'm not about to say that it's to be dismissed because it conflicts with Genesis. What I'm going to say is that it doesn't conflict with Genesis.

You must be joking!

Physics says that the universe developed over billions of years; Genesis says it took six days. Evolution says life forms developed slowly over millions of years; Genesis has them all appearing in three days. There is a ton of evidence that humans gradually evolved, whereas Genesis says that at one moment there were no humans and at the next there were. If that isn't enough, Genesis says the first woman was formed from the body of the first man! Whatever faults you may accuse evolutionary theory of having, no version of it ever said anything that unbelievable!

I'm familiar with those accusations, and I promise to address every one of them. But if you're to appreciate the full force of my answers, I need to preface them with some preliminary remarks. Only then can I deal with each of the points you've raised.

I'm all ears.

My preliminary remarks concern the specifically *religious* focus of the Scriptures I've mentioned several times now. This includes Genesis, of course. Genesis is a prologue to the covenant with Moses intended to connect the Mosaic covenant with previous covenants God had made, the covenants with Adam and Eve, Noah and Abraham. Chapter 1 starts by identifying the God who is making the covenant as the Creator of everything other than himself and the only divine reality. In contrast to the pagan creation myths, Genesis neither regards any natural thing or force as divine nor thinks of God as merely one among many bearers of divine power.

Chapter 2 then focuses on the covenant receivers. It stresses that God created humans for fellowship with himself and gives that as the reason for establishing merciful covenants with us. It records the first covenant of probation, the fall into sin and God's merciful second redemptive covenant. What then follows is a brief synopsis of the subsequent major editions of the covenant in order to connect them all with the covenant with Moses, which follows in Exodus, Leviticus, Numbers and Deuteronomy. The point is that the early chapters of Genesis are not to be read as science. They constitute a birth announcement of the universe and the human race, including the announcement of their Father's loving covenant promises.

Most of the objections you have raised utterly miss this religious, covenantal focus of the text and assume that Genesis is an attempt to do science, or at the very least to say what we would have seen had we been there to observe the origins of the universe and humans. That's a serious mistake; there is plenty of evidence *in the text* to show that it was not intended to be taken that way. That evidence convinces me that if we could bring Moses back and ask him how old the universe is, how long it took God to bring about all the life forms, how old the human race is, and what processes God used to accomplish his purposes, he'd be amazed. He'd say something like "I just brought you the greatest news anyone could possibly hear! I've told you that the Creator of the world is offering you his love and forgiveness, and look what you ask me! Are you crazy?"

Please don't take this criticism personally. It's understandable that you missed this point; many scholars have also missed it. Part of the reason they missed it is worth recounting, since it will help us to avoid the same mistake.

Before the modern era no one even dreamed there could be a way to discover answers to questions such as how, or how long ago, the universe and life originated. So those who believed Scripture to be God's revelation thought that their only chance to get such information was if Scripture contained hints about it. Thus instead of concentrating on Scripture's religious focus, they succumbed to what I call "the encyclopedic assumption." They treated the Scriptures as an encyclopedia packed with infallible information on virtually every topic. It was no surprise, then, that they subsequently "found" information on physics, astronomy, geology, biology, medicine and a host of other disciplines.[9] But the encyclopedic assumption resulted in their failing to fully appreciate the religious import of the text of Scripture, putting burdens on the text that it cannot bear, and distorting science.

To sum up, early Genesis forms a prologue to the covenant that God gives to Moses. It is to be read as profound religion and not as crude and faulty science. It's now time to back that up with a closer reading of the text.

I think I'm following you, but I still don't see how examining the text is going to help. You're not simply going to allegorize it or dismiss everything incompatible with science as poetry, are you?

Not at all. It's not poetry, as you can see by comparing it with some of the references to creation in the Psalms, which *are* poetry. Nor am I going to allegorize anything. My purpose is to try to understand the text on its own terms and see from its own structure, vocabulary, historical setting and so on what it is trying to say. If there is symbol, poetry or allegory in it we need to *find* them there, not impose them on the text for the sake of making it look acceptable.

Let's start by discussing the part of the Genesis account that you referred to which says creation took place in six days. Did you ever notice how days one, two and three correspond to days four, five and six?

What do you mean?

After God calls creation into being,[10] the first three days go like this: On day one God separates light and darkness, on day two God separates seas and atmosphere. On day three God separates dry land from the sea and orders it to produce plant life. Look at how that matches up with days four, five and six. On day four God forms sun, moon and stars; on day five God orders the sea to produce sea life and forms birds; animals and humans are formed on day six.

See the correlation? Each set of three days corresponds to the other; the first set speaks of God's bringing about the preconditions for what he forms in the second set. Light is a precondition for sun, moon and stars; atmosphere and sea are preconditions for birds and sea life; and dry land is a precondition for the appearance of plants, animals and humans.

Now, I have a question for you: are you prepared to argue that this matchup is accidental? Can you doubt that such a prominent feature of this text—the obvious correspondence of the two sets of days—was intended by its author?

I suppose not. There's no way to prove it one way or the other beyond a doubt. But if we have to assume one rather than the other, then it does look intentional.

I agree. In that case the "days" being spoken of here appear to be a way of stating God's creative purposes. They are a framework for conveying an *order of purpose* rather than an *order of time*. Although the basic meaning of the word "day" is a twenty-four-hour period, it can also be used to refer to other things, as it does in "every dog has his day" or as Scripture does elsewhere when the prophets speak of "the day of the Lord." Here it stands for a division of God's creative purpose rather than a period of twenty-four hours. St. Augustine noticed this last point over fifteen hundred years ago when he said that "day" couldn't be intended as a literal twenty-four-hour period since, according to the text, the sun wasn't created till the fourth day!

The upshot is that the "days" of creation are not trying to convey a chronological order or supply a scientific description of the early stages of the universe. If you ask me why the term "day" was used at all, the answer is also fairly obvious. The Mosaic covenant includes the command that God's people work six days and rest the seventh. Thinking of God's creative work in this way made it a model for humans to emulate. Thus speaking of God's accomplishing his purposes as taking place in six "days" does (at least) two things at once. It expresses God's creative work in temporal, creational terms we can understand and expresses it in a way that can make God's work a model for our own.[11]

I find that the intent of the text, then, is to teach truth about God rather than supply scientific information about the universe. It teaches that there is no blind chance or fate involved in the origin of the universe, nor was God limited by any other force or by the material he had to work with. The purposes are God's, as is the accomplishment of those purposes. Virtually no attention is given to the processes God used or the length of time those processes took. The only thing the text says about the results of God's command for each purposive stage of creation is "and it was so." Thus there's no justification for reading the text in isolation from the covenant account that follows it, for mistaking its order of purpose for an order of time, or for missing its essentially religious character. It's simply religious through and through, and attempting to read it as science is a blatant distortion that obscures its religious significance.

That may be right about how to understand the days of creation, but it won't save the story of Adam and Eve. That still sounds mythological to me!

OK, let's also consider that account bit by bit. First, let's look at the statement that God formed Adam out of the dust of the ground. It's possible, of course, to read that as the description of a single act by which Adam came to exist. But it's also possible to read it as a comment on Adam's *nature:* he is made of the same stuff that everything else is made of, and consequently he is subject to death. I find that the rest of the story confirms the second as the right way to read the intent of the expression "the dust of the ground." Notice that after Adam transgresses the covenant he is told that he may no longer live under God's special protection in the garden of God but will have to struggle with the ground for his living. Because of his disobedience, he will lose that struggle and will ultimately return to the ground: "out of the dust you were taken; you are dust, and to the dust you shall return" (Gen 3:19 RSV). Moreover, the rest of the Hebrew Scriptures confirm this understanding of the expression, since it is always used to refer to human mortality.[12] It conveys the important teaching that humans never are, nor ever can be, more than creatures of God. They are not bits of divinity stuffed into physical bodies, nor are those bodies merely as a house for the soul as, for example, the ancient Egyptians and Greeks thought. Humans are by nature subject to death, and whether they live or die depends ultimately on God; there is the strong intimation that had they remained in proper relation to God, God would have continued to sustain their lives forever.

Relative to what bothers you, however, what we need to notice is that the account does not describe humans as coming into existence because God made a mud mannequin and breathed on it so that it hopped up and ran around.

Even if that's right, you can't deny that the story unavoidably gives the reader the impression that at one moment there were no humans and at the next there were.

That's surely so, and I think it means to do that.

Well then, it's still hopelessly at odds with evolutionary theory. No matter what version of that theory you take, wouldn't we expect many nearly human creatures to develop into human beings at roughly the same time?

Let's take that as true and consider the rest of the Genesis account in relation to it. Does it create a hopeless inconsistency? I think not.

To see why it doesn't, we need to raise an issue that is crucial to any discussion of human origins: how to define what counts as a human. No one can avoid this, troublesome though it may be. If we are trying to interpret skeletal remains and the question is whether these bones belonged to *humans*, then we are going to employ some idea of what it means to be human, whether we acknowledge it or not.[13] Do we mean a being that makes tools? Do we mean one that lives in community and shares food and protection? There are animals that do these things. Remember, what we really want to know when we examine skeletal or cultural remains is whether these beings were essentially like *us*. So we can't avoid the question of the defining features of a human. Rationality? The use of language? There is evidence that gorillas and chimps can learn and use sign language. Apparently they carry on limited conversations with their trainers and even with each other. In that case they too may have some conceptual and linguistic abilities.[14]

The point of view of Genesis, however, is that humans are beings created in the image of God for fellowship with him. They are *religious* beings. They exist in dependency on God, whether they believe that or not. If they don't believe in God, it's because they believe in something else as divine instead. We've discussed this already, and I tried to show you why it makes sense to think of humans this way once you understand what religious belief is and how it influences all of life.

And I told you I'm not convinced of that.

Right. I'd not forgotten. But for now that doesn't matter. Whether *you* agree or not, that's the way *Genesis* sees humans.[15] So from its viewpoint, the origin of the human race is identical with the origin of beings in the image of God, a very significant part of which is their capacity for fellowship with God.[16] From the biblical point of view, then, the origin of humans is the same as the origin of beings with religious consciousness, that is, beings with an innate disposition to know what is divine and to respond to God when he reveals himself as the divine Creator on whom they depend. Genesis does not view a human as a being with a certain skeletal structure or brain size in comparison to body, nor as a being with certain rational and linguistic capacities. Though all of these (and more) may be preconditions for the appearance of religious consciousness, it is the religious consciousness that is the defining difference. Given the religious focus of the text, that can't be much of a surprise.

No, I guess it's not. But how does it help to alleviate the conflict with science?

The Genesis account of human origins is written from a commonsense point of view, not a scientific one. In commonsense speech we speak of one event as the "cause" of another without ever trying to distinguish as many causal factors as we would in science. For example, if we're asked how a fire started, we ordinarily give an answer such as "Somebody threw a cigarette butt onto those rags." We don't say, "Those rags were exposed to sufficient oxygen," "The flash point of the oil on them was lower than the temperature of the cigarette butt," and "The cigarette butt came in contact with the rags." Even in science we are rarely called on to list *all* the relevant causes of a fire; a complete list would include our continent's being above sea level!

The point is that no matter how many causal factors there may be for an event, ordinary speech usually gives only the last one or two as its cause. That is, in commonsense speech, we use "cause" to mean the last event of a series which, when added to all the other conditions needed, was sufficient to produce the effect we're trying to explain.

That is what Genesis is doing. It neither suspects nor is interested in all the causes that it took to produce humans. It neither affirms nor denies that a long evolutionary process was involved. It's interested only in the last step, the step before which there were no humans and after which there were. That step was God's revealing himself to the first beings in whom he simultaneously brought about the capacity for religious consciousness. In other words, God's speaking to Adam and making his covenant with him was the last causal step in Adam's becoming fully human. That is, God's breathing on him "the breath of life" was God's speech, which made Adam's biological life into a life that was fully human. The breath and spirit of life for humans is not merely a matter of bodily metabolism but of the gracious word of God, which both makes them and sustains their lives in relation to God. This is why Jesus said humans do not live by bread alone but by the word of God. So God's speaking to Adam and his offering of the covenant was the step by which God made him fully human. Adam was a human rather than an animal the moment he responded to God.

On this view there was indeed a real person who was the first human. But on almost any view there would have to be, wouldn't there? Suppose there were many beings on the threshold of becoming human at about the same time. No matter what you choose as the defining difference, there would have to be some individual who was the very first to meet the definition![17] On the view I'm sketching here, the full humanity of those other nearly-human beings would have been brought about by their learning of the covenant from Adam and Eve.[18] And the fact that they would learn it from Adam and Eve rather than directly from God makes sense of the Christian doctrine that Adam was the (first) religious head of the human race.[19]

Does that mean you accept that the first woman was made of the rib of the first man?

I believe there is a parallel between the way the text uses "Adam's rib" and the way it uses "dust of the earth." We already saw that although "dust of the earth" basically refers to material, it was used to symbolize human nature. I think the same thing happens again with "Adam's rib." It's a term that literally designates a body part and is said to be the material from which Eve was fashioned. But here it symbolizes the common human nature she shares with Adam; it's why she is said to be the only one among all God's creatures who is a proper mate for him, and why she is held equally responsible for covenant disobedience. Of course, it also means that in some way Eve's humanity depends on Adam's. But on the view I took of how other nearly-human beings became fully human, this makes sense: because Adam received the covenant from God directly, he was directly made fully human by God;

because Eve received the covenant from Adam rather than directly from God, her becoming human depended on Adam in a way that his did not depend on her.

Are you saying there was a long evolutionary process that ended with God's giving some nearly-human hominoids both the capacity for religion and a revelation of himself?

Yes. I think the evidence for an evolution of life forms—including humans—looks strong. It doesn't, as some zealots have claimed, have such overwhelming evidence that it has ceased to be a theory at all and should be regarded as an uncontrovertible fact.[20] It has a number of snags that still need a good bit of work and may yet need to undergo some important revisions. At a number of points it's still in need of supplementary evidence, the way recent work in genetics has supplied evidence in answer to several questions that used to have no good explanation. But on the whole I think some version of it is probably right.

But let's not get sidetracked. Please remember that the point of what I've been saying is not to arrive at an evaluation of the truth of evolution as a biological theory, but to see whether that theory is in "hopeless conflict" with the teaching of Genesis. I have just shown you that it's not.[21]

This seems especially clear if—once again—we are careful to keep in mind the *religious* focus of Genesis. Genesis has no interest in or inkling of the physical and biological processes involved in the development of animals that led to the emergence of humans any more than biology has of the states of consciousness and beliefs of the creatures whose remains it discovers. Given that each has a distinctive focus and purpose, I find the two accounts to be complementary rather than in conflict; the only way to make them appear inconsistent is to misread Genesis as trying to do the same things that science tries to do.

Let me add that mistaking the difference between the religious and the scientific accounts as conflict has been done not only by theists who succumbed to the encyclopedic assumption but by scientists as well. Some of them have gone out of their way to make gradual evolution appear as incompatible with belief in God as possible. They have spoken as though the fact that physics and biology examine creation and don't discover an obvious pattern of purposive planning is reason to think there is no God who superintended the evolutionary process to produce just what he wanted produced. But confining our attention to physical and biological properties, laws and processes can't possibly show that there's no transcendent Creator they depend on.[22] And the claim that the properties, laws and processes that science studies have independent reality is itself a (contrary) religious belief! So any scientist who claims that an evolutionary process *shows* there was no purpose of God involved in the development of life has either made a logically invalid inference or is actually preaching an alternative religion.[23] Ditto for any claim that science *shows* humans are "only higher animals" without a soul or religious center to their consciousness. It's either a blatant logical mistake or the dogmatic assertion of a contrary religious belief (or both). Science can't show anything about what lies outside its scope, and anyone who asserts that nothing lies outside its scope has simply offered a confession of a contrary religious belief in place of an argument.

But wouldn't the fact that evolutionary history looks chaotic and random support the inference that it is unplanned? Why is that unreasonable?

It's unreasonable precisely in relation to belief in God! If no one had ever even thought of the idea of God, then it *might* seem reasonable to assume there was no purpose behind the course of evolution. Even then, however, not finding evidence of purpose wouldn't conclusively show that none is there, as everyone knows who has ever been fooled by camouflage or has mistaken a beaver dam for an accidental pile of brush. As long as no one ever thought of the possibility of a personal Creator, the lack of conclusive evidence would entitle us to say that there is no purposive order to the course of evolution *as far as anyone can see*. It wouldn't be definitely ruled out, but there would be no reason to think it true.

In relation to the possibility that God exists, however, it's sheer dogmatism to say we know that only blind chance guides the evolutionary process. For if God's providence did superintend evolutionary history to accomplish his purposes, there would be no grounds whatever for thinking those purposes would have to be obvious to us when we examine the course of that history.[24] That is explicitly denied in Scripture; in fact, we are warned that what looks random to us is nevertheless under God's control (Prov 16:33). This is a point that theologians have recognized for a long time.[25] After all, the Scriptures insist that God superintends the course of human history too, and that looks at least as chaotic as the course of evolution! So finding that evolution did not unfold the way we would have planned it shows nothing about whether or not God planned it. Contrary to what some theologians and philosophers have said, there is no particular way in which God would have to work or in which we could expect him to do things. He's not obliged to be as efficient or as rational or as beneficent as possible. God can work his purposes any way he chooses.

The upshot is that in relation to the possibility that God is real, and to the fact that if God is real then neither he nor his purposes could be expected to be discovered by the scientific examination of creation, it's sheer dogmatism to say that God is not real because you don't find God's purposes in the course of doing physics or biology. Not being able to find something by doing science doesn't show it can't be discovered any other way, let alone that it doesn't exist at all.

But there are still other things that seem unscientific in Scripture, even if you're right about Genesis. Miracles, for example. Surely no scientist can accept Moses' parting of the Red Sea or Jesus' turning water into wine, to say nothing of raising someone from the dead. There's no misunderstanding of the text involved in those stories, is there?

No, certainly not. Those stories report just what they seem to report: out-of-the-ordinary events performed by the power of God to call attention to God's covenant dealings with humans. They are startling, to be sure; if they weren't, they wouldn't do the job of getting our attention. But whether they're unscientific depends on what you mean by that. If you mean they can't be accounted for by science, then that's true but irrelevant. How could science explain what comes about when the power of God is added to the forces in creation? If you mean, however, that the possibility of such events *conflicts* with science, then I disagree.

First, let me make clear that I agree with Augustine, Calvin, C. S. Lewis and others that a miracle doesn't violate the laws of nature. The power of God can do things that we can't do or even think of any way of doing, but that doesn't mean the laws God has set over creation are violated by God's acting in nature. If I hold up a book, for example, the fact that it doesn't fall isn't a violation of the law of gravity because the book is not an unsupported object. If I remove my hand and God suspends the book in midair, it's still not an unsupported object. No law would be violated by such an event, even though there is no explanation that science could give of it.

There is nothing derogatory to science in saying that there are events it can't account for. The scientific enterprise is one of explaining the world in terms of the properties, laws, patterns, functions, processes and so on that we find in it or postulate it to have. The fact that it's the best way we have of discovering new information about the world doesn't guarantee that nothing can happen in creation that is beyond its scope. Whether or not we believe there can be events that can't be explained scientifically depends on whether or not we believe in God. If God exists, then surely he can bring about miracles. What reason could there be for thinking that an almighty Creator can't change water into wine? (Grapes and bacteria do it regularly!) Or for thinking that the Creator and Sustainer of the universe and its laws can't raise the dead? It all turns on what you take to be divine. If you reject God and take some aspects of the creation as divine, you are then bound to say that those aspects are the ultimate explainers of everything and that nothing can occur that can't be explained by them.

The upshot is that no one really rejects belief in God because of the miracle stories; they reject the miracle stories because they don't believe in God and have put something else in God's place. Calvin once observed that if the Bible recorded no miracles, people would say that it couldn't be from God because God would have done miracles to attest Scripture as his word. But since it does record them, people say they can't believe Scripture is from God because it reports miraculous and so is unbelievable![26]

You suggest that no scientist believes the miracle stories. Not so. Many scientists have done so and still do, depending on whether or not they believe in God. Again, the only way a science can rule out miracles is by assuming that the only reality is what that science studies. But believing that there is nothing beyond what one or another of the sciences study is itself a religious belief; it's a belief that all reality is basically physical, or whatever else the thinker is regarding as divine. (Notice again how such divinity beliefs are brought *to* science instead of being derived from it or justified in the course of doing it, as was shown by our thought experiment.) Thus theists have as much right to view science in the light of their belief in God as nontheists have to view it in the light of whatever they believe to be divine.

I see I'm not getting anywhere with this line of attack, so I'm going to go on to my next objection, which I think is the strongest. Surely you can't deny that the Scriptures say God is good, and you've already admitted that they teach God superintends the course of history. So what more do you need to see? Either God doesn't care enough to stop the suffering caused by injustice and cruelty, or he does care but hasn't the power to stop it. This shows conclusively that there couldn't be any being that is both all-good and all-powerful, as the Scriptures say God is. Surely you can't elude this criticism by some clever construal of the biblical texts! You do admit that Scripture teaches God to be all-good and all-powerful, don't you?

Yes, though we need to be careful about exactly what those terms mean. Some writers have construed them in ways that are not what I understand the Scriptures to teach. So we really need to examine some of the sections of Scripture that deal with the existence of undeserved suffering in the world.

OK. But before you do that, let me say that I've been reading up on this objection to belief in God and don't think the usual replies to it succeed; it may save us some time if I say right away why they fail. One standard reply is to say that God gave humans free will, that free will would be meaningless unless he let them exercise it, and that much of the suffering in the world is the result of human choices to do evil rather than good. That doesn't succeed for several reasons.

First, even if it's true that people have free will, it doesn't explain why God didn't create people so that they have good natures and so always (freely) choose what is good. That has to be possible on your view, since the New Testament says Jesus was sinless (Heb 4:15) and that in heaven everyone will be (Rom 7:7—8:30). So presuming that Jesus and the redeemed in heaven have free wills, God can create people who are free but good. If he's going to do it later, why didn't he do it from the beginning? Why doesn't he do it now?

Second, why doesn't God prevent (at least the worst cases of) the suffering that stems from the evil use of free will? It seems to me that it could be done without violating anyone's freedom. He could intervene to protect an intended victim or just cause the evildoer to drop dead! Hitler could have been run over by a beer truck in Munich before coming to power, for example, or Stalin could have choked on a fish bone.

Third, evil free choices don't explain the great deal of suffering caused by natural disasters—earthquakes, droughts, epidemics, tidal waves and so on. Not only are these not the products of creatures' exercise of their evil free wills, but your Scriptures say God causes them himself (Is 45:7; Mt 10:29)!

In addition, there are choices that are not evil that result in suffering, which could have been avoided had anyone had the knowledge and power to stop them. For example, not long ago someone had a heart attack at the wheel of his car and crashed into another car, killing an entire family. You and I might have prevented that from happening had we only known of the impending heart attack. But if God exists then he did know of it, did have the power to stop it, and yet did not! For all these reasons, even if free will is a fact it doesn't explain God's not preventing suffering.

I could say at this point is that God does prevent a great deal of suffering; in fact, he probably prevents far more than he allows. Notice that your own way of putting the accusation accepts that God superintends the whole of creation, which is why you see God as responsible for the undeserved suffering that results from both. But that same point would also mean that every time someone could have suffered but didn't, God is responsible for that too. And surely it is no exaggeration to say that there are hundreds of possibilities for suffering by every person on earth every day that do not ever occur. That amounts to hundreds of billions of prevented occasions of suffering daily!

Cold comfort to those who suffer!

No doubt you're right. I didn't mean to sound uncaring about those who do suffer. I was simply pointing out that every one of us has far more for which to be thankful to God than we ever realize. But that's not what you're interested in at the moment.

No, I'm not, and for good reason. If you say that God sometimes prevents suffering, then you're admitting that God has the power to do it all the time. So

I'm asking, what about the other times?

OK, I think I understand your position.

I'm not sure you do. You phrased this objection as questioning how there can be undeserved suffering in the world, but it's not only the undeserved suffering that's the problem. So let me restate the objection by repeating a point I made in connection with free will but this time giving it a wider application. According to your Scriptures, God will one day bring heaven to earth. Life in God's kingdom will be everlasting and will be free of wrongdoing and suffering because those who inherit that everlasting life will be given natures that are good. They will live lives of happiness and love, at peace with God and their fellow humans, right?

If that's true, then it shows that God can make humans who have free will but are good and thus can make a life for humans that's entirely happy. So there won't be any suffering, period. No one will deserve any, and God will prevent there being any that is undeserved. But if that's possible, then why didn't God do it from the beginning? Why doesn't God do it now?

I don't see how anything you can say is going to get out of this dilemma! Either God can do it or he can't. If God can't, he's not the Creator on which everything other than himself depends. If God can but won't, then how can he be good?

That's why I'm convinced that if it's really true that for any being to be God that being has to be maximally good as well as maximally powerful and all-knowing, there can be no getting round the point that such a being would prevent (almost all) the terrible suffering that ravages the whole world every day. Since that doesn't happen, there is no being that has all three of those qualities. Since your Scriptures say God has them all, they lie.

You've certainly posed this objection as forcefully as I've ever heard it put! Moreover, I think you're right about the usual replies to it. Although it is appropriate to mention human free choice in certain contexts, or God's having reasons for allowing specific sufferings such as using suffering to produce greater good, you have pressed the issue to its most profound level by asking why God made the world and humans the way he did. At this most basic level the straightforward answer to your questions is that there is no answer. But although we don't know why God made the creation as it is, his having done so does not make him evil. My position is that what the

Scriptures say about God implies that it is beyond our ability to judge God when it comes to why he made the world the way he did.

Let me start with an important point. You have been speaking of God's goodness in a way that is importantly different from what I find in Scripture. You're understanding it in a way that derives from the Greek philosophical idea of perfection, which is not what I find to be the biblical idea of what it means to say that God is good. For Plato a "perfection" meant the greatest conceivable degree of some admirable quality such as the highest possible goodness, justice, mercy or whatever. And many theologians have jumped on that idea and have identified it with God. God, they say, is the being who has all the perfections and has only perfections. This is what you assumed when you said God would have to have perfect goodness to be God.

But Scripture never speaks of God that way. And indeed doing so would compromise the doctrine that God called into being everything found in creation, including goodness and all the other admirable qualities that creatures have or lack. According to Scripture, God created everything whatever—visible or invisible (Col 1:16)—and that would include goodness. This means that God's goodness is not a perfection that God can't help having so that it compels how he treats humans. It is instead a quality attaching to how God freely relates to us as revealed by the covenant he offers us. In order to make his covenant with us, God established relations to creation in which he is loving, just, merciful, forgiving and so on and has promised to remain in those relations everlastingly "to those who love him." But there is nothing in those created relations that could oblige him to create the world one way rather than another.

I admitted that my position on this was very different from the usual answers, so, as you can imagine, it would take a lot of time to lay out even the major points of the arguments for and against it. All I can do now is summarize it in a bit more detail so you can see how it contrasts to the answers you found unconvincing.

Go ahead.

God is the only absolute being, the one on whom all else depends. According to Scripture, God called into existence everything found in creation with no exceptions. In that case, God is the Creator not only of every thing and every event, but also of every kind of property they have and every law that governs them. This means that God transcends time and space and is above all laws.[27] That is not a widely held view in theology. Most theologians have found ways to understand the biblical doctrine of creation so that it doesn't regard God as the Creator of every kind of property and all laws.[28] The reason for this is that accepting the doctrine that God created everything found in the universe means that the uncreated being of God doesn't have to have any property found in creation. This is why when Scripture says that God is personal, loving, just, forgiving, all-knowing and so on, it doesn't say he *must* have those characteristics to be God or that he just can't help having them. On the contrary, the doctrine that God brought into existence everything found in creation strongly suggests the reverse.[29] So I take it that the attributes ascribed to God in Scripture, which he shares in common with creatures, are created qualities God has assumed to himself in order to relate to us.

In other words, because it is God who called these qualities into existence, we should not suppose that any of them have to be true of God's uncreated being. Nor should we suppose that any law governing creatures must apply to God. Rather, God's having the attributes he does is the result of his accommodating himself to us so as to enter into the covenant. Ditto for the way any law found in creation applies to God: he freely abides by it for the sake of relating to us. On this position, then, God became for us personal, loving, wise, just, merciful and all the other attributes that constitute the nature he reveals himself to have.

The view I just described is not the prevailing view found among theologians, so let me cite a few of the Christian thinkers who have taken this position, lest you think it a totally idiosyncratic idea with no precedent. The Cappadocian Fathers of the fourth century—Sts. Basil, Gregory of Nazianzus and Gregory of Nyssa—held that God's own being is "incomprehensible to human reason" and that "all that is rational belongs to creation."[30] They explicitly deny that God is to be identified with his attributes[31] and insist instead that prior to creation the being of God was "free of qualities altogether."[32] Hence the oft-quoted saying of Basil: "We do not know what God is but what God is not and how he relates to creatures."

Luther and Calvin took the same position in the sixteenth century. According to Luther,

> God does not manifest himself except through his works and Word, because the meaning of these is understood in some measure. Whatever else belongs to the Divinity cannot be grasped and understood ... such as being outside time.[33]
>
> Now God in his own nature and majesty is to be left alone; in this regard we have nothing to do with him, nor does he wish us to deal with him. We have to do with him as clothed by his word, by which he presents himself to us.[34]
>
> We know no other God than the God clothed with his promises. ... When he is clothed with the voice of a man, when he accommodates himself to our capacity to understand, I can approach him.[35]

And likewise Calvin:

> There is nothing more peculiar to God than eternity and self-existence.[36]
>
> Every perfection [ascribed to God in Scripture] may be contemplated in creation so that ... in the enumeration of his perfections, he is described not as he is in himself, but in relation to us.[37]

More recently Karl Barth has taken a similar view, contending that the only way there can be intercourse between God and creature is by God's "entrance into its form of existence."[38] He takes God's freedom—God's not being bound by laws of creation—to mean that God has freely taken on the nature he reveals himself to have. On this view God really has the attributes and really stands in the relations he reveals, and he promises to do so forever. But he was not bound by them prior to creating them, nor are we entitled to suppose he had to take to himself the nth degree of every attribute that constitutes his nature.

I'm not sure it makes sense to say God took on obligations if he wasn't already bound by moral laws. When you and I make promises, they're binding because we're already under moral obligation, no?

On the view I just sketched, that could still be true of God's obligations. God could have taken on a created nature in order to "enter into the form of existence" of creatures in such a way as to freely abide by moral laws in just the ways he wished, and then have made his promises. Or he could have freely subjected himself to those laws and made his promises simultaneously. Either way his abiding by them is limited to exactly the ways and to the extent he wished.

But where is all this going? How does it supply an answer to my objection?

It answers the charge of inconsistency between the goodness of God and the existence of suffering, since God is not mandated by his own nature to be as good as we can possibly conceive or wish; his creating and taking on the characteristic of being good to us means he is good in just the ways he promises to be, not in every way we can wish or imagine. Chief among the ways he swears to be good are the covenant promises to forgive those who turn to him and to grant them his love, his fellowship and everlasting life. (Of course, we can observe that he is also good to those who stand outside his covenant in ways he is not obliged to be by those promises. As Scripture says, he sends the rain on the just and the unjust.)

But nowhere in Scripture does he promise to be as beneficent as possible to as many people as possible. He does not promise to prevent all suffering or alleviate all pain. Since he never promised any such things, he is not obliged to do them. In short, Scripture never claims that God is maximally perfect in the sense Anselm and other theologians adopted from the ancient Greeks.[39] So the fact that God made the world and humans the way he did does not show that he isn't good in the senses and ways Scripture asserts him to be, nor is the way he made the world inconsistent with that goodness.

I know I've been a bit long-winded already, but let me briefly refer to the way the biblical story of Job confirms this view. Job is a man who loves God and is good to other people; nevertheless God decides to test him. God allows Satan to bring a series of disasters on Job. He loses his fortune, his children are killed, his wife leaves him and, finally, he is put under quarantine for coming down with a terrible disease. Three old friends then come to visit him and offer their advice. Their conversations go through several cycles of repeating basically the same things in different words. They admonish Job to confess to God whatever wrong he has done so that God will restore him to health and happiness. Job denies any wrongdoing; they say they know Job must have done something wrong because God is perfect and so *couldn't* allow him to suffer unless he deserved it. Job again denies any wrongdoing, and the cycle starts anew. After a number of rounds like that, Job wishes aloud that God were present because he'd tell God to his face that he has nothing to confess. Then he adds that it would have been better had he never been born.

At that point God does appear to Job and gives him a good tongue lashing. But he berates Job only for saying it would have been better had he never been born, not for saying he'd done nothing to deserve to suffer. God says that Job's last remark was incredibly presumptuous because it meant that he knew better than God what should have been. It is interesting that God does not indict Job for any wrongdoing; he lets Job's protest of innocence stand. More than that, God expresses great indignation at the advice of Job's friends! He orders them out of his sight, tells them to offer sacrifices and ask to be forgiven, and then adds that he will not forgive them until Job prays for them.

So what is going on here? Why is God angry with Job's friends? What did they say that was so bad? The answer, I believe, exactly coincides with the point I have been making. They were regarding God as good in the sense of completely conforming to the rules that bind humans. God simply couldn't be allowing Job to suffer unjustly, they said, so Job must be deserving of his suffering. No doubt they considered their belief to be pious; after all, they were praising God, weren't they? But God saw it differently: They were regarding him as one more creature in the universe subject to its laws rather than the Creator of all its laws. The position of Job's friends required that if God allowed unjust suffering he would be unjust himself. And that's exactly what the story of Job teaches to be wrong! God is not whatever we want him to be, but whatever he has freely become toward us. It's he who must tell us what that is, not we who get to tell him what we want.

The upshot is that *we cannot judge God by the standards that apply to us.*[40] God allows Job to suffer. If you or I did that when we could have prevented it, we would be evil. God commands Abraham to sacrifice his son. If you or I did that, we would be evil. God has determined the time and cause for the death of every person. If you or I did that, we would be evil. (Notice what Job said in regard to the death of his children: The Lord gave and the Lord took away; blessed be the name of the Lord.) God says that he "sends a strong delusion" to those who oppose him "to make them believe what is false" (2 Thess 2:11 RSV). If you or I did that, we would be doing something evil. Ditto for God's not preventing all the suffering that results from evil choices, natural disasters, or accidents resulting from heart attacks. But God is not bound by the laws of morality in the ways that bind us, and God's goodness does not consist in doing what we would have to do to be good. Since God is the Creator of the norms of ethics and justice, they do not apply to him except insofar as he has freely bound himself to them by making covenant promises.

The greatness of God's goodness, then, does not consist in his perfectly obeying the norms of justice and morality or in having the most beneficent character we can imagine, but in the fact that although he was not obligated to us at all, he in fact made wonderfully loving and merciful promises to us anyway! Promises aside, he would owe us zilch. But he freely made the promises when under no obligation, and so now has just the obligations he has sworn himself to uphold. So can you see how wildly off it is to suppose that God can't be real if there's suffering in the world?[41]

This still doesn't explain why God doesn't stop more of the suffering if he has the power to do it. Even if he doesn't have to do it to be good in the ways he has promised, it still seems to me that he should do it.

I'm afraid I can't help you with why he doesn't. That's not something God has let us in on, and I have no idea. But notice that when you say that God *should* do it, you are once again applying to God the standards that apply to us. Like Job's friends, you are reducing God to the status of being one more creature in the universe subject to the same laws in the same ways we are. That's just what angered God about their advice to Job. You and I may not like it that God hasn't made the world a better place than it is; in one sense that's a natural thing to wish for, and the Psalms frequently express the same yearning. My point is only that we have no intellectual right to extend that wish into an indictment of God or a rejection of his reality on the ground that God is obliged to be and to do what we would like. And in that case, this objection does not succeed in defeating belief in God; it is not good evidence that the experience of the biblical message as self-evident is a spurious one.

Well, this doesn't make me any happier with belief in God, I can tell you! Your reply may remove the logical conflict between belief in God and the reality of suffering, but what kind of God does it allow for? Why would anyone worship a God who made this *world?*

The Scripture's own answer to that is "we love him because he first loved us." God made a world that is often a harsh place, yes. But he has also made himself known to us, offered his love and forgiveness and promised us everlasting life. From the Christian point of view, he also came incarnated in Christ and shared with us the sufferings of this life. To those who encounter him in their own experience, that encounter brings self-evident knowledge of God's love. That's more than enough to induce worship.

It sounds to me as though your last question *still* assumes that we can judge God by our standards. You are not fully grasping that we're talking about the Absolute Being, who would be quite beyond anything we could conceive had he not freely entered into created relations we can understand. In that case the only judgments we're entitled to make about God concern whether he has kept the promises he has made, and those promises are enough to counterbalance the worst sufferings that people can endure.[42] The New Testament puts it this way: "What God has planned for people who love him is more than eyes have seen or ears have heard. It has never even entered our minds" (1 Cor 2:9 CEV), and "I am sure that what we are suffering now cannot compare with the glory that will be shown to us" (Rom 8:18 CEV). God promises to stand with us in our suffering, and he experienced one of the worst forms of suffering in Christ's passion. But in the final analysis it's God's offer of everlasting love and happiness that answers how—and in what sense—God can both be good and not prevent all suffering.

Of course that doesn't explain why the world is constituted so that there is such a thing as suffering at all. You may not find that *palatable*, but how does that affect its truth? I'm not trying to sell belief in God by making it look more attractive; I'm trying to answer your question as to how and why anyone can believe in God. Those of us who believe do so because we've encountered God, not because everything about what God has revealed is so pleasant that we would simply prefer to believe it.

You just spoke of "encountering God" when all along I thought you'd been saying that nothing in creation is the uncreated God, so that what people experience is something God created to reveal himself. So which is it?

Can you see what I'm getting at? It's a point I made very early in our discussions: how can any experience be of God if God transcends the world? If you say it's not of God but something God created to reveal himself, then you're admitting you don't experience God but some part of the world you take to be God's revelation. The problem is that you'd have to already believe God exists to believe anything could be God's revelation. So your claim begs the question.

The view of God I just sketched answers this objection, I think. No one experiences God's uncreated being, but they can and do experience him as he has accommodated and revealed himself to us through his Word and by the experienced presence of his Spirit. It is God's accommodation that makes it possible for us to encounter him in the various sorts of religious experiences we've been talking about, including the simple intuitive experience of finding his word to be his word. When we experience the revelation of God as God's speaking to us, we have encountered *God.* Let me explain this with an analogy.

If we set up a reflecting telescope and look at the moon, we can describe our experience in two different ways. We could say that what we're seeing is a tiny image of the moon on the surface of the telescope's mirror an inch or so from our eye. We could also say that we're seeing the moon—a huge object that is 240,000 miles from our eye. I can't think of any reason to believe one of those is true and the other false; in fact, we can actually experience our act of seeing either way, depending on our own attitude. We can see it *as* the moon or only *as* an image of the moon.[43]

It's the same with coming into contact with God's Word. We can see it only as a set of stories and teachings collected in a book that are no more than ways some ancients thought about what is divine. Yet when that contact includes the quality of self-evidency with respect to its truth, in a very real sense we have experienced the One who intended to make himself known through it. For we then hear the message as God's speaking to us, and hearing someone speak is a way of experiencing that person.

Moreover, for that to happen, we need not beg the question; we need not already be assuming the truth of what we hear. On the contrary, when someone experiences the self-evidency of the biblical message as the truth about God from God, the resulting belief in God's reality is part of that message and so arises simultaneously with it.

I see you have that one covered, so I'm going to go back to an objection I raised earlier and put it another way. I earlier asked, if you rest your belief in God on the experience of self-evidency, what's to prevent anyone from claiming that virtually any belief is self-evident?

Your reply admitted that they could. You wanted to acknowledge self-evidency wherever people actually have it. But if so, doesn't that mean conflicting intuitions of it can't be knowledge? Since contrary beliefs can't all be true, they can't all be knowledge either, and that would mean your account (even if it's right) hasn't shown belief in God to be knowledge—which is what I thought you've been trying to do!

If you define "knowledge" as justified *true* belief, you're right. But why is that the right way to define knowledge? It's not the way we ordinarily speak of knowing something. In commonsense speech we say we know, rather than merely believe, something when we're sure (or nearly sure) of it. In other words, we say we "know" when we think we're justified in being certain.

The traditional philosophical view of knowledge you're invoking requires that for a belief to be knowledge it must not only have powerful or even overwhelming justification but also be really true independently of that justification. But that would mean that no matter how good our reasons are for a belief and no matter how certain we are of it, we're not entitled to say we know it unless we can find out whether it's true independently of our reasons for it. Do you see the problem? Since the only way a belief can be known to be true is by its justification, then adding that a belief must be true independently of that justification is to insist on a condition we can never satisfy! For if *every* belief needs to be true independently of our grounds for it in order for it to count as knowledge, then we can't claim to "know" we have evidence or grounds for a belief any more than we can know the belief itself. So short of claiming that either the belief or its justification was obtained in a way that just couldn't yield false belief (that is, by an infallible method), the additional requirement that the belief *be* true over and above its justification will never be fulfilled.

This is why I see the requirement that a belief must in fact be true in order for it to be knowledge as a legacy from the desire to have some capacity of ours turn out to be infallible. It's a way of saying that either we don't know anything at all or we have infallible truth! But those are not the only possibilities. We can have justification for a belief that warrants our being certain of it, without its having been obtained in a way that couldn't be wrong. This is why it seems to me that if we take a fallibilist position about our belief-forming capacities, we also need to give up the insistence that a belief must really be true (over and above all the grounds we could ever have for thinking it is) in order to count as knowledge.

But doesn't your proposal create the paradox that knowledge can be false? You admit that we can have good grounds for a belief—even for being certain of it—and still be wrong. In that case you had knowledge that wasn't true! Isn't that a weird thing to say?

There's nothing weird about that from a fallibilist point of view. It only sounds odd because we're so used to the view that "knowledge" must be restricted to what's in fact true independently of our grounds for believing it. And *that* sounds far weirder to me! It has the paradoxical consequence that we can be absolutely sure of something but not be entitled to call it knowledge. Does that make any sense?

Consider this analogy. Suppose we were to say that a perception is veridical (reveals a real object to us) only if that object is really there independently of any perceptions we have of it. How could we ever claim to show and thus know that? With that requirement laid on us, we could never claim to know any object is real because all we would ever have as grounds for believing its reality are more perceptions, each of which would have the same requirement placed on it. My point is that just as we can't step outside of our perceptual relation to objects to see if they're *really* there independently of our perception (and even if we could, our "seeing" that they are would be yet another perception!), just so we can't step outside of the relation of our grounds for believing and the beliefs they are grounds for. We can't check on truth from the standpoint of God's omniscience.

So the view I'm proposing is that when we have good grounds for certainty we have knowledge, and that a belief's being intuitively self-evident is one of the best grounds we can have for such certainty (provided it comports well with the rest of our experience). This is much closer to the commonsense use of "knowledge," and I'm taking that to be on the right track as opposed to the prevailing philosophical definition. It's why in ordinary speech we say things like "As a youngster I just *knew* such and such was true; as I grew older, I found out how wrong I was." Similarly, we sometimes speak of a belief as something that was known in an earlier century but is now known to be false. In each case it means a belief once had such strong justification that it was regarded as certain (or nearly certain) despite the fact that we now have good grounds to say it was false.

The assumption behind our talking this way is that we regard a belief as knowledge depending on the degree of certainty we have for it—provided we don't mean only a *feeling* of certainty but a *judgment* about its justification. So I'm saying that what makes a belief knowledge is not whether it meets a condition we can never know it to meet, but whether we have such strong grounds for believing it that we are either completely certain or very close to completely certain of it. (Of course, the belief is really *true* only if it corresponds to how things are independently of our believing.)

For these reasons, I think belief in God can also be knowledge when it is founded on an intuition of the truth of the biblical message and confirmed by the way it comports with the rest of our experience. It is then as certain as any belief we have because it's completely certain. So we are entitled to say we *know* it even if someone else is entitled to say the same about a contrary religious belief. We can't both be right, of course, but we may both have grounds for our assertions that are as good as it is possible for humans to have.

But this is the same as saying that many—perhaps most—people's intuitions of self-evidency are wrong when it comes to what is divine! Is that really what you want to say? Are you really claiming that others don't see God to be the genuine and only divinity because there's something wrong with them? If so, why do humans have such a serious defect?

Yes, that is what I'm saying, and your question shows that you've understood me correctly. In fact, it is a Christian teaching that owing to the fall people are all born with the defect that their self-evidency antennae are not in proper working order when it comes to what is unconditionally real.[44] Our antennae are generally reliable when it comes to perceptual and a host of other nonreligious beliefs. But there are wide and deep divergences when it comes to what is divine.

The fact is, some version of this answer is taught by every major world religion. Each says that the reason there are people who do not share its beliefs is that those people suffer from a spiritual (intuitive) blindness that prevents them from seeing the truth about what is divine. They further hold that only correcting that blindness will allow such people to see both the truth about what is divine and the truth about how to properly relate to the divine. Their accounts of the nature of that blindness, how it gets corrected and the nature of the correction differ, but all give the same basic explanation for why people have different divinity intuitions.

At the same time, however, no one has any answer for your second question as to *why* humans are religiously blind and need to be enlightened. Even Genesis, with its account of the first humans' fall into sin, doesn't explain why God didn't make them so that they would respond to him as they should have, or so that their lapsed condition would not subsequently be the common nature of all humans. But this lack of explanation is not peculiar to Genesis. The question as to why people do not all share correct intuitions about what is divine is one with no answer from any point of view I know of.[45]

But the fact that no one can answer this question is beside the point of our discussion. My lack of an answer does nothing to make it any less worth your while to do what you can to put yourself in a position to have the sort of experience which alone can answer the question we began with.

It's bad enough that you leave religious beliefs hopelessly deadlocked this way, but that's not all you're doing. If the appeal to self-evidency is allowed, then why wouldn't that justify crazy beliefs? For example, why couldn't someone claim to know self-evidently that there is a great pumpkin that rises out of the pumpkin patch every Halloween and rewards all good boys and girls?[46]

If you mean a real vegetable pumpkin that is spatial, physical, sensory and so on and does those things, then the first part of my answer is that such an object is the sort of thing we should be able to perceive—to see and touch. The fact that no one claims to have done so, or would fail to perceive it if they tried, disconfirms that claim. Of course, the claim is also prima facie absurd because of what it attributes to a pumpkin; in that respect it's similar to someone's claiming to know of a rock that can speak or a tree that can fly.

On the other hand, if we take your question in the context of religious belief and think of a great pumpkin as the symbol of a divine power, then the answer is very different. There could indeed be a Great Pumpkin cult whose devotees wear little pumpkin images around their necks and on armbands called pumpkin patches. They could eat pumpkin pie as a sacramental meal and celebrate Halloween as their high holy day. If such a person told me in all sincerity that this idea of divinity looked self-evidently true, then I'd be perfectly willing to accept that as a genuine deliverance of his (malfunctioning) intuitions about divinity. In fact, such a religious belief would not be very different from many that have existed or still do exist.[47] So although your concern is well taken, it does not defeat the appeal to intuition of self-evidence as the real ground of religious belief. It doesn't show that this account of it leads to any absurdity.

I'm not sure what to say to this except that I remain unconvinced. As I've said several times, I'm going to have to think about this at greater length. I know I don't like much of what I've heard; but as you say, that doesn't show it's not true.

Of course! Think it over. But I can tell you in advance that no amount of thinking it over will, all by itself, show you whether it's true. The experiment I described, however, can. Read the Scriptures with as open a mind as you can muster. Listen to them as written from a commonsense point of view and as possible records of God's encounters with humans. Attend worship and Scripture study with a congregation of believers. Give yourself the best possible opportunity to have the same experience that I and millions of others have had. Only if that happens will you know why we believe in God.

6

Some Loose Ends

I'M STILL THINKING ABOUT WHETHER THE POSITION YOU'VE OUT-*lined is possible. I must admit that it's hard to think of reasons why it's* impossible, *and I suppose I've little to lose by trying your so-called experiment.* *But I'm also feeling a bit swamped by all the new information and some of the* *more difficult arguments. So before I decide what I'm going to do, there are a* *number of scattered loose ends I'd like to tie up from our previous talks. Can we* *start by running down my list?*

Sure. Fire away.

The first has to do with self-evidency and doubt. If a belief is self-evidently *true to someone, does that make it impossible for that person to doubt it? And* *how serious is doubt for belief in God, anyway? Is doubting a sin or something?*

The question of doubt is more complicated than you might think. There are several kinds of it and different reasons for them. From the Christian point of view, there are cases in which doubt *is* a sin. Those are the cases where someone is sure God is real and has offered his love and forgiveness in the covenant, but then (either in attitude or in practice) doubts that God will keep those promises. This is related, by the way, to how Bible writers use the term "faith"—never to refer to belief that God is real, but to mean our trust in and reliance on his word. When they admonish us to have faith, then, it never means to take God's reality on blind trust but to wholeheartedly trust the promises we *know* God has made. So the kind of doubt I'm speaking of can properly be called lack of faith.

Other kinds are not serious in the religious sense. For example, after experiencing any belief to be self-evident, we may reflect on the possibility that we may be mistaken. Merely reflecting on the fact that we are fallible amounts to nothing more than admitting the abstract possibility of error; it's not the same as actually doubting the belief. In connection with belief in God, this kind of doubt often arises from considering an alternative divinity belief. We can reflect on what it would be like to hold the other belief and notice its more attractive features. For example, we might admire the dedication and integrity of its advocates or appreciate the art it has inspired. There's nothing wrong with this sort of reflection and appreciation. In fact, I'd say that those who never reflect on other divinity beliefs in this way have failed to take them seriously.

In itself this sort of doubt is no threat to belief in God. For anyone whose belief in God is grounded in a genuine experience of the kind I've described, taking alternatives seriously will only lead to strengthening their own belief.

What about the doubt that can arise from criticism? You've obviously thought a lot about the objections I raised against belief in God. Don't any of them ever make you doubt—even a little bit?

Yes, but only in the weak sense I just mentioned. This is because the strong objections—objections trying to show that belief in God conflicts with other self-evident beliefs—all seem to me to fail, for reasons like those I gave when you raised the most famous examples of them in our last discussion. I find the replies far more plausible than the objections. Moreover, a great many of those replies have stood the test of time; they have been around for centuries and been examined and reexamined time and time again. The result, in my opinion, is that they're stronger than ever.

But remember: even if a believer can't effectively counter a claim that belief in God is in conflict with another self-evident or strongly confirmed belief, that fact doesn't settle the matter against belief in God. As with conflicts between nonreligious beliefs, discovering the conflict still leaves a choice as to which belief to retain and which to give up. What usually happens in those cases is that people retain a self-evident belief over one that has a lot of evidence but is not self-evident. And where the conflict is between self-evident beliefs, they retain whichever self-evidency seems to have the broadest scope (as when mystics reject all we perceive and conceive as illusion in favor of what they experience as self-evidently divine).

What of probability arguments? I've seen a number of those lately, and they seem to draw their conclusions more cautiously and to be quite reasonable. Maybe that's the way to deal with religious belief rather than looking for certainty!

That doesn't sound right. Consider this analogy. Suppose I read an article containing a number of convincing reasons why it's improbable that a woman can bench-press over 350 pounds. I can find nothing wrong with the reasoning, but twice a week when I go to the gym I see Jane bench-press 360. Do I refuse to believe what I see? Do I feel compelled to find rebuttals to the reasons in the article? No. There may be nothing wrong with the article's arguments; what Jane does may be highly improbable, yet it's still true that she does it. The point is that the improbability of something's being true can never trump our direct experience that it *is* true.

The writer C. S. Lewis has commented on this same point. Most of his life he was an atheist, but then he became a Christian. Even after his conversion he thought Christianity looked improbable; by his conversion experience, he said, he was "dragged kicking and screaming into the Kingdom of God."

You must admit, though, that a number of writers who defend belief in God don't see the issue of doubt the way you're describing it. They think the objections and probabilities are more important than you're allowing them to be.

True enough. I think this happens when believers succumb to assuming that belief in God should be treated as a theory that depends on its evidence. If someone does that, they're treating belief in God like a large-scale explanation to be accepted because of how well it solves intellectual puzzles—as, say, atomic physics does. Such a person is going to agonize endlessly over a host of arguments and counterarguments and take them more seriously than I think they should be taken. This is why it's so important to recognize that belief in God is not a hypothesis but is grounded in direct experience. It's not based on arguments, so we don't have to solve every difficulty or answer every question for it to be justified.[1]

But getting back to your question, we can notice other forms of doubt besides these. For example . . .

I'm not sure it's worth going on with this. You've answered what I had in mind.

OK. But there's one more sort I'd like to mention just in case it applies to you. This is a more subtle form of doubt I'll call "practical doubt." It arises from being surrounded by unbelief rather than from wrestling with definite reasons for rejecting God's reality. For some it begins when their belief is ridiculed in college by religion-bashing professors or fellow students. Or it may come not from outright bashing so much as from the fact that everyone seems to regard belief in God as passé and not worth worrying about. A believer can be seduced by the vague impression that being educated and up with the times requires that belief in God be abandoned—at least in practice. It rarely occurs to those who are affected this way that the bashings and godless lifestyles presuppose an alternative divinity belief; it seems instead that religion as a whole is simply not in vogue.

Others fall into the same sort of doubt from cultural osmosis rather than schooling. From their workplace and the popular media they gradually absorb attitudes and values that conflict with, or simply ignore, belief in God. Perhaps at the same time they are turned off by a bad experience with the church or with someone who professes belief. They begin to drift away. Over time the very fact that they seem to be able to get along without belief in God playing an active role in their lives leads them to doubt that such a belief is relevant to modern life.

In this case too, it probably doesn't occur to them that their new attitudes and values presuppose belief in some alternative divinity—a belief they would find false were it to be consciously articulated and examined. The sad thing is that they continue to see belief in God as true (provided they had a genuine experience of the self-evidency of the biblical message). They've simply given in to cultural and peer pressure;

they've allowed those pressures to make them feel embarrassed about the social acceptability of their belief, and so have ceased to put it into practice.

In relation to your original question about self-evidency and doubt, then, practical doubt can afflict belief in God even while the belief is experienced as self-evidently true.

Doesn't that show a weakness in such people's experience of self-evidency? Isn't the fact that this happens evidence that their experience isn't the same as the self-evidency of normal sense perception or rational axioms?

Not at all. Practical doubt can afflict any self-evident belief and isn't unique either to belief in God in particular or to religious belief in general. The fact is, we are the kind of creatures who can at times repress what we know to be true or be talked out of almost any belief—at least at a superficial level. There are many examples of this: the alcoholic who denies his addiction, the eyewitness whose certainty is shaken under cross-examination in court.

This is why all along I've been urging you to be self-conscious about your own convictions, seek to enlarge your experience, and have the courage to live by whatever you end up experiencing as divine. Caving in to cultural and peer pressure is the most unjustified sort of doubt there is.

I can assure you my doubts are not of that type! I've never had any experience that has left me the least inclined to believe in God. So we can go to my next loose end, if you don't mind.

I have lingering misgivings about the whole topic of "self-evidency." Most people hardly ever use that expression and aren't even sure what it means! So why is that the right way to think about religious experience?

Well, yes, the expression is not part of our everyday speech.[2] But the fact that most people don't have a precise understanding of it or rarely use it doesn't matter so long as you now have a clear definition of the way I've been using it, which is the way it's been traditionally used in science and philosophy. Once that's clear, and the three theories that have burdened it are exposed and cleared away, I think it's the most helpful way to see what is going on in the formation of divinity beliefs.

But please don't take me to be insisting on a particular term! If you don't like *self-evident*, use some other word. It doesn't really matter what you call the experience of intuitively recognizing the irresistible certainty of a belief. So long as it's clear that's what we're talking about, call it what you like.

I don't want to waste time arguing about terms either. So let's go to what I believe is a more important issue.

You've proposed that I make the "experiment" of reading the Bible to see if I experience it as revelation from God. But couldn't anyone make the same proposal on behalf of some other divinity belief?

If you say they could, then why wouldn't I have to read them all in order to be fair to all the other possibilities? If that's right, then your proposal is actually biased in favor of belief in God. What's more, it would then turn out that in order to eliminate the bias, I'd have to spend the rest of my life doing nothing but reading religious works that teach or defend virtually every divinity belief! Needless to say, I haven't got the time for that. So your "experiment" is either unfair or impractical; either way I'm led down the garden path.

You're right, of course, that believers in other divinities could advise you to read their scriptures or other works advocating their beliefs. What could prevent them? And even were you to read only the scriptures of the divinity beliefs that have had the most followers, it would, as you say, take a huge amount of time. With all that I fully agree.

What I don't agree with is your suggestion that it would somehow be unfair to the other beliefs if you made the experiment I recommend vis-à-vis belief in God. First, because it was belief in God you asked about. If you want to know why we who believe in God find that to be the truth, then it's not necessary to read everything else in order to have the experience of seeing it to be true—which is the only thing that can show you the answer. Second, there's the reason you brought up at our last session. You noticed that the three theistic traditions are anchored on the idea that God has revealed himself and has preserved a record of that revelation in Scripture. The Scriptures therefore have a unique role relative to belief in God in contrast to the sacred writings of other traditions. For example, in Hinduism or Buddhism the sacred writings are aids to achieving one's mystical experience, but they lack any binding, authoritative content such as the Jewish-Christian-Muslim Scriptures claim to have. As a Brahmin priest once said to me, "I read the Upanishads or the Gita or whatever only to aid my own experience. If my experience differs from them, *it* is the final authority—not them."

So there's nothing unfair about starting with the Scriptures, since they're *supposed* to be a message from God with definite authoritative content, and because the Scriptures themselves say that finding God is especially tied to encountering the record of his revelation in them (Rom 10:1-17). The sacred writings of most other religions don't make that strong a claim. The contrast can be summarized this way: whereas in the pantheistic traditions the role of sacred writings is to aid you to achieve an experience that authoritatively reveals the divine, in theism the experience is that of finding the biblical message to be the revelation of God. The experience is not itself the authority; it is the subjective side of experiencing Scripture's teaching as the objective source of revealed truth.

The same thing holds for the way theism contrasts to pagan divinity beliefs. In their cultic versions, the most influential pagan sacred writings had the form of myths that were not supposed to be authoritative revelation from the gods but the work of religious and literary geniuses like Homer or Hesiod. Even where tribal myths were believed to have been handed to ancestors by the gods themselves, there is no accompanying belief that the gods control the course of history in such a way as to superintend the preservation of its oral or written record, as theists believe. So I think there are prima facie reasons for at least starting with the theistic Scriptures: what they claim for themselves would make them, if true, more reliable and important sources of truth relative to belief in God than the writings of other traditions are supposed to be *according to those traditions.*

Needless to say, the noncultic versions of paganism that pick out particular kinds of properties and laws as the nature of the divine have never claimed to be based on revelation; they aim to justify their choice by arguments. Perhaps you recall that we talked about this earlier. I gave you two reasons why arguments can't really justify these beliefs: (1) the arguments presuppose the divinity belief they're intended to defend, and (2) we can't even conceive of any kinds of properties and laws as independent of all others, and so we can't successfully argue that any of them have that status.

Oh yes—the "experiment in thought" argument we discussed the first time we met. I have a loose end there too!

I thought I got the point when you gave it, but now I'm not so sure. Just how does it show there can be no arguments to justify pagan divinity beliefs like the ones you were just talking about? Can you run it by me again?

I'd be glad to. Do you recall the basic idea? We attempted to think of some particular kind of properties and laws as the only kind anything really has, or as the basic nature of whatever produces all other things along with any other kinds of properties and laws they may have. Ascribing either status to any kind of properties and laws makes that kind to be the nature of whatever is supposed to be independently real (divine).

Yes, I've got that part all right. And I still get nothing at all whenever I try to conceive of any of those kinds apart from all the other kinds. But why does that all by itself show we couldn't successfully argue for any of them as the nature of what has independent reality and is what everything else depends on?

This is one of the more difficult points of our discussion, so I don't blame you for wanting to go over it.

Let's approach it from a slightly different angle this time. Start by recalling that pagan religious belief takes some part or aspect of the world as divine. When this happens in theories, it is phrased as the claim that there's a particular kind of properties and laws that is the nature of the divine part of reality. It's by settling on the *kind* of properties and laws that are basic that a theory picks out and identifies what is supposed to have independent (divine) reality.[3] We already noticed that in the history of theories some of the most popular pagan candidates for the nature of divinity have been mathematical, physical, sensory, logical, etc. Let's call any such identification X. In that case whatever is believed to exist independently—is what everything else depends on—is said to be of the X-type.

Now a claim that X identifies what's divine can be argued for in either of two ways. The first is to try to show all reality has *only* X-type properties and is governed by X-type laws. In that case there are no other kinds of things than X-type things, and so nothing for them to depend on. They are thus divine. The other way is to allow that there really are non-X-type things or non-X-type properties, but to argue that they all depend on things that are X-type. So once again, X marks the spot! It locates what's divine.

The significance of the thought experiment is that if you can't actually form a concept of any of these kinds as independent, then nothing you could put into an argument could be thinking and speaking of them that way. You can't give an argument for the truth of a belief that you literally can't think of! The result is that an argument for the real independence of any X requires us to think of that X not as independent but as connected to other kinds of properties and laws. That's the only way we can conceive of them at all. That doesn't prevent the making of divinity claims on their behalf, of course. Anyone can always claim that although we can't conceive of X apart from a host of non-X properties and laws, it's really X that picks out what's independent in reality anyway. But that's not an argument.

As we saw, the closest anyone could come to an argument in defense of such a claim is to argue that the X nature of things is the precondition for the appearance of all the non-X kinds of properties and laws. That can often be done, but it's too weak to establish that X is the *cause* of all the other kinds. It doesn't rule out the possibility that both X and the precondition relations, together with the other kinds X is a precondition for, depend on God.

The situation is even worse for the theories claiming X is all there is—that there are no other kinds of properties and laws at all. Any argument for that conclusion would have to be an exception to its own conclusion. An argument has to have non-X properties and appeal to non-X laws in order to be understood or to be persuasive. For example, any argument would have to have a linguistic meaning to be understood and would have to establish its conclusion by mathematical and/or logical laws. The argument would also have to be represented by physical marks on paper or sounds we make with our mouths, and these require spatial arrangement. An argument also has to be able to be sensorily perceived. So an argument made for concluding that there are only X-type properties and laws must itself be experienced to have a multiplicity of kinds of properties to be understood at all!

But I fear this explanation has been too abstract, so let me apply it all to an actual example.

Please do! Especially the part about X-type things being preconditions for anything non-X.

Suppose the X someone wants to defend is the *physical* kind of properties and laws. The theory is then some version of materialism, and its central claim is that it's things whose nature is physical that are the cause of any nonphysical properties or of any nonphysical things that may exist. That is, the essentially physical realities are the reason there are such things as nonphysical properties, laws or things.

Now suppose further we succeed in amassing tons of evidence that physical properties are always preconditions for other kinds: that nothing has biological life that isn't physical; that nothing is conscious, perceives, or feels that isn't alive; that nothing thinks logically that isn't conscious and perceives; and that nothing that lacks logical thought can develop an economy or a politics, etc.[4] Would that show it's the physical properties and laws of things that cause all the other kinds of properties things can have? That is, would it show that although things actually have many kinds of properties, their physical nature is independent of those other kinds? Would it establish the physical nature of reality as independent and divine? Not by a millon miles!

Even if we could show that certain physical properties are always preconditions for any nonphysical property, that wouldn't prove the others are *generated* by the physical. Why not? Because it wouldn't rule out the possibility that physical properties and laws, along with their relations to all the nonphysical properties and laws, are all caused by something else. Being a necessary precondition for nonphysical features of things won't make the physical features also *sufficient* to produce the nonphysical. For example, the presence of oxygen is a precondition for fire, but oxygen alone won't cause a fire. So even if the physical features are preconditions for nonphysical ones, that doesn't show the physical alone *produces* the nonphysical. To show *that*, you'd have to prove the physical is not only a necessary but also a sufficient precondition for anything nonphysical. That is, you'd have to show not only that nothing can have nonphysical properties without having physical properties, but also that the physical is all you need to have in order to produce the nonphysical.

(Please remember that "physical" is being used here only as our example; all the same points apply to arguing for any other kind of properties and laws as picking out what has independent reality and is what everything depends on.)

But why worry about the strange abstract possibility of some "other reality" being what everything really depends on? If things can have biotic life or sensory perception or logical thought only if they're physical, what more do you need to know in order to conclude everything is basically physical?

It's not an abstract possibility at all; it's God. If God is the real Creator of everything other than himself, then what everything depends on isn't matter, space, logical laws, numbers or sensations, or any of the other pagan candidates selected from creation and presupposed by philosophical or scientific theories in place of God. This is why arguing for an X selected from this world as the precondition for everything else is not the same as establishing its independence. It simply begs the question to respond: what else could it be? Relative to belief in God, that's no more than the confession of a contrary religious belief, the belief in the divinity of X! It already assumes there's no transcendent Creator. And it does so not because of arguments but, as I've been saying, because those who argue that way already experience X as divine.

I think I see more clearly now why you've been contending that the noncultic pagan ideas of divinity are actually believed because they just look (self-evidently) right rather than because of the arguments. But if that's so, I'm just going to have to try harder to find a way to avoid all religious belief whatever!

So how about this? Let's set aside the question whether everyone has such a belief and talk about whether anything really has to be divine at all. I propose that to avoid all religious beliefs whatsoever, we should replace them with the belief that nothing whatsoever has independent reality! In that case there just is nothing to stand in proper relation to or use as the ultimate basis of explanations in theories. Everything depends on something. What's wrong with that?

What's wrong is that there's no way to understand this proposal that doesn't still imply that something is nondependent and thus divine. Here's why.

Both in commonsense speech and in science, we at times talk about "the whole ball of wax" or "everything whatever" or "all reality." There doesn't seem to be anything silly about that; nobody flinches at such expressions because there doesn't seem to be anything incoherent in talking about "all that is." But if that's right, this alone shows something is slotted as divine! The sum total of all there is can't depend on anything. If it's all there is, then there's nothing else for it to depend on.

So we can't even think of an alternative to these two possibilities: either the totality of reality is nondependent, or some part of it is.[5] In that case the proposal that nothing is divine has no coherent interpretation; there's just no way to think of its being so.

Maybe that's just a quirky fact about the way we think rather than showing the way things are.

Of course people can always take different interpretations of this fact. They can say it's due to the way our brains happen to have evolved or a result of our psychological makeup. And those who believe in God have an explanation for it too: we say God created us for fellowship with him, so that we have an innate sense of divinity and an impulse to discover and direct ourselves toward God (or whatever surrogate we put in his place). But notice that our explanation, and every other explanation of religious belief anyone adopts, explains in terms of what it presupposes is divine.

So what sense does it make to propose that everyone try to repress their intuitions about divinity? That's especially futile if we can't so much as conceive of an alternative so that even our theories can't avoid presupposing something in that role![6]

Why, then, try to avoid the unavoidable? Why not instead try to become acquainted with the ideas of divinity that have seemed intuitively right to millions of people, rather than to ignore them all?

I find it curious that you engage in considerable logical analysis and argument, yet you have a fairly low opinion of the arguments for God's existence. I understand that's because you're convinced that all divinity beliefs are grounded on and justified by experience. But how then do you see the relation of rational thinking to belief in God? I suspect there's some inconsistency between your position and the way you're defending it.

Not really. The fact that belief in God is grounded in experience rather than argument doesn't mean there has to be any conflict between experience and thinking. After all, the beliefs we acquire by perception are also grounded in experience, and many of them are even self-evident. But the fact that they have no rational proof doesn't create a tension between what we believe on the basis of normal sense perception and the practice of thinking rationally about those beliefs. Even the fact that it's possible for rational thought to construct theories that can correct specific perceptions, or for it to enlarge our knowledge beyond what is directly perceivable, doesn't put them in conflict. As I indicated in the essay on self-evidency, the appearance of inconsistency arises between them only if a theory tries to give a logical argument that concludes perception is generally unreliable or fails to reveal realities independent of us.

By the same token, the fact that belief in God is a justified certainty even without arguments doesn't mean we can't think about it. Our belief doesn't require that we'd be better off with no upper brain when it comes to religion. Reason is indispensable for understanding and explaining the biblical idea of God, for contrasting it to other ideas of divinity, and for defending it from attack and criticism. Often the criticisms are based on a mistaken notion of biblical teaching or on arguments that contain a mistake in reasoning. It's important to be able to point those out, as well as to think through the relations between the teachings that make up the content of biblical revelation. For those tasks we need all the rationality we can muster.

Nevertheless, I don't think rational argument can—all by itself—turn a person to genuine belief in God. Remember that the biblical requirement that we believe in God is not the same as mere intellectual consent that God exists;[7] it is the commitment of our whole being. As the first commandment puts it, we're to "love the Lord with all our heart, soul, mind and strength." Scripture's own account of how that happens is that the Spirit of God removes the blindness of our hearts and minds so that we directly experience its message as God speaking to us. As I've pointed out, that experience is equivalent to having our self-evidency antennae restored to proper working order when it comes to what is divine. Without that, an argument for belief in God is an argument against whatever else appears to a person to be self-evidently divine instead of God. So it's every bit as futile to attempt to dislodge that self-evidency by an argument as it is to dislodge belief in God by argument in the case of a person who's experienced God.[8]

Of course that doesn't mean God can't use an argument to aid in the process of bringing a person to a change of heart and experience. But it seems unlikely that an argument trying to prove God's existence would do that; it would more likely be an argument that exposed difficulties with the divinity belief the person already holds. That could be instrumental in getting that person to take belief in God seriously—to make the experiment I've recommended to you, for example. But it's the change in experience that alters the belief, not the argument.

For the same reason I don't think there's any one right way to deal with people like you who are searching for the truth about religion in general or about belief in God in particular. There's no one approach that will be helpful or convincing to all or even most people; the entire matter is highly idiosyncratic, since it has to do with many factors in each person's past experience and present condition, many of which may be unknown to the person himself or herself.

I'd like now to switch to another loose end. What do you say about those who follow other religions? I'm thinking now of other major world traditions rather than of the pagan divinity beliefs that appear in theories (I'm sure you'll say those are just wrong!). The other world religions all agree with belief in God in saying that no part of the world is divine, but each has a different description of the transcendent divine reality on which the world depends. I know you've been emphasizing the differences of those other ideas from theism, but can't they be considered true also?

Belief in God often sounds so harsh in the insistence that it alone is true!

The quick, straightforward answer to your question is "No, they can't all be true." You're right in pointing out that the major world religions all reject the pagan deification of any part of the world. But since the descriptions of divinity in Hinduism, Buddhism and Taoism are logically contrary to theism, it's not possible that they're all true. You say this sounds harsh, but the fact is that every religious tradition recognizes this point. Many forms of Hinduism and Buddhism hold that all people will, given sufficient lifetimes, come to see their teachings as true and so attain Nirvana. However, it is still *their* truth everyone will have to believe in order to attain the experience of enlightenment that will deliver them from being reborn into further lifetimes of suffering. Even according to those traditions, therefore, all competing ideas of divinity and human destiny are false.[9]

But this may not answer what you really had in mind. It occurs to me that you may not have been interested so much in which idea of the divine is true as in the ultimate destiny of those who don't believe the one that is.

Right. I'm thinking of the biblical teaching about a day of judgment for all who have a different idea of God or who lack what you call the "proper relation" to him. My real question is whether it's a nonnegotiable part of belief in God that those who adhere to other religions will be condemned.

Once again you've raised a question I can't presume to answer on behalf of Jews or Muslims; so I will only speak here as a Christian.

The answer is not so simple as you might suppose. The Bible does, of course, teach that there will be a Day of Judgment at which all will give account of themselves to God and those who do not love God will be judged. However, that's not the whole of what Scripture says on the matter, and it must be balanced with other scriptural teachings. Christian theology has long recognized that while only the life, death and resurrection of Jesus Christ fulfilled the demands of God's covenant with the human race, there may be many people who will benefit from what Christ did though they've never heard of him.

Almost all Christians, for example, have believed that infants and the mentally incompetent are included in God's mercy. And these are not the only examples. The New Testament explicitly says that those who died before Christ but who related to God via earlier editions of the covenant—the covenants with Adam, Noah, Abraham and Moses—have obtained the promises of God's love and everlasting life. Their proper standing with God is actually secured by the work of Christ, even though they didn't know about that work or about the doctrines of the Trinity and incarnation that were revealed in connection with it.

In addition, the first chapter of Romans (verses 20-25) says that God has created the world in such a way that, if viewed rightly, it would appear nondivine and thus dependent on a powerful, divine reality that transcends the world. The text makes clear that while that divine reality is in fact God, it is possible for people to see the world's dependence though they may not have any further description of what the world depends on other than "divine," "powerful" and "not the world." Romans then speaks of this as constituting a "witness" God has made to himself that is available to everyone (reminiscent of Psalm 19:1, 4: "The heavens are telling the glory of God; and the firmament proclaims his handiwork.... Their voice goes out through all the earth" [RSV]).

The most interesting part of this text is therefore directly related to your question. It's a clear statement that although people can know very little about God from noticing the nondivinity of the world, God will hold people responsible for whether they believe that witness of nature. This clearly implies that anyone who had only that much information available and believed it would come under God's mercy and have applied to them the covenant benefits secured by the work of Christ.

So does that mean it's not that either you're a conscious, practicing Christian or it's curtains for you come Judgment Day?

Right. It's that and a good bit more. This text also teaches that *some* truth about God is available to everyone, that no one is held accountable for more than was available to him or her, and that anyone may still have God's forgiveness by believing whatever truth about God was available. As we have seen, that can be as little as "something other than this world is the divine on whose power I and the world depend," so clearly it need not include the demands and promises of God's covenant and their fulfillment by Christ. It's not ignorance but the rejection of whatever truth was available to a person which the text says God will condemn, because it results from believing some aspect of the world to be divine instead of God. What is condemned is having a false god.

On this basis I believe there are now, and have been throughout history, a great many around the world who have believed this minimal witness to God despite never hearing the good news about Christ and despite outwardly remaining adherents of some other religious tradition.

Some Christian theologians have gone even further. The Swiss theologian Karl Barth argues that there are scriptural grounds for saying it is possible that God will ultimately show his mercy to everyone. He is careful to add, however, that we are not entitled to state this as firm doctrine; he only says there is enough scriptural basis for it that we may take comfort in the *hope* that it may be so.[10]

I won't go on about this issue, since Christians have held a number of differing interpretations of its details and trying to decide between them would take an extensive exegetical study of the Scriptures.[11] Perhaps it's a topic you'll want to investigate further if and when you study the Bible!

OK, OK. Don't press me. I'm thinking about it.

Let's go to my last loose end. I'm worried about what I fear may result from your contention that rational thinking isn't the basis for religious beliefs. I mean, if that's so, how can there be real dialogue between people of differing faiths? Won't those who accept your position wall themselves up in faith communities? Won't that lead to worsening relations between them? Couldn't it even incite hatred and warfare?

Just the reverse! The position I've maintained is, I believe, the best way to *prevent* people from being walled up, unable to communicate, and in strife over both their religious belief and the differences in practices and other beliefs which it inspires.

You are right, of course, in thinking that one consequence of my position is that reason, for all its importance, is neither infallible nor "autonomous"; it is not self-sufficient or a law unto itself.[12] Rather, as we sow our premises so we reap our conclusions. Reasoning must always be based on beliefs we don't reason to—many of which we experience as self-evidently true. Among these self-evident beliefs is some pivotal belief as to what is divine. In that sense reasoning is always faith-directed. So regardless of whether the divinity belief is an unconscious presupposition or a conscious, fervent commitment, it guides the formation of other beliefs such as the nature of reality, human nature, destiny, happiness and ethical values. So you're right that my position makes religious belief responsible for a lot of the differences people have over a great many things, and I can see why you might be tempted to jump to the conclusion that acknowledging that fact could intensify strife over those differences.

But in my view that conclusion is a seriously misguided jump. Recognizing the root of religious differences or the existence of faith communities stemming from them is not the cause of strife between people. The cause of the conflicts between people is not that they *have* different beliefs and lifestyles but that they take certain *attitudes* toward them. In that respect I think the view of religious belief I've defended is the best possible hedge against the misunderstanding, hatred and strife you fear. Let me explain.

I think my view of religion—that people can't help but experience something or other as divine but have contrary experiences of what that is—promotes the chance that those of differing beliefs will live in peace with one another. This is because it allows members of each faith community to see that the ground on which those in other communities hold their divinity beliefs is the same sort of experience as their own. That allows and encourages the insight that were we ourselves to experience as divine what the other person does, we too might well be inclined toward the same (or similar) further attitudes, beliefs and practices.

At a more general level, this helps reinforce the teachings of every major world religion to the effect that everyone owes tolerance and respect to all people. And—need I add it?—belief in God specifically prescribes not merely tolerance but *love* toward those of other religious beliefs and lifestyles. So I think my view of religious belief in general, as well as the requirements of belief in God in particular, ought to generate attitudes that make for peace and goodwill rather than strife.

Maybe they ought *to, but surely you can't deny that they very often* don't!

Of course not. I don't live with my head wrapped in a blanket! We both know that these attitudes are sorely lacking in the world and are often violated even by those who do, or claim to, believe in God. This position is no panacea for all that's wrong with the world. But that, in a way, is my point: it's neither this view of religion nor belief in God that generates strife. It's the failure to live up to them that generates evils ranging all the way from petty snobbery to war.

Remember: no teaching can guarantee that all who believe it will live up to it. To be sure, there have been people who have done horrible things in the name of religion, including belief in God. But the same is true of other beliefs; great evils have been done in the name of justice, democracy and the advance of science, for example.

On the other hand, there are views of religion in general and of specific religious teachings which *when lived up to* produce horrible results!

You mean religions that taught human sacrifice and things like that?

That's an example, but it's not the only one. Consider, for instance, the view that what is divine are the rational principles which both order the universe and make human reason possible. This view was held by the ancient Greeks, modified and partially incorporated into medieval thought, revived by the Renaissance and ensconced by the Enlightenment. So it's an idea of human nature that has been and continues to be enormously influential in Western culture and that has often been praised for the effect it has had in encouraging the development of mathematics, logic and science.

On that view, humans are deemed essentially rational beings: a rational being is a human, and a human is a rational being. Human reason is affirmed to be self-sufficient (autonomous), but in order to deliver truth it needs to be insulated as much as possible from all other influences. It is present in all people—though not to the same degree (obviously some are more intelligent than others)—and is the sovereign authority by which all decisions are to be made. If there are questions it can't decide, then they can't be decided at all and we should form no belief about them. As Alfred North Whitehead once put it, "The appeal to reason is to the ultimate judge, universal and yet individual to each, to which all authority must bow."[13]

The difficulty arises when this view of humans attempts to explain why people have such profound disagreements. Why do they come up with such widely differing beliefs and then draw consequences from them so diverse that their cultures surprise and even shock one another? If reason is divine, autonomous and the essential nature of humans, there can be only one answer: people disagree because they don't have the same rational capacities or are allowing their reason to be trumped by nonrational influences. According to rationalism, if people were being truly rational they would come to largely the same beliefs, and if they were all guided by those beliefs they would live in much more similar ways. This is not to say they would all have the same subjective tastes and preferences, of course. But they would hold most of the same objective matters to be true or false, and largely the same courses of action to be the correct ways to behave.

It follows from this view that when one person differs sharply from another concerning how to identify the divine, human nature and destiny, what constitutes happiness and so on, at least one of them must have made a mistake in reasoning. And when a large group of people differs from another about almost all such beliefs, it's hard to avoid the conclusion that one group must be more rational than the other. This conclusion is especially tempting when the community that deifies rationality contrasts its beliefs and practices to those of another that does not.

This, however, is a fateful conclusion. For if being rational is the essential characteristic of being human, it will then follow that those who are less rational are also less human. And that is exactly the conclusion the ancient Greeks drew. Their mottos included "Whoever is not a Greek is a barbarian" and "Barbarians are fit only to be slaves to Greeks." Such beliefs inspired Alexander's attempt to conquer the world.

Unfortunately, the Greeks are not the only ones to have drawn that conclusion, nor is rationalism the only religious belief that can yield it. In the twentieth century some of the most horrific evils—think of the Holocaust—have been perpetrated on the grounds that those being eliminated, enslaved or colonized were either less human or not human at all. This result arises because the deification of an aspect of the world means that aspect is divine in humans as well as in the rest of reality. Whether that's reason, emotion, will or whatever, it then follows that those who are superior in that respect are more human than those they judge to be inferior in that respect.

So you think that denying the divinity of any aspect of the world can help to avoid dehumanizing people?

Yes. As I admitted, whether people live up to this point is often another matter. But at least theism discourages dehumanizing others, whereas deifying some facet of human nature encourages it.

So it's important that the general view of religious belief I've presented to you, as well as belief in God specifically, implies no such horrific conclusions. Correctly understood, belief in God implies that although reason, emotion and will are important components in human nature, they are all led and guided by what is experienced as divine. What people see as divine is a product of their experience of self-evidency rather than of their being superior in reason, will or any other facet of human nature; there is nothing about humans that is divine, and so nothing about them that entitles anyone to enslave or eliminate others.

In short, the view I've taken about religion in general regards all people as equally human because capable of religious belief, while belief in God teaches that all people are equally human because created in the image of God—and there are no degrees of that! So while those who believe in God may regard their neighbors of differing faith as mistaken, for that very reason they are urged to be all the more just and loving toward them rather than regard them as less human.

Once again you've given me a lot to think about, and I'll do just that.

I still don't like a lot of what I've heard—and I'm not sure about trying the "experiment" you've recommended. But I do see why you think that only something like it could lead to changing my mind.

Thank you for taking the time to talk about this.

I was happy to do it.

I'll be praying that you make the experiment, and that through your reading, study and contact with a believing community, God will make himself known to you. If that happens, you will be in direct contact with the greatest love it is possible for humans to know, and your knowledge of it will have the greatest certainty humans can possess.

Notes

Chapter 1: What Is Religious Experience?

[1]For further clarification:

    1. An experience *deepens* a religious belief in case it makes the contents of the belief clearer, adds to its contents or intensifies the resolve of the believer to be guided by it.

    2. An experience *confirms* a belief when it is what one would expect if the belief were true.

    3. A belief is an acquired disposition to regard a state of affairs as in fact the case, and the statement of it as true. I will be using the term "belief" in the sense which allows that it may or may not also be knowledge, not in the sense of mere belief in contrast to knowledge.

[2]This shows that atheism and religion are not opposites and that a person's not believing in God or gods does not mean that person has no religion at all. Atheism has a relation to religion like the one that vegetarianism has to eating. The fact that someone does not believe in any god tells us what that person does *not* believe is divine, just as someone's being a vegetarian tells us what that person does *not* eat. The question of what an atheist *does* believe to be divine is not answered by knowing he's an atheist, any more than knowing what a vegetarian *does* like to eat is settled by knowing she's a vegetarian.

[3]For an account of yet other difficulties with this definition, see Roy Clouser, *The Myth of Religious Neutrality* (Notre Dame, Ind.: University of Notre Dame Press, 1991), pp. 28-30 (henceforward referred to simply as *Myth*).

[4]For a discussion of why many of the prominent scholarly attempts at a definition fail as badly as the popular ones reviewed here, see Clouser, *Myth*, chap. 2.

[5]For example, W. C. Smith, *The Meaning and End of Religion* (New York: Harper & Row, 1978), esp. pp. xiv, 11-14, 141-46.

[6]Differences among believers in the same divinity about how to stand in proper relation to it are also religious disagreements, of course. Here I am concerned only with different identifications of the divine.

[7]After arriving at this definition, I found that many before me had also done so, including Plato and Aristotle. Werner Jaeger, in *The Theology of the Early Greek Philosophers* (New York: Oxford University Press, 1960), showed that it was the common property of a number of pre-Socratic Greek thinkers as well. In the twentieth century alone it has been held by William James, *The Varieties of Religious Experience* (New York: Longmans, Green, 1929), pp. 31, 33; A. C. Bouquet, *Comparative Religion* (Baltimore: Penguin, 1973), pp. 21, 38, 45, 48; Mircea Eliade, *Patterns in Comparative Religion* (New York: New American Library, 1974), pp. 24-30; Hermann Dooyeweerd, *A New Critique of Theoretical Thought* (Philadelphia: Presbyterian & Reformed, 1955), 1:57; N. K. Smith, *The Credibility of Divine Existence* (New York: St. Martin's, 1967), p. 396; Paul Tillich, *Systematic Theology*

(Chicago:University of Chicago Press, 1951), 1:9, 13; Hans Küng, *Christianity and the World Religions* (Garden City, N.Y.: Doubleday, 1986), p. xvi; C. S. Lewis, *Miracles* (New York: Macmillan, 1948), pp. 16-20, 99-107.

[8]This is the case in religions that regard demons and jinn as minor deities (gods) and in religions that have malevolent divinities, such as the Dakota evil Great Spirit. See James Fraser, *The Golden Bough* (New York: Macmillan 1951), p. 308. Plato is also an example, since he insisted on an evil world soul as well as a good one (*Laws* 10.896).

[9]This is an important point even for Hinduism and Buddhism, despite their teaching that only the divine really exists. For although that doctrine seems to preclude any dependency relation, drawing a distinction between the divine reality and the illusory world still leaves their relation to be explained. Hinduism explicitly deals with the issue, teaching that Brahman-Atman generates the illusion. Buddhism generally avoids the issue on the grounds that it is spiritually unhealthy to think about the illusory world at all. Compare Robert Neville's remarks in *The Tao and the Daimon* (Albany: State University of New York Press, 1982), p. 116.

[10]Other "isms" do the same. Positivism, for example, takes either perceptions or their causes to be divine instead of matter. As Ernst Mach put it, "One must not attempt to explain sense perception. It is something so simple and fundamental that the attempt to trace it back to something simpler, at least at the present time, can never succeed" (*Knowledge and Error* [Dordrecht: Reidel, 1975], p. 441).

John Stuart Mill, on the other hand, did take their explanation back one step. When asked what caused sensations, Mill replied that actual perceptions are the product of realities he called the "permanent possibilities of sensation." These he regarded as metaphysically ultimate: "There exist in nature a number of permanent causes which have subsisted ever since the human race has been in existence and for an indefinite and probably enormous length of time previous. . . . But we can give no account of the origin of the permanent causes themselves. . . . All phenomena without exception which begin to exist, that is, *all except the primeval causes,* are effects either immediate or remote of those primitive facts or some combinations of them" (*The Philosophy of Scientific Method,* ed. Ernest Nagel [New York: Hafner, 1950], pp. 202-3).

For Mach, then, sensation is so fundamental in reality that it cannot be explained by anything else, whereas all else is explained by it. For Mill, the primeval permanent possibilities of sensation did not begin to exist and are the causes of all that does. But on either version something is regarded as divine despite Mill's claim to be "one of the few . . . who has not thrown off religious belief, but never had it." From Mill's *Autobiography,* in *The Essential Works of John Stuart Mill,* ed. Max Lerner (New York: Bantam, 1961), p. 39.

[11]Again, this is true not only of materialism but of theories of reality generally. Take Aristotle's theory as an example. In the *Metaphysics* he sets out to find what has utterly independent existence and argues that it is not just matter but form in addition to matter (*Metaphysics* 1042.a.25-33). But he also insists that only the forms be called "divine," despite admitting that matter has independent reality. The reason is that he insists "divine" be defined not only as nondependence but also as changelessness. So he says about forms, "Therefore about that which can exist independently and is changeless there is a science. . . . And if there is such a kind of thing in the world here surely must be the divine, and

this must be the first and dominant principle" (*Metaphysics* 1064.a.33-38).

He then goes on to say that although all forms are divine, some have more "dignity" than others in that they are combined with less matter and are capable of thought. It is the highest of these, the prime mover, which he calls "god." This "unmovable first mover" is a single individual, an astronomical body devoid of all matter (*Metaphysics* 1074.a.3-39) and capable of self-knowledge (*Metaphysics* 1075.a.5-11). But because the prime mover neither knows nor cares about humans, Aristotle rejects the secondary beliefs usually attached to the gods in the Greek religious traditions. His theory is thus an example of taking a religious divinity belief and attempting to strip it of its traditional cultic accompaniments. He says, "Our forefathers in the most remote ages have handed down to their posterity a tradition in the form of a myth, that these bodies are gods and that the divine encloses the whole of nature. The rest of the tradition has been added later. . . . But if one were to separate the first point from these additions and take it alone, that they thought the first substances to be gods, one must regard this as an inspired utterance and reflect that . . . these opinions have been preserved until the present like relics of ancient treasure" (*Metaphysics* 1074.b.1-13).

Thus even though the prime mover is not an object of worship for Aristotle, he did not succeed in divesting the divinity of it and all other forms from every belief about the right way to relate to them. He still thought it essential to *know* that forms are divine, based his view of human nature and destiny on that belief, and advocated a way of life in accord with the ideas of ethical virtue and happiness it implied. Thus his metaphysics included belief in divinity and in how to relate to divinity. The latter carried enormous personal implications.

[12]I believe this can be convincingly demonstrated to be the case for theories in every discipline without exception; none can fail to have metaphysical, and thus religious, assumptions. See Clouser, *Myth,* chaps. 7 (on mathematics), 8 (on physics) and 9 (on psychology).

[13]It has also been suggested that for all its breadth, my definition is actually still too narrow! The trouble is supposed to be that in Buddhism there is no such notion of the divine as I define it. This is simply mistaken. In the famous dialogue from the Buddhist scriptures called "The Questions of King Milinda," we find the following: "One can point out the way to the realization of Nirvana, but one cannot show a cause for its production. And what is the reason for that? Because that dharma, Nirvana, is unconditioned. . . . It is not made by anything. . . . it is something that is" (*The Buddhist Scriptures* [Baltimore: Penguin, 1968], p. 159).

And the Pali Canon *Udana* 8.3 asserts that Nirvana "is without any foundation, without development, without foothold." In commenting on this, Lambert Schmithausen has pointed out that "some passages even speak of Nirvana as a transcendent metaphysical state or essence. . . . According to these passages there is a metaphysical reality . . . which is also called nirvana and preexists the nirvana that is a spiritual event. . . . Most of the Hinayana schools [think Nirvana to be] a positive metaphysical entity. They take the spiritual event of Nirvana to be participation in this metaphysical entity" (in *Christianity and the World Religions,* ed. Hans Küng [Garden City, N.Y.: Doubleday, 1986], pp. 301, 327.

The nearest thing I know to a rejection of my definition of the divine in Buddhism is the teaching of Nagarjuna, a master of the Shunyavada branch of Mahayana Buddhism who lived about eighteen hundred years ago. He laid great emphasis on the ideas of emptiness and the Void and insisted, in contrast to other Buddhist schools of thought, that even the dharmas were "empty" of reality. By itself this is no problem for my definition, but some commentators have wondered whether this is a nihilist rejection of every reality whatever, divinity included. The fact is, however, that Nagarjuna never said any such thing. His claim was simply that individual things are empty of reality because they have "no essential nature of their own, and are thus impermanent. . . . They arrive in and vanish from the world of appearances in keeping with the law of 'dependent origination' " (Heinz Beckert, "Buddhist Perspectives," in *Christianity and the World Religions*, p. 363).

None of this shows that the divine as I define it is utterly lacking in Nagarjuna's teachings. Far from it; the divine as I define it is a necessary assumption to the contrasts he drew. If the world of everyday experience is unreal because it is "impermanent," "changeable" and "dependent," this clearly assumes that there is a genuine reality that contrasts to it as permanent, changeless and nondependent. I conclude therefore that the divine as I have defined it is *presupposed* by the Shunyavada position, even if it is not explicitly asserted.

The same conclusion has been reached by other scholars as well, such as David Dilworth in "Whitehead's Process Realism, the Abhidharma Dharma Theory and the Mahayana Critique," *International Philosophical Quarterly* 18, no. 2 (1978): 162-63, and Robert Neville, *The Tao and the Daimon* (Albany: State University of New York Press, 1982), p. 116.

[14]William F. Albright, *From the Stone Age to Christianity* (Garden City, N.Y.: Doubleday, 1957), pp. 15-16.

[15]Joseph Addison Alexander, *Commentary on the Prophecies of Isaiah* (Grand Rapids, Mich.: Zondervan, 1953), p. 147.

[16]Some translations render the word *elements* as "elemental spirits," but that is not what the Greek texts say. They speak of belief in "the elements of the cosmos" (στοιχεῖα τοῦ κόσμου) as both false philosophy and false religion, in opposition to belief that all depends on Christ. The same term is used in 2 Peter 3:10, where it makes no sense whatever unless it means physical elements.

[17]An outstanding example of holding a belief unconsciously is the way the law of noncontradiction is assumed by people who have never articulated it to themselves or have never heard it stated. More than that, many of them express doubt or actually reject it on first hearing it stated, even though it continues to be presupposed by all their concept-forming and reasoning—including their denial of it!

[18]Theories of knowledge have proposed or assumed a list of candidates for the nature of knowledge that is largely the same as the list I cited earlier from the history of metaphysics. The basic nature of knowledge has been held to be sensory, physical, logical, mathematical, historical and so on. The alleged metaphysical innocence of even the simple statement "Knowledge is justified true belief" is unmasked as soon as any explanation is attempted as to exactly what "justified," "true" and "belief" mean.

[19]Arguments purporting to show the dependency of the rest of reality on X usually attempt to establish that certain Xs are preconditions for the occurrence of certain non-Xs. The trouble with such arguments is that even if correct, they do not establish the conclusion that X is nondependent. To do that, the arguments would have to show that Xs are the sufficient as well as necessary conditions for all non-Xs and that there could not be any other reality on which Xs and the order of preconditonality depend. We will return to this point in chapter six. See also Clouser, *Myth,* chap. 10.

[20]Some philosophers have recognized the experiential ground of their belief about nondependent reality. Paul Ziff once put it this way: "If you ask me why I'm a materialist, I'm not sure what to say. It's not because of the arguments. I guess I'd just have to say that reality looks irresistibly physical to me" (lecture on philosophy of language at the University of Pennsylvania, March 1962).

[21]Compare Dooyeweerd, *New Critique of Theoretical Thought*, pp. 57ff., and the insightful comments with which Calvin begins his *Institutes of the Christian Religion* (1.1.1-3).

[22]This point is the key to understanding Psalm 14:1, "The fool has said in his heart there is no God." It does not mean (as Anselm thought) that one who denies God exists is a fool because he contradicts himself. Rather, it means those who deny that anything whatever is divine are blind to that fact that they are simultaneously regarding something as divine.

[23]Compare the remarks of biologist Richard Lewontin: "It is not that the methods and institutions of science somehow compel us to accept a material explanation of the . . . world, but on the contrary, that we are forced by our *prior* adherence to material causes to create an apparatus of investigation and a set of concepts that produce material explanations, no matter how counterintuitive, no matter how mystifying to the uninitiated. Moreover, that materialism is absolute, for we cannot allow a Divine Foot in the door. . . . To appeal to an omnipotent deity is to allow that at any moment the regularities of nature may be ruptured, that Miracles may happen" (*New York Review of Books*, January 7, 1997, p. 31).

Chapter 2: Types of Religious Belief & Experience

[1]It also avoids confusing surface similarities with genuine agreement. Various forms of worship and rites involved in acquiring the right relation to the divine can be remarkably similar, can arise in similar cultural conditions, and can even be phrased in similar wording but still have very different meanings when understood from the standpoint of different conceptions of the divine and of how the nondivine depends on the divine.

[2]"Theism" simply signifies belief in one Creator God who transcends the universe and who reveals his will to humans. The term *transcendent,* when applied to God, denotes God's distinct existence or "otherness" with respect to creation: creation is not made out of (or made up of) the being of God. For theists, there is only God and creation, and creation is all that is not God. Though the being of God is not the being of creatures, God shares properties with creatures.

"Deism" is the view that there is probably some sort of divine being who created or formed the universe but no longer sustains or cares for it, and whose nature can't be known by us at all. "Atheism" is the belief that there is no personal divine being. It is also sometimes intended to connote the belief that there is nothing whatever divine, whether personal or not.

[3]To say that God created something does not require that there ever was a *time* when it didn't exist and another at which it began to exist. What distinguishes anything as created is solely its dependency on God. As Thomas Aquinas put it, even had the world always existed, it would have always depended on God (*Summa Theologica* Q46.a1).

[4]Will Herberg, "The Fundamental Outlook of Hebraic Religion," in *The Ways of Religion*, ed. Roger Eastman (New York: Canfield, 1975), p. 283.

[5]The ancient Pythagoreans, for example, worshiped numbers as divine. Here is their prayer to the number ten: "Bless us, divine number, thou who generatest gods and men! O holy, holy tetraktys, thou that containest the root and source of eternally flowing creation! For divine number begins with the profound, the pure unity until it comes to the holy four; then it begets the mother of all, the all-encompassing, the all-bounding, the first born, the never swerving, the never tiring holy ten, the keyholder of all" (Tobias Danzig, *Number: The Language of Science* [Garden City, N.Y.: Doubleday/Anchor 1954], p. 42).

A contemporary version of Pythagorean religious belief without the involvement of worship is found in Werner Heisenberg: "In modern quantum theory there can be no doubt that the elementary particles will finally also be mathematical forms, but of a much more complicated nature. . . . The mathematical forms that represent the elementary particles will be solutions of some eternal law of motion for matter. Actually this is a problem which has not yet been solved. . . . If we follow the Pythagorean line of thought we may hope that the fundamental law of motion will turn out as a mathematically simple law. . . . It is difficult to give any good argument for this hope. . . . [It] fits with the Pythagorean religion, and many physicists share their belief in this respect, but no convincing argument has yet been given to show that it must be so" (*Physics and Philosophy* [New York: Harper & Row, 1958], pp. 71-73).

[6]This is the position ascribed to Socrates in Plato's *Phaedo* 103.B.105-6. Many theists accept this Greek dualistic view of humans as properly Jewish or Christian or Muslim when in fact it is not. As Herberg says, "However familiar and plausible [the] dualistic view may seem to many religious people today, it is nevertheless utterly contrary to the Hebraic outlook. In authentic Hebraism, man is not a compound of two 'substances' but a dynamic unity. . . . The body, its impulses and passions are not evil; as parts of God's creation, they are innocent and, when properly ordered, positively good. Nor, on the other hand, is the human spirit the 'false divinity' of the Greeks. Spirit is the source of both good and evil, for the spirit is will, freedom, decision" (Herberg, "Fundamental Outlook," p. 284).

[7]For example, Norman Kemp Smith, *The Credibility of Divine Existence* (New York: St. Martin's, 1967); John Smith, *Experience and God* (New York: Oxford University Press, 1968); Caroline Franks Davis, *The Evidential Force of Religious Experience* (New York: Oxford University Press, 1989); William Alston, *Perceiving God* (Ithaca, N.Y.: Cornell University Press, 1991).

[8]B. H. Streeter and A. J. Appasamy, *The Sadu* (London: Macmillan, 1921), pp. 5-7.

[9]From Mircea Eliade, *Gods, Goddesses and Myths of Creation* (New York: Harper & Row, 1974), pp. 16-18.

[10]It would take us too far afield to discuss the many issues surrounding miracles. But for the record, I hold that miracles are events directly caused by divine agency for the purpose of calling attention to God's covenantal dealings with humans. And I side with Augustine in holding that although many miracles can't be explained or duplicated by us, they do not violate the laws of nature.

[11]Rudolf Otto, *The Idea of the Holy* (New York: Galaxy, 1958). Otto himself did not distinguish this type of experience from the others we're considering but tried to reduce them all to this kind. His position was that the other alleged sorts of experiences are really all different interpretations of this type, which are devised subsequent to the experiences themselves. In other words, he held that the experiences are all purely emotional and are identical, whereas the interpretations are the products of an overlay of later rationalization.

That, however, does not accord with most experience reports. While there are experiences that are vague and thus come to be interpreted later, most are *at the time* experienced as mystical union, a divine power in all things, a personal presence or contact with God. The differences are not all devised upon later reflection.

Caroline Franks Davis makes the same point and adds the supporting observation that some of the most distinctive features of the experiences reported are contrary to the cultural background and expectations of those having them and thus are unlikely to have been subsequent rationalizations. See Davis, *Evidential Force,* pp. 176-77.

[12]Otto, *Idea,* pp. 12-13.

[13]Ibid., pp. 8-11.

[14]Alston says of this type of experience: "Many people find it incredible, unintelligible, or incoherent to suppose that there could be something that counts as *presentation* [experience] . . . but is devoid of sensory content. So far as I can see, this simply evinces a lack of speculative imagination. Why suppose that the possibilities of experiential givenness . . . are exhausted by *our* five senses? . . . The point is that there is no good reason to doubt that phenomenal content may be very different from any that is produced by our external senses and may not result from the stimulation of any sense organ. It is this possibility that [those reporting these experiences] suppose themselves to have realized" (Alston, *Perceiving God,* p. 17).

[15]William James, *The Varieties of Religious Experience* (New York: Longmans, Green, 1929), pp. 66-67.

[16]Simone Weil, *Waiting on God* (Glasgow: Collins, 1959), pp. 5-6.

[17]Davis distinguishes four subtypes. See *Evidential Force,* pp. 54-65.

[18]James, *Varieties,* pp. 380-82. Compare Davis, *Evidential Force,* pp. 18-19.

[19]James, *Varieties,* pp. 213-14, 399.

[20]Compare James's comments in ibid., p. 248. Once again, I speak here only of experiences that *produce* religious beliefs, because we are confining our discussion to them and skipping experiences that deepen or confirm beliefs already held.

[21]James, *Varieties,* pp. 72-73. See also Davis, *Evidential Force,* p. 41.

[22]James, *Varieties,* pp. 59-62.

[23]Ibid., pp. 221-22, 246 n., 238-39, 382; compare also Davis, *Evidential Force,* p. 42.

[24]See James, *Varieties,* p. 399.

[25]Abraham Kuyper, *Encyclopedia of Sacred Theology* (New York: Scribner's, 1898), pp. 128-29.

Chapter 3: Self-Evident Knowledge

[1]Quoted by Alvin Plantinga in *Warrant: The Current Debate* (New York: Oxford University Press, 1993), p. 26. On the same page Plantinga cites other advocates of this view: Sigmund Freud, Brand Blanshard, H. H. Price, Bertrand Russell and Michael Scriven.

[2]There are also probability arguments in which the conclusion has a degree of likelihood rather than certainty relative to its premises. But even these assume a broader, tacit, deductive context that encompasses the rules of probability. In other words, probability arguments depend at some level on deductive certainty; their conclusions are certainly probable, not probably probable.

[3]Compare Aristotle *Posterior Analytics* 72b20-24.

[4]Compare Aristotle's remarks in *Prior Analytics* 64.b.28-38. What are called truth tables in books of logic are not really proofs of logical rules, since they assume the truth of the rules already. Rather, they are devices for exhibiting the rules to our logical intuition.

[5]In most endeavors a mistake is simply called a mistake, but logic and theology have special names for them. In logic, an inference incorrectly drawn is called a "fallacy," and in theology false teaching is called "heresy." The special names appear to reflect the belief these mistakes are more important to avoid than other kinds, since fallacies affect all reasoning and heresies end in divine judgment. There have long been special (human) punishments for each as well. Heresy used to result in excommunication (or worse) but is nowadays generally praised. Fallacies, however, have retained their ancient punishment: crushing embarrassment in the face of wild, uncontrollable laughter.

[6]Two clarifications: First, self-evident beliefs are not the only noninferential beliefs. Guesses are also noninferential, for example, but are uncertain. Second, *noninferential* here means that the belief is not learned by deriving it from any other belief, not that it *can't* be inferred. Trivially, any belief can be inferred if one disjoins it to a falsehood and denies the falsehood.

[7]In this respect self-evidency is like rationality and justification generally. See Nicholas Wolterstorff, "Can Belief in God Be Rational If It Has No Foundations?" in *Faith and Rationality*, ed. Alvin Plantinga and Nicholas Wolterstorff (Notre Dame, Ind.: University of Notre Dame Press, 1983), esp. pp. 155, 165; also Alvin Plantinga, "Reason and Belief in God," in *Faith and Rationality*, p. 56.

[8]There is an impressive list of thinkers who have described the experience this way: Aristotle *Metaphysics* K.5-6; Aristotle *Posterior Analytics* 1-2; Aquinas *Disputations* 14; Aquinas *De Veritate;* Aquinas *Summa Theologica* 1.q2.1.obj.2; René Descartes *Rules for the Direction of the Mind,* rule 3; John Locke *Essay* 4.2.1, 4.7.2; G. W. von Leibniz *New Essays* 4.7, 9; Roderick Chisholm, *The Foundations of Knowing* (Minneapolis: University of Minnesota Press, 1982), pp. 27, 57-58; Karl Popper, *Objective Knowledge* (Oxford: Clarendon, 1972); Plantinga, "Reason and Belief in God," pp. 55-59.

[9]Compare Thomas Aquinas: "The intellect knows that it possesses truth by reflecting on itself." From *The Disputed Questions on Truth,* trans. Robert Mulligan (Chicago: Henry Regenery, 1952), 1.9.

[10]Compare Descartes: "By intuition ... I [mean] ... the apprehension which the mind ... gives us ... so that we are ... freed from all doubt as to what we are apprehending. ... Thus each of us can tell by intuition that he exists, that he thinks, that the triangle is bound by three sides only." From *Descartes' Philosophical Writings*, trans. N. K. Smith (New York: Random House, 1958), p. 10. See also Alvin Plantinga's remarks in *Warrant and Proper Function* (New York: Oxford University Press, 1993), pp. 105-6.

[11]Conflict with another self-evident belief is not, however, the only ground on which an intuited belief may come to be doubted. I may, for example, become persuaded on less than self-evident grounds that I have gone insane or that I am suffering some other serious malfunction when others I trust assure me that they know the belief to be false and remind me that in my normal state I did too. We will return to this point in a later chapter.

[12]The experience of intuiting a belief as self-evident normally triggers in us the response of believing it unless it is somehow blocked. Such blocking factors can include beliefs we already hold that are incompatible with the experienced self-evidency, powerful emotions and so on. For more on this point, see Wolterstorff, "Can Belief in God Be Rational?" pp. 148-55, and Plantinga, *Warrant and Proper Function*, 108-9.

[13]Aristotle *Posterior Analytics* 100.b.5-14. See also *Topics* 100.a.31-b.21.

[14]*Descartes' Philosophical Writings*, p. 73.

[15]Ibid., p. 10.

[16]It will not get around this point to suggest that we could accept all the beliefs that appear self-evident if only we would give up the logical law that two incompatible beliefs cannot be true at the same time. The reason is that the logical law is also self-evident. In that case there are three self-evident beliefs involved, some one of which will still have to be rejected as false.

[17]J. Van Heijencourt, *From Frege to Gödel* (Cambridge, Mass.: Harvard University Press, 1976), pp. 124-25.

[18]Bertrand Russell, *Mysticism and Logic* (Garden City, N.Y.: Doubleday/Anchor), p. 73.

[19]Aristotle *Posterior Analytics* 71.a.11-15.

[20]Michael Dummet, *The Logical Basis of Metaphysics* (Cambridge, Mass.: Harvard University Press, 1991).

[21]Morris Kline, *Mathematics: The Loss of Certainty* (New York: Oxford University Press, 1980), p. 6. Kline further adds that "the developments in the foundations of mathematics since 1900 are bewildering, and the present state of mathematics is anomalous and deplorable. The light of truth no longer illuminates the road to follow. In place of the unique, universally admired and universally accepted body of mathematics whose proofs, though sometimes requiring emendation, were regarded as the acme of sound reasoning, we now have conflicting approaches to mathematics. Beyond the logicist, intuitionist, and formalist bases, the approach through set theory alone gives many options. Some divergent and even conflicting opinions are possible even within the other schools. Thus the constructivist movement within the intuitionist philosophy has many splinter groups. Within formalism there are choices to be made about what principles of metamathematics may be employed. ... At the very least what was considered to be illogical and to be banished is now accepted by some schools as logically sound" (pp. 275-76).

[22]There is no contradiction in saying that a belief can be self-evident but not infallible,

given what we have seen about the experience of self-evidency. A belief is infallible if and only if satisfaction of the conditions for its being a justified belief and failure of the conditions for its being true is not possible, which is obviously not yielded by the experience of self-evidency. This is not even true for incorrigible beliefs that have what Alston calls "self-warrant." These are such that satisfaction of their belief conditions and failure of their justification conditions is not possible. See William Alston, "Self-Warrant: A Neglected Form of Privileged Access," *American Philosophical Quarterly* 13, no. 4 (1976): 257ff.

[23]Compare Saul Kripke's comment about Leibniz's law: "Already when I worked on modal logic it had seemed to me, as Wiggins has said, that the Leibnitzian principle of the indiscernibility of identicals was as self-evident as the law of contradiction." Saul Kripke, *Naming and Necessity* (Cambridge, Mass.: Harvard University Press, 1980), p. 3.

[24]This point is the more significant since Aristotle claimed not only that the law is infallible but also that no one can fail to believe it (*Posterior Analytics* 76.b.23-24). This shows that he simply didn't know about Hindu and Buddhist mysticism.

[25]On the other hand, some writers have denied not only that incorrigible beliefs are infallible but even that we have the right to be certain of any of them. They think they *can* see how it's possible for such beliefs to be false. For example, Louis Pojman says, "Suppose Ruth is sad, and considers whether she is. Her psychiatrist, . . . believing . . . it . . . better for Ruth to overcome her depressive moods through positive thinking, assures her on the highest authority that the feelings she is having really are feelings of deep peace and well-being. Ruth, having a great deal of misplaced faith in her psychiatrist, believes him and consequently, whenever the 'sad' feelings come over her, gets herself to believe that these are feelings of deep peace and well-being." Louis Pojman, *What Can We Know?* (Belmont, Calif.: Wadsworth, 1994), p. 126.

First, I'd like to say that I find the example preposterous. The likelihood that anyone could be persuaded that depression is peace is on a par with the likelihood of persuading someone that fire feels cold to the touch or that red is blue. But that aside, the example still fails. It does not show that there is nothing Ruth believes that couldn't be falsified. For even if she can be swayed to call her experience by another name, what she feels remains the same; her belief that she has *this* particular feeling—whatever she calls it—still couldn't be shown wrong.

Moreover, there's nothing significant at stake about her changing the name she gives an experience. We have many feelings for which we have no name at all, but we know ourselves to have them when they occur and recognize them as familiar when we reexperience them. Whether we have names for them at all, and whether we ever change those names, is irrelevant to the self-evidency of the feeling experienced.

Pojman's argument really shows two things. First, Ruth's experience led to the formation of more than one belief. One belief, about the feelings she suffered, didn't change and was certain; the other belief, about what to call the feelings, changed (assuming she is incredibly gullible) and was not certain. But how does that defeat the claim that she has every right to be certain she really had the feeling she seemed to have?

Second, the argument reminds us that people can be talked out of what they believe. In fact, they can even be talked out of what appears self-evident to them (although this example is not a case of that); think of what happens in jury rooms! The power that various motives can have on the human belief-forming capacities are at times truly astounding, and people have the ability to repress almost any belief in favor of another; Hindu and Buddhist mystics are extreme cases of this.

[26]If this much is right, then the main objection to counting (many) beliefs formed by normal sense perception as knowledge is removed. Many, though not all, beliefs produced in that way exhibit the quality of self-evidency every bit as much as do logical and mathematical beliefs. We will return to this point later.

[27]This claim is strongly suggested by Descartes, Leibniz and Locke, since they all insist that intuitive certainty is part of "the natural light of reason" and hence the property of all rational adults. More recently Anthony Quinton has endorsed it explicitly: "What is significant is the fact of universal agreement, amongst all but the muddled or deliberately perverse, that a particular set of such beliefs are true. The dialectician who claims to deny the law of excluded middle is insincere" (*The Nature of Things* [London: Routledge and Keagan Paul, 1973], p. 125).

[28]This was held by Aristotle in *Posterior Analytics* 88.b.30-89.a.10, and seems to be endorsed by Aquinas when he identifies self-evident truth with what is instantly recognized true because it is analytic (*Summa Theologica* 1.a.2.1). In the *Meditations* and *Rules for the Direction of the Mind* Descartes also seems to hold this, since all the examples he gives of intuitively certain beliefs are (either incorrigible or) necessary truths of logic and mathematics. Nicholas Wolterstorff has noticed that Locke does the same thing in "The Migration of Theistic Arguments: From Natural Theology to Evidentialist Apologetics," in *Rationality, Religious Belief and Moral Commitment*, ed. Robert Audi and William Wainwright (Ithaca, N.Y.: Cornell University Press, 1986), pp. 46-48. In *The Foundations of Knowing* ([Minneapolis: University of Minnesota Press, 1982], p. 73) Roderick Chisholm points out that Leibniz as well as Locke held this view.

[29]This refers, of course, only to those truths I will call per se necessary: those that express a lawlike relation and so are both universal and necessary. It does not include truths that are per se contingent but are necessary in the sense that they cannot be altered because they state past events.

[30]Not only thinkers of the past have held this view (such as those mentioned in note 28); it has contemporary advocates as well. See, for example, Plantinga's *Warrant and Proper Function*, p. 106, where he links self-evidency with both necessity and being known a priori.

On the view I'm defending here necessary truths are *among* the self-evident beliefs known by intuition and are also a priori in the sense of not being inference from inductive instance counting. But my position is that they are not the only beliefs known intuitively and that "a priori" can't mean "independent of *all* experience."

[31]The nonreductionist force of the experiment in thought offered in chapter one applies here. Experience isn't purely *sensory* any more than concepts are purely logical or objects purely physical. Sensory, logical and physical qualities are among many kinds exhibited by all the things and events we experience. See Roy Clouser, *The Myth of Religious Neutrality* (Notre Dame, Ind.: Notre Dame University Press, 1991), chaps. 10-11.

[32]Letter to William Graham, Down, July 3, 1881, in *The Life and Letters of Charles Darwin*,

Including an Autobiographical Chapter, ed. Francis Darwin (London: John Murray, 1887), 1:315-16. Cited in Plantinga, *Warrant and Proper Function*, p. 219.

[33]Patricia Churchland, "Epistemology in an Age of Neuroscience," *Journal of Philosophy* 84 (October 1987): 548.

[34]I explained this in more detail and distinguished it from self-referential and self-performative incoherency in *Myth*, chap. 4. The same chapter also distinguishes a strong version and a weak version of each of these three incoherencies.

[35]In principle, discoveries of this sort are no more serious than our learning that a stick that appears bent in water isn't really bent or that the shimmer in the road on a hot day isn't really water. These are instances of better perceptions correcting poorer ones, from which no skeptical conclusion can be drawn that is not guilty of self-assumptive incoherence.

[36]Ernest Nagel, *Sovereign Reason* (Glencoe, Ill.: Free Press, 1954), p. 130.

[37]Ibid.

[38]Ibid., p. 304.

[39]Ibid., p. 305. In the surrounding paragraphs Nagel shifts freely between speaking of the "first principles" of science and the "hypotheses of science" in a way that requires all first principles to be hypotheses. This is typical of pragmatism.

[40]This is nevertheless the advice Richard Rorty gives us about intuitions of self-evidency: "What really needs debate between the pragmatist and the intuitive realist is *not* whether we have intuitions. . . . *Of course* we have . . . intuitions. . . . But it begs the question between pragmatist and realist to say that we must find a philosophical view which 'captures' such intuitions. The pragmatist is urging that we do our best to *stop having* such intuitions" (*Consequences of Pragmatism* [Minneapolis: University of Minnesota Press, 1982], p. xxx).

[41]See Karl Popper, *Conjectures and Refutations* (New York: Harper & Row), pp. 113-14.

[42]Ibid., p. xix. I have critiqued Rorty's position in more detail in Roy Clouser, "A Critique of Historicism," *Crítica* (Mexico) 29, no. 85 (April 1997): 41-63.

[43]Compare George Pappas, "Lost Justification," in *Midwest Studies in Philosophy*, ed. Oeter French, Theodore Uehling and Howard Wettstien (Minneapolis: University of Minnesota Press, 1979).

[44]One theory of knowledge into which this position on self-evidency could easily by integrated is that developed by Plantinga in *Warrant and Proper Function*. In note 30 I mentioned that Plantinga restricts self-evident beliefs to necessary truths and so argues for a distinct class of beliefs which are basic but not self-evident.

Although there may well be such a class of beliefs, on my position most of those whose basicality Plantinga is concerned to defend are actually self-evident. If that is correct, however, it would only serve to strengthen his overall position.

Chapter 4: Belief in God & the Axiom of Equals

[1]Augustine *Confessions* 10.6. A contemporary thinker who holds this view is Alvin Plantinga ("Reason and Belief in God," in *Faith and Rationality*, ed. Alvin Plantinga and Nicholas Wolterstorff [Notre Dame, Ind.: University of Notre Dame Press, 1983], pp. 16-93). Paul Helm has given a helpful exposition of this understanding of "faith" as it is found in John Calvin and John Owen. See *The Varieties of Belief* (New York: Humanities,

1973), chap. 6.

[2]John Calvin *Institutes of the Christian Religion* 1.7.2.

[3]Ibid. 1.7.4.

[4]Ibid. 1.7.5.

[5]Blaise Pascal, *Pensées*, trans. A. J. Krailsheimer (London: Penguin, 1966), p. 58. Obviously Pascal is referring to the rational intuition of truth when he speaks of knowing with the heart, and not to hunches or feelings.

[6]The biblical teaching about the acquisition of belief in God is always in terms of the typical visual metaphors associated with intuition and self-evidency. This is true of the Hebrew Scriptures but is even more prominent in the New Testament. Here are just a few examples. In Ephesians 4:18 those who do not believe are said to be suffering from "ignorance" due to "blindness of the heart," whereas the first chapter of that same book addresses those who do believe as those in whom "the eyes of your understanding [are] opened" (Eph 1:18). Second Corinthians 4:6 speaks of the light of the knowledge of God. In Hebrews 10:32 the turning of unbelievers to God is called the result of their being "illuminated," and chapter 11 begins by calling faith in God the "foundation" and "evidence" for believers' trust in God's promises. (Notice that faith in God doesn't *need* foundations and evidence; it *is* the foundation and evidence.)

[7]Nor would it help if they were to perform a miracle. For any event, no matter how strange, there is always another possible explanation than that it is the result of God's acting directly in the world in order to call attention to his covenant. So unless you already believed in God, you would not regard any event as his activity. Compare Jesus' remark in Luke 16:31.

[8]See William Alston, *Perceiving God* (Ithaca, N.Y.: Cornell University Press, 1991), pp. 228-34, and Nicholas Wolterstorff, "Can Belief in God Be Rational If It Has No Foundations?" in *Faith and Rationality*, ed. Alvin Plantinga and Nicholas Wolterstorff (Notre Dame, Ind.: University of Notre Dame Press, 1983), pp. 153-55.

[9]Compare the example given by Alister Hardy: "It was while listening to a sermon in St Mary's, that I became convinced of the reality of God. Emotion was at a minimum. . . . This sense of being convinced was not basically intellectual either. It was just that I knew the preacher was speaking the truth." *The Spiritual Nature of Man: A Study of Contemporary Religious Experience* (Oxford: Clarendon, 1979), p. 100.

The point is that although feelings may accompany such an experience, as they did for Wesley or Pascal, they are not what warrants a belief. They should not be identified with the testimony of God's Spirit to the truth of the biblical message as, for example, the Mormons do.

[10]Compare Matthew 13:5-6.

[11]Compare William James's remark: "The effect of conversion is to bring with it a changed attitude towards life, which is fairly constant and permanent, although the feelings fluctuate." *The Varieties of Religious Experience* (New York: Longmans, Green, 1929), p. 258.

[12]For a more detailed criticism of the strong historicist position and attempts to avoid its self-defeating character, see Roy Clouser, "A Critique of Historicism," *Crítica* 29, no. 85 (1997): 41-63.

[13]George Gamow, *One, Two, Three, Infinity* (New York: Mentor, 1955). See also Tobias Danzig, *Number: The Language of Science* (New York: Doubleday, 1954), pp. 5-7.

[14]Compare N. K. Smith's insightful article "Is Divine Existence Credible?" in *The Credibility of Divine Existence and Other Essays* (New York: St Martin's, 1967), pp. 375-97.

[15]For the sake of accuracy I take note here that the intuitionist school of thought in mathematics holds that we should not start mathematical reasoning with axioms at all. But clearly it takes other truths as self-evident in place of them, so the main point here is not affected.

[16]Some forms of Hinduism and Buddhism do take the tack of rejecting the law of noncontradiction. The trouble is that this leaves no difference between truth and falsehood and thus no way of conceiving or asserting that the rejection itself is *true*. The rejection thus cancels its own claim.

[17]Bernd Heinrich, *Bumblebee Economics* (Cambridge, Mass.: Harvard University Press, 1979), p. 39.

[18]George Mavrodes, *Belief in God* (New York: Random House, 1970), pp. 83-85.

[19]There are a great many such works, but for a beginner perhaps it's best to stick with the classics. For example, I have always found Augustine, Luther and Calvin particularly helpful, while others have said the same about Aquinas or Wesley. Author John Updike once commented on the great help he received from reading the theology of Karl Barth.

[20]Mavrodes, *Belief in God,* p. 87. The only comment I would like to add to this quote is the point I've been making all along. The intuition of the self-evidency that the biblical message is God speaking to us is an additional element of our experience to that of reading Scripture or finding a theology to be helpful. Many people find the message of Scripture or a theological systematizing of it to be comforting, beautiful and so on but still fall short of seeing for themselves that it is certainly *true*.

Chapter 5: Objections to Belief in God

[1]It is significant in this connection that a few years ago a joint committee made up of Roman Catholic, Anglican and Lutheran theologians concluded twenty years of discussions by issuing a statement saying that the only doctrinal points on which they disagreed were the authority of the pope and whether the pope is infallible when speaking on doctrine—the same issues that caused the split between the Roman Catholic and Greek Orthodox churches in the eleventh century.

[2]This point was also missed by John Wisdom in his famous essay "Gods" (reprinted in *Classical and Contemporary Readings in the Philosophy of Religion,* ed. John Hick [Englewood Cliffs, N.J.: Prentice-Hall, 1970], pp. 434-35). Wisdom supposes that belief in God is a hypothesis analogous to the belief that there is an invisible gardener who cares for a particular garden. Someone who believes in the invisible gardener finds features of it to be evidence for the gardener's existence, whereas the unbeliever does not. Wisdom worries over whether such a difference can be rationally resolved, since is it a difference over attitude, not fact. Thus, according to Wisdom, both believer and unbeliever have exactly the same experience of the garden but interpret that experience differently.

But Wisdom's position is wrong on both counts. Belief in God is not a hypothesis, and it is not imposed on the garden (world), which is experienced in exactly the same way by the believer and the unbeliever. The believer in God experiences part of the garden to be (self-evidently) revelation from God; the unbeliever finds that something about it (self-evidently) reveals another divinity.

[3]This translation brings out the force of the different forms of the verb "to talk" (λαλήσας, ἐλάλησεν) as they appear in the passage. The first indicates ongoing action while the second indicates completed action. See also John Calvin *Institutes of the Christian Religion* 4.8.7, and Geerhardus Vos, *The Teaching of the Epistle to the Hebrews* (Grand Rapids, Mich.: Eerdmans, 1956), pp. 70-71.

[4]This idea of progressive revelation has been developed extensively in Geerhardus Vos's *Biblical Theology* (Grand Rapids, Mich.: Eerdmans, 1948) and Ernest Wright and Reginald Fuller's *The Book of the Acts of God* (Garden City, N.Y.: Doubleday/Anchor, 1960). See also Vos's address "The Idea of Biblical Theology," reprinted in *Redemptive History and Biblical Interpretation,* ed. Richard Gaffin (Philadelphia: Presbyterian & Reformed, 1980), pp. 3-24.

[5]For example, Paul Tillich once claimed that "biblical research in Protestantism has shown the many levels of biblical literature and the impossibility of considering the Bible as containing the infallible truth of faith." *The Dynamics of Faith* (New York: Harper & Brothers, 1958), p. 98.

[6]For an excellent exposition of this point, see Henry Vander Goot's *Interpreting the Bible in Theology and the Church* (New York: Edwin Mellen, 1984).

[7]In fact, the practice of reconstructing history from one's armchair has resulted in a staggering variety of wildly conflicting theories. In the nineteenth century one New Testament scholar produced no fewer than four different reconstructions of the life of Christ, the third of which argued that Jesus never lived, while the fourth took that back!

Such armchair history was roundly rejected by the great archaeologist William F. Albright. Albright maintained that there was no substitute for archaeological investigation and that the latter had convinced him—contrary to his expectations—that the biblical literature was remarkably accurate. Toward the end of his life he summarized his position this way: "I still insist on the primacy of archeology in the broad sense, including the interpretation of written documents recovered by archeologists as well as the excavation and reconstruction of material ·ulture. I continue to maintain . . . that we must approach history [by following] the general principles of . . . empiricism. . . . Turning to Israel, I defend the substantial historicity of the Patriarchal tradition. . . . I have grown more conservative in my attitude toward the Mosaic tradition. . . . I now insist much more vigorously on the pattern of prophetic thinking which made the Prophets such successful predictors of the course of history. . . . The prophetic message was validated . . . by the truth of its predictions. . . . There seems to be hardly a single 'prophecy after the event' in the whole extant prophetic literature of Israel. . . . [I] insist on an early date of the Gospels, including John . . . [and] now lay more stress on the continuity of Old and Testaments." *From the Stone Age to Christianity* (Garden City, N.Y.: Doubleday, 1957), pp. 2-3.

[8]This has been recognized by virtually every major theologian. W. J. Bousma has pointed it out about John Calvin: "Calvin was little troubled . . . by discrepancies among [the Gospels'] accounts; indeed he was scrupulous to identify them. The authors of the Gospels . . . had not written 'in such a way as always to preserve the exact order of events,

but rather to bring everything together so as to place before us a kind of mirror or screen on which the most useful things about Christ could be known.' He argued, indeed, that the differences among the Gospels, given their general agreement, increased their credibility [by proving] there had been no collusion among their authors. . . . Nor did it disturb him that the biblical narrative contains inaccuracies and instances of carelessness on the part of its human authors. 'It is well known,' he observed, 'that the Evangelists were not sufficiently careful with their time sequences, nor even bothered about the details of what was done or said.'" *John Calvin* (Oxford: Oxford University Press, 1988), pp. 121-22.

[9]It is this encyclopedic assumption, rather than a strictly literal interpretation of Scripture, that characterizes fundamentalism. The literal meaning of any text must at least *begin* with ascertaining the intent of its author, and knowing what that is requires (1) information about the text's historical setting, (2) knowledge of to whom it is addressed and (3) knowledge of its language. In these respects fundamentalism is not literal enough. Often what fundamentalists call the "literal" meaning of Genesis is whatever they happen to have thought of when they first read it, however uninformed that was.

An especially painful consequence of this assumption was the attempt to deduce from Genesis the age of the earth and the human race. Early Genesis says absolutely nothing on either topic, offering only a synopsis of the major editions of the covenant. In the course of doing that, it names people who played an important role in connection with those covenants and also mentions their age at death. And in a style typical of the ancient world, it calls one of those people the "father" of another where we would use *ancestor.* Only the encyclopedic assumption could induce a reader to suppose that adding up those ages yields the age of the human race—let alone the age of the earth.

[10]The idea of God's calling all else into being out of nothing is unique to the biblical doctrine of creation and distinguishes it from other creation stories. But it is worth noting that after the universe is called into being, the various life forms are not created out of nothing. In fact the wording of the text suggests that they resulted from natural processes, since the *waters* bring forth swarms of living creatures. Of course that happens according to the plan, and at the command, of God.

[11]We can form no concept of how God called the universe into being, since all our concepts are formed in accordance with laws God created. Hence they could not have applied to God's creating *them*. We have only the limiting idea that all depends on God, without being able to analyze the dependency.

[12]For example, Psalm 22:15, 29; 30:9; 44:25; 103:14; 104:29; Ecclesiastes 3:20; 12:7; Isaiah 26:19; Daniel 12:2.

[13]Until recently this point was not fully appreciated in most discussions of human origins, since the definition of "human" was raised largely as an afterthought. That will not do, since it largely *controls* the conclusions reached. Roger Lewin recognizes this point briefly in *Human Evolution* (New York: W. H. Freeman, 1984), p. 25, and I have developed it at some length in "Genesis on the Origin of the Human Race," *Perspectives on Science and Christian Faith* 43, no. 1 (1991): 2-13.

[14]Francine Patterson, "Conversations with a Gorilla," *National Geographic,* October 1978. I am not suggesting that apes have shown anything close to human abilities in these respects. There is nothing to suggest they have abstract concepts, for example, and they

never originate questions. But the abilities displayed are, to say the least, startling, and they show that it is not humans alone who have them. This makes it extremely difficult to say at what point these abilities become distinctly human.

[15]This isn't true of Genesis alone, of course, but all of the Hebrew Scriptures and the New Testament. It's why Bible writers never try to prove the existence of God but everywhere presuppose that all people have some religious belief. Rather than argue that God exists, they always admonish their readers to turn from their false gods to the one true God.

[16]The expression "image of God" does not, of course, mean that God *looks* like us. Many theologians have taken it to refer chiefly to human rational capacities, whereas others have taken it to refer chiefly to the human ability to love. Both are important parts of the human makeup, but neither captures the intent of the Hebrew text, where the imaging consists in the way humans are reflections of God *as he is described in the account:* God is the One who creates. Of course God calls creation into being by divine power, whereas humans can be creative only within their creaturely limitations. But in the story that appears chiefly as their ability to create other humans. The text is explicitly sexual in its wording concerning Adam's need for a mate.

[17]The only alternative to this would be a view that makes the defining feature of humanity a relational one, as did Aristotle and Marx. These views have severe difficulties, however, as it seems clear that prehumans already lived in groups. In that case it couldn't just be interaction with others that made humans human; there would have to be some change of capacity in specific individuals, even if that could only manifest itself socially.

[18]This fits beautifully with the Genesis account, which has Adam and Eve's children traveling among other people! On hearing that part of the story, every schoolchild asks where those other people came from. But if an evolutionary view is taken together with the Genesis account, the question is answered.

[19]This view makes Adam the head of the race in a religious sense but *not* in the biological sense of being the actual ancestor of all people, as most Christian theologians have held him to be. I have looked extensively for scriptural support for the view that Adam was the biological father of all people but have found none. The closest Scripture comes to saying anything like that is Adam's own remark when he refers to Eve as the "mother of all living." In context, however, that also seems to have a religious rather than a biological connotation. The title is conferred on Eve because she is to be the mother of someone who will be the covenant hero, or Messiah, who will perfectly keep the covenant and thus restore to the human race the promise of eternal life, which was lost in the fall (Gen 3:15).

In Christian theology Jesus is that Messiah. So it seems decisive for the question that the New Testament calls him the "second Adam," the one who gives a new (religious) start to the human race. This strong parallel between Jesus and Adam allows that Adam's covenant status needn't depend on his being the biological ancestor of everyone, since Jesus' covenant status certainly didn't.

[20]Microevolution, the gradual development of new species, has been directly observed and is a fact. That *all* life forms developed in the way new species have and have a common descent remains a hypothesis with difficulties yet to be solved. See Michael Denton's *Evolution: A Theory in Crisis* (Bethesda, Md.: Adler & Adler, 1986).

[21]Here Paul Tillich's observation is well taken: "The famous struggle between the theory

of evolution and the theology of some Christian groups was not a struggle between science and faith, but between a science whose faith deprived man of his humanity and a faith whose expression was distorted by Biblical literalism. . . . A theory of evolution which interprets man's descendence from older forms of life in a way that removes the infinite, qualitative difference between man and animal is faith not science." *The Dynamics of Faith* (New York: Harper & Row, 1957), p. 83.

It should also be noted that on the position I'm defending, the term *Homo sapiens* would not be synonymous with the term *human* even if both classifications had all the same members. *Homo sapiens* is a strictly biological classification, whereas *human* means much more. To assume that they mean the same is to insist uncritically that humans are essentially biological creatures. Since that view presupposes a nontheistic belief about what is divine, it is (as Tillich notes) the expression of a religious belief and so begs the question against the biblical account.

[22]It is instructive to see why Darwin missed this point. In his case it was the assumption that whatever happens gradually is natural, whereas whatever happens suddenly needs a supernatural explanation. This faulty theology had been taught him at Cambridge and stayed with him throughout his life, as Howard Gruber points out in his book *Darwin on Man: A Psychological Study of Scientific Creativity*. "*Natura non facit saltum*—nature makes no jumps—was a guiding motto for generations. . . . Darwin encountered it in a sharp and interesting form, posed as an alternative of terrible import: nature makes no jumps but God does. Therefore if we want to know whether something that interests us is of natural origin or supernatural, we must ask: did it arise gradually out of that which came before, or suddenly without any evident natural cause? . . . Among the pages of his student notes . . . there are a few sheets outlining the argument of *The Evidence of Christianity Derived from Its Nature and Reception* by John Bird Sumner. . . . Sumner's central argument is that if something is found in the world that appears suddenly, its origins must be supernatural. . . . Darwin made a chapter-by-chapter outline of Sumner's *Evidence*" ([Chicago: University of Chicago Press, 1981], p. 242).

From a properly theistic view, both central claims of this view are false. God is the reason for the fact that the universe exists at all, including whatever gradual processes, jumps or anything else it exhibits. It is simply false that if something happens suddenly it must be a miracle, just as it is false that if something happens gradually it happens without God.

More recently Stephen Hawking missed this same point when he said that if the universe is infinite in space and time, it would "just Be," and there would be no reason to believe in God (*A Brief History of Time* [New York: Bantam, 1988], p. 136). God is the reason there is something rather than nothing, the Creator of everything other than himself whether it is finite or infinite. As was pointed out earlier (p. 183, n. 3), that the universe is created means it *depends* on God, not that it had to have a beginning in time. Even if it always existed, said Aquinas, it would always have existed in dependence on God (*Summa Theologica* Q46.a1).

It is interesting that although Hawking acknowledges Aquinas's point as an afterthought later in the book (pp. 174-75), Carl Sagan endorses only the mistake in his introduction to it (p. x).

[23]In *Adventures of Ideas* (New York: Mentor, 1955), Alfred North Whitehead notes that when the Bible raises the question "Canst thou by searching find out God?" it expects a negative answer. Whitehead doesn't like that answer and wittily quips that "it is good Hebrew but it is bad Greek" (p. 108). But at least he recognizes that on the biblical view one would not expect to find God by examining creation and thus not be entitled to conclude that God doesn't exist upon failing to do so.

[24]Great mischief has been caused on this point by those who have misread Romans 1. There Paul says that creation (somehow) witnesses to the existence of God. Many theists have taken that to mean that we should be able to infer the statement "God exists" from statements about characteristics of creation, such as its appearing designed.

This is a serious mistake. Romans 1 says that *if* we rightly interpreted nature, we would see that it is not self-existent but dependent on God, but the text immediately adds that our fallen nature blinds us to that fact. Because of the Fall, our natural inclination, it says, is to "turn the truth about God into a lie and worship or serve something God made." Moreover, even if we didn't turn a blind eye to the witness of nature, all we would see from creation, according to the text, is that the world would look dependent on God. There is nothing in the text to suggest that we would be able to read out God's purposes or discern his nature, or that we'd need belief in God to fill gaps in our theories about nature.

[25]For example, Calvin says, "Who does not attribute [casting lots] to the blindness of Fortune? Not so says the Lord, who claims the decision for himself (Prov. 16:33)" (*Institutes* 1.16.6).

Later he adds, "Though all things are ordered by the counsel and certain arrangement of God, to us, however, they are fortuitous. . . . The order, method, end and necessity of events are, for the most part, hidden in the counsel of God [though] they have the appearance of being fortuitous. . . . What seems to us contingence, faith will recognize as the secret impulse of God. . . . At the same time, that which God has determined, though it must come to pass, is not . . . in its own nature, necessary. [This is the difference between] necessity secundum quid, and necessity absolute, also between the necessity of consequent and of consequence" (*Institutes* 1.16.9).

[26]Notice that there is no argument here *from* miracles *to* belief in God. David Hume was right in saying that such an inference won't work. But it doesn't need to, since the relation between the two is quite the other way round.

[27]Though there is not room for a defense of this view here, I have defended it elsewhere. In addition to chapter 10 of *The Myth of Religious Neutrality* (Notre Dame, Ind.: University of Notre Dame Press, 1991), see my "Religious Language: A New Look at an Old Problem," in *Rationality in the Calvinian Tradition*, ed. Hendrik Hart, Johan Van der Hoeven and Nicholas Wolterstorff (Lanham, Md.: University Press of America, 1983), pp. 383-407; and "The Uniqueness of Dooyeweerd's Program for Philosophy and Science: Whence the Difference?" in *Christian Philosophy at the Close of the Twentieth Century*, ed. Sander Griffioen and Bert Balk (Amsterdam: Kok-Kampen, 1995), pp. 113-25.

[28]Some notable exceptions are the Cappadocian Fathers, Luther, Calvin and Barth. See note 35.

[29]Proverbs 8:22-31 specifically says this about God's wisdom. After asserting that God created wisdom, it says it was then a property he possessed and "delighted in." (This

passage could not have been written by an Anselmian while roaring drunk, let alone sober.)

[30]Jaroslav Pelikan, *Christianity and Classical Culture* (New Haven, Conn.: Yale University Press, 1993), p. 84.

[31]Ibid., p. 55.

[32]Ibid., p. 242. To this Basil added that when negative terms are used of God they signify "the absence of non-inherent qualities rather than the presence of inherent qualities" (see ibid., pp. 40-42). I take this to head off the objection that to deny God has a property P is to assert he has not-P. They mean to say that God had neither prior to creating and taking on the properties he has.

[33]Jaroslav Pelikan, ed., *Luther's Works* (St. Louis: Concordia Publishing House, 1955), 1:77.

[34]John Dillenberger, ed., *Martin Luther* (Garden City, N.Y.: Anchor, 1961), p. 191.

[35]Paul Althaus, *The Theology of Martin Luther* (Philadelphia: Fortress, 1966), p. 20.

[36]Calvin *Institutes* 1.13.21.

[37]Ibid. 1.10.2.

[38]Barth *Church Dogmatics* 3.1.14.

[39]The only place Scripture uses the term *perfect* in connection with God is one that makes no sense on the Anselmian view. In Matthew 5:48 Jesus tells his disciples that they should "be perfect as their Father in heaven is perfect." It should be clear, therefore, that his use of *perfect* did not have the meaning it did for the ancient Greeks (and Anselm). It did not mean "the highest degree of a great-making property." Rather it had the Hebrew connotation of "unfailing faithfulness." On the Anselmian view, Jesus would have been telling his disciples to be God! In context, he's actually telling them to be as faithful to their end of the covenant as God is to his end of it.

[40]Calvin is one of the clearest on this point: "Not that God should be [regarded as] subjected to the law, unless insofar as He is a law unto himself" (*De Aeternal Praedestinatione* C.R. 36.361). "And therefore He is above the laws because he is a law to himself and everything" (*Comm. [spell out] in Moses Libros 5*, C.R.[spell out] 52.131). "It perverse to measure [the] Divine by the standard of human justice" (*Institutes* 3.24.17). "[It is] sinful . . . to insist on knowing the causes of the Divine will, since it is itself, and justly ought to be, the cause of all that exists. . . . If you proceed farther to ask why He pleased [what he did], you ask for something greater and more sublime than the will of God, and nothing such can be found" (*Institutes* 3.23.2).

[41]It's worth noting that if the existence of undeserved suffering really entails that God doesn't exist, then even a single instance of the slightest disappointment would yield that conclusion! The argument is thus tantamount to insisting that either everyone's life be one of uninterrupted bliss or belief in God is irrational. That alone should be sufficient to show that the argument does not attack a *biblical* idea of God.

[42]Simone Weil has called the worst sort of suffering "affliction," which she distinguishes as suffering that tends to crush and degrade those who bear it by producing in them self-disgust, guilt and worthlessness. Even these forms of suffering, she says, are counterbalanced by the love that God offers to the afflicted. See Diogenes Allen, "Natural Evil and the Love of God," and Marilyn McCord Adams, "Horrendous Evils and the Goodness of God," in *The Problem of Evil*, ed. Robert Adams and Marilyn McCord

Adams (New York: Oxford University Press, 1994).

[43]See George Mavrodes's *Belief in God: A Study in the Epistemology of Religion* (New York: Random House, 1970), p. 58.

[44]Compare Alvin Plantinga, *Warrant and Proper Function* (New York: Oxford University Press, 1993). Plantinga has made a convincing case that in any account of knowledge it is crucial to include the requirement that our information-gathering and belief-forming capacities be in proper working order.

[45]This is the case not only with respect to formal, cultic religious traditions but also with the noncultic religious beliefs presupposed by theories. For example, what is the materialist explanation for why not everyone sees materialism as true?

[46]The reference is to a fictional Great Pumpkin in the comic strip *Peanuts*, by Charles Schultz. Alvin Plantinga has used it as an example of a crazy belief. See "Reason and Belief in God," in *Faith and Rationality*, ed. Alvin Plantinga and Nicholas Wolterstorff (Notre Dame, Ind.: University of Notre Dame Press, 1983), p. 74.

[47]Compare, for example, "The Worship of Trees," in James Fraser's *The Golden Bough* (New York: H. Wolff, 1951). See also G. F. Moore's *History of Religions*, vol. 1 (New York: Scribner's, 1913), chap. 6.

Chapter 6: Some Loose Ends

[1]Although we may need argument to *show* a belief is justified, we do not need to know how to justify it in order for it to *be* justified. Compare the comments of William Alston (*Perceiving God* [Ithaca, N.Y.: Cornell University Press, 1991], p. 79) and Roderick Chisholm (*The Foundations of Knowing* [Minneapolis: University of Minnesota Press, 1982], p. 69).

[2]Most people know the expression *self-evident* only in connection with the American Declaration of Independence, where Thomas Jefferson wrote, "We hold these truths to be self-evident . . ." and then listed the beliefs that all humans are created equal before the law and have been endowed with natural rights—neither of which is really self-evident! As Jefferson used the expression, then, it merely indicates that he would not argue for those beliefs in the Declaration. It should be clear that *self-evident* has not been used in that sense in this book. Given our meaning, it would have been more accurate had Jefferson written, "We *premise* that all men are created equal and are endowed with inalienable rights . . ."

[3]Earlier (chapter two, note 5) I pointed to the example of the ancient Pythagoreans, who worshiped numbers, as compared to Werner Heisenberg, whose view of math lacked worship but still regarded mathematical principles as divine. And note 10 in chapter one made the same point about the theories of Mach and Mill.

[4]This order of preconditions has a lot of intuitive plausibility, so let me add that it's actually very difficult to show it's correct. It's difficult because it is hard to identify exactly what sorts of conditions are *always* necessary to what sort of results. For example, it seems plausible that certain wavelengths of light hitting the retina are preconditions for seeing red. But in a totally darkened room you can see red and many other colors by pressing on your eyeball. The presence of light is therefore not a necessary precondition for seeing any of those colors at all!

[5]If it is replied that reality may consist of an infinite series of dependent entities, the argument given remains unaffected. For even if each and every individual were dependent, the entire series could not be, since there would be nothing for it to depend on. The only answers to the question "Why does this series exist?" would be (1) no reason, it's just there (in which case it's divine), and (2) we don't know (in which case it's divine so far as we can know).

It won't do to object that the series depends on the contingent entities that make it up. What I'm calling "the series" is not a distinct individual whole that depends on those entities as its parts; it is simply a name for the total array of them. The series doesn't then *depend* on that array; it *is* that array.

[6]The role of divinity beliefs in theory making is defended at length in Clouser, *Myth*, chaps. 7-11.

[7]Scripture's own comment on simply accepting that God exists is "You believe that there is one God. Good! Even the demons believe that—and shudder" (James 2:19 NIV).

[8]This paragraph assumes two things I've been maintaining all along. The first is that everyone has some divinity belief, and the second is that divinity beliefs are never deliberately chosen but are produced by our experience of their self-evidency. Compare the remarks of Paul Tillich in *The Dynamics of Faith* (New York: Harper & Row, 1957): "The certitude of faith is 'existential,' meaning that the whole existence of man is involved. . . . [It is] certainty about one's own being, namely . . . [its] being related to something ultimate or unconditional" (pp. 34-35). By contrast, Tillich says, a voluntarist view of faith assumes that "faith is . . . an act of knowledge with limited evidence and that the lack of evidence is made up for by an act of will. . . . This does not do justice to the existential character of faith" (p. 35).

He then points out that our will can play a role in genuine faith, but the role isn't that of producing belief but of living up to it: "We are often *grasped by* something, e.g., Biblical passages, as expressions of [objective faith], but we hesitate to accept them as our subjective [faith] for escapist reasons. In such cases . . . the appeal to will is justified . . . but such an act of will does not produce faith—faith . . . is already given" (p. 37, italics mine).

[9]Wilfred Cantwell Smith has long taken the position that all religions are equally efficacious in bringing people into proper relation to the divine (*The Meaning and End of Religion* [New York: Harper & Row, 1978]), and more recently John Hick has defended the same position (*An Interpretation of Religion* [New Haven, Conn.: Yale University Press, 1989]).

It is noteworthy, however, that even for Smith and Hick the beliefs of the different traditions are not all *true;* they admit that is impossible. What they contend is that all people experience the same Divine Reality but then conceptualize, explain and theorize differently about that Reality. The conceptual overlays disagree, but that fact doesn't matter for anyone's ultimate destiny.

I have already commented on this position in connection with Otto. It is false to religious experience-reports that all people experience the same thing but then concoct differing explanations of it. I pointed out that many people actually experience the divine to be all there is, a force in nature, matter or God, and many of the descriptions of these experiences are contrary to the cultural background and expectations of those who had them, so that it is highly unlikely they can be attributed to subsequent rationalization.

Moreover, the importance of truth cannot so easily be dismissed in connection with either what is divine or what is the right relation to the divine. Either we think of the divine and our relation to it in ways that correspond to them, or we do not. And every religion insists that it's imperative to be correct rather than wrong about those matters. By denying this point, Smith and Hick actually hold that all religions are *false* but that it doesn't matter. They have not, therefore, found a way to reconcile all religions but have invented a new one instead. And the irony is that their new one is just as logically incompatible with all the others as any of the others are with one another.

[10] Karl Barth, *Church Dogmatics* 4/3, pt. 1, trans. Geoffrey Bromiley and T. F. Torrance (Edinburgh: T & T Clark, 1961), pp. 477-78.

[11] For a brief discussion of several Christian positions on this issue, see Gabriel Fackre, Ronald Nash and John Sanders, *What About Those Who Have Never Heard?* (Downers Grove, Ill.: InterVarsity Press, 1995).

[12] Regarding reason to be autonomous is usually a sign that its principles are believed to have divine status. On this point compare Karl Popper's remarks about the "irrational faith in reason" in *The Open Society and Its Enemies* (London: Harper & Row, 1988), 2:321.

[13] Alfred North Whitehead, *Adventures of Ideas* (New York: Free Press, 1964), p. 165.

Index